ENGLISH COSTUME

ENGLISH COSTUME

BY

IRIS BROOKE

A series of seven books, each with 8 plates in
colour and 32 pages of line drawings.

"These volumes fill a need so long felt that all designers of theatrical
costumes have reason to be grateful to the publishers. They are
inexpensive and they are very complete. The text is adequate without being needlessly elaborate. The reproductions are excellent, and
the drawings, without being needlessly stiff or tight, give an excellent
idea of dressmaking construction." LEE SIMONSON in THE STUDIO.

ENGLISH COSTUME OF THE EARLY MIDDLE AGES
The Tenth to the Thirteenth Centuries

ENGLISH COSTUME OF THE LATER MIDDLE AGES
The Fourteenth and Fifteenth Centuries

ENGLISH COSTUME IN THE AGE OF ELIZABETH
The Sixteenth Century

ENGLISH COSTUME OF THE 17TH CENTURY

ENGLISH COSTUME OF THE 18TH CENTURY*

ENGLISH COSTUME OF THE 19TH CENTURY*

ENGLISH CHILDREN'S COSTUME

* Text by James Laver

A. & C. BLACK, LTD : LONDON, W.1

A MAN OF THE TIME OF GEORGE IV.   1820-1830

ENGLISH COSTUME
1066-1820

BY

DION CLAYTON CALTHROP

WITH SIXTY-ONE PLATES IN COLOUR
BY THE AUTHOR
AND MANY OTHER ILLUSTRATIONS

ADAM & CHARLES BLACK
4, 5 & 6 SOHO SQUARE LONDON W.1
1950

PRINTED IN GREAT BRITAIN

First published in four volumes, 1906
Reissued in one volume, 1907
Reprinted, 1913, 1917, 1923, 1926, 1931, 1941, 1946 and 1950

AGENTS

New York
THE MACMILLAN COMPANY

Toronto
THE MACMILLAN COMPANY OF CANADA

Melbourne
THE OXFORD UNIVERSITY PRESS

Bombay   Calcutta   Madras
MACMILLAN AND COMPANY, LTD.

INTRODUCTION

THE world, if we choose to see it so, is a complicated picture of people dressing and undressing.
The history of the world is composed of the chat
of a little band of tailors seated cross-legged on
their boards ; they gossip across the centuries,
feeling, as they should, very busy and important.
Someone made the coat of many colours for Joseph,
another cut into material for Elijah's mantle.

Baldwin, from his stall on the site of the great
battle, has only to stretch his neck round to nod
to the tailor who made the toga for Julius Cæsar ;
has only to lean forward to smile to Pasquino, the
wittiest of tailors.

John Pepys, the tailor, gossips with his neigh-
bour who cut that jackanapes coat with silver
buttons so proudly worn by Samuel Pepys, his
son. Mr. Schweitzer, who cut Beau Brummell's
coat, talks to Mr. Meyer, who shaped his panta-

loons.   Our world is full of the sound of scissors,
the clipping of which, with the gossiping tongues,
drown the grander voices of history.

As you will see, I have devoted myself entirely
to civil costume—that is, the clothes a man or a
woman would wear from choice, and not by reason
of an appointment to some ecclesiastical post, or
to a military calling, or to the Bar, or the Bench.
Such clothes are but symbols of their trades and
professions, and have been dealt with by persons
who specialize in those professions.

I have taken the date of the Conquest as my
starting-point, and from that date—a very simple
period of clothes—I have followed the changes of
the garments reign by reign, fold by fold, button
by button, until we arrive quite smoothly at Beau
Brummell, the inventor of modern clothes, the
prophet of cleanliness.

I have taken considerable pains to trace the
influence of one garment upon its successor, to
reduce the wardrobe for each reign down to its
simplest cuts and folds, so that the reader may
follow quite easily the passage of the coat from its
birth to its ripe age, and by this means may not

only know the clothes of one time, but the reasons for those garments. To the best of my knowledge, such a thing has never been done before; most works on dress try to include the world from Adam to Charles Dickens, lump a century into a page, and dismiss the ancient Egyptians in a couple of colour plates.

So many young gentlemen have blown away their patrimony on feathers and tobacco that it is necessary for us to confine ourselves to certain gentlemen and ladies in our own country. A knowledge of history is essential to the study of mankind, and a knowledge of history is never perfect without a knowledge of the clothes with which to dress it.

A man, in a sense, belongs to his clothes; they are so much a part of him that, to take him seriously, one must know how he walked about, in what habit, with what air.

I am compelled to speak strongly of my own work because I believe in it, and I feel that the series of paintings in these volumes are really a valuable addition to English history. To be modest is often to be excessively vain, and, having made an exhaustive study of my subject from my own point of view, I do not feel called upon to hide my knowledge under a bushel. Of course, I do not suggest that the ordinary cultured man should acquire the same amount of knowledge as a painter, or a writer of historical subjects, or an actor, but he should understand the clothes of his own people, and be able to visualize any date in which he may be interested.

One half of the people who talk glibly of Beau Brummell have but half an idea when he lived, and no idea that, for example, he wore whiskers. Hamlet they can conjure up, but would have some difficulty in recognising Shakespeare, because most portraits of him are but head and shoulders. Napoleon has stamped himself on men's minds very largely through the medium of a certain form of hat, a lock of hair, and a gray coat. In future years an orchid will be remembered as an emblem.

I have arranged, as far as it is possible, that each plate shall show the emblem or distinguishing mark of the reign it illustrates, so that the continuity of costume shall be remembered by the arresting notes.

As the fig-leaf identifies Adam, so may the chaperon twisted into a cockscomb mark Richard II. As the curled and scented hair of Alcibiades occurs to our mind, so shall Beau Nash manage his clouded cane. Elizabeth shall be helped to the memory by her Piccadilly ruff; square Henry VIII. by his broad-toed shoes and his little flat cap ; Anne Boleyn by her black satin nightdress ; James be called up as padded trucks ; Maximilian as puffs and slashes ; D'Orsay by the curve of his hat ; Tennyson as a dingy brigand ; Gladstone as a collar ; and even more recent examples, as the Whistlerian lock and the Burns blue suit.

And what romantic incidents may we not hang upon our clothes-line ! The cloak of Samuel Pepys ('Dapper Dick,' as he signed himself to a certain lady) sheltering four ladies from the rain ; Sir Walter Raleigh spreading his cloak over the mud to protect the shoes of that great humorist Elizabeth (I never think of her apart from the saying, 'Ginger for pluck') ; Mary, Queen of Scots, ordering false attires of hair during her captivity — all these scenes clinched into reality by the knowledge of the dress proper to them.

And what are we doing to help modern history —the picture of our own times—that it may look beautiful in the ages to come? I cannot answer you that.

Some chapters of this work have appeared in the *Connoisseur*, and I have to thank the editor for his courtesy in allowing me to reproduce them.

I must also thank Mr. Pownall for his help in the early stages of my labours.

One thing more I must add: I do not wish this book to go forth and be received with that frigid politeness which usually welcomes a history to the shelves of the bookcase, there to remain unread. The book is intended to be read, and is not wrapped up in grandiose phrases and a great wind about nothing; I would wish to be thought more friendly than the antiquarian and more truthful than the historian, and so have endeavoured to show, in addition to the body of the clothes, some little of their soul.

DION CLAYTON CALTHROP.

Contents

CONTENTS

Illustrations in Colour

Illustrations in Black and White

WILLIAM THE FIRST

Reigned twenty-one years : 1066—1087.
Born 1027.   Married, 1053, Matilda of Flanders.

THE MEN

Why France should always give the lead in the matter of dress is a nice point in sartorial morality — a morality which holds that it takes nine tailors to make a man and but one milliner to break him, a code, in fact, with which this book will often have to deal.

Sartorially, then, we commence with the 14th of October, 1066, upon which day, fatal to the fashions of the country, the flag of King Harold, sumptuously woven and

1

embroidered in gold, bearing the figure of a man fighting, studded with precious stones, was captured.

William, of Norse blood and pirate traditions, landed in England, and brought with him bloodshed, devastation, new laws, new customs, and new fashions.

Principal among these last was the method of shaving the hair at the back of the head, which fashion speedily died out by reason of the parlous times and the haste of war, besides the utter absurdity of the idea. Fashion, however, has no sense of the ridiculous, and soon replaced the one folly by some other extravagance.

William I. found the Saxons very plainly dressed, and he did little to alter the masculine mode.

He found the Saxon ladies to be as excellent at embroidery as were their Norman sisters, and in such times the spindle side was content to sit patiently at home weaving while the men were abroad ravaging the country.

William was not of the stuff of dandies. No man could draw his bow ; he helped with his own hands to clear the snowdrift on the march to Chester. Stark and fierce he was, loving the solitudes of the woods and the sight of hart and hind.

When some kind of order was restored in England, many of the Saxons who had fled the country and gone to Constantinople came back, bringing with them the Oriental idea of dress. The Jews came with Eastern merchandise into England, and brought rich-coloured stuffs, and as these spread through the country by slow degrees, there came a gradual change in colour and material, and finer stuffs replaced the old homespun garments.

The Jews were at this time very eminent as silk manufacturers and makers of purple cloth. The Britons had been very famous for their dyed woollen stuffs. Boadicea is said to have worn a tunic of chequered stuff, which was in all probability rather of the nature of Scotch plaids.

The tunics worn by the men of this time were, roughly speaking, of two kinds: those that fitted close to the body, and those that hung loose, being gathered into the waist by a band. The close-fitting tunic was in the form of a knitted jersey, with skirts reaching to the knee; it was open on either side to the hips, and fell from the hips in loose folds. The neck was slit open four or five inches, and had an edging of embroidery, and the sleeves were wide, and reached just below the

elbows. These also had an edging of embroidery, or a band different in colour to the rest of the tunic.

The other form of tunic was made exactly in shape like the modern shirt, except that the neck opening was smaller. It was loose and easy, with wide sleeves to the elbow, and was gathered in at the waist by a band of stuff or leather.

The skirts of the tunics were cut square or V-shaped in front and behind. There were also tunics similar in shape to either of those mentioned, except that the skirts were very short, and were tucked into wide, short breeches which reached to the knee, or into the trousers which men wore.

Under this tunic was a plain shirt, loosely fitting, the sleeves tight and wrinkled over the wrist, the neck showing above the opening of the tunic. This shirt was generally white, and the opening

A MAN OF THE TIME OF WILLIAM I.   1066-1087

A WOMAN OF THE TIME OF WILLIAM I.   1066-1087

at the neck was sometimes stitched with coloured or black wool.

Upon the legs they wore neat-fitting drawers of wool or cloth, dyed or of natural colour, or loose trousers of the same materials, sometimes worn loose, but more generally bound round just above the knee and at the ankle.

They wore woollen socks, and for footgear they wore shoes of skin and leather, and boots of soft leather shaped naturally to the foot and strapped or buckled across the instep. The tops of the boots were sometimes ornamented with coloured bands.

The cloak worn was semicircular in shape, with or without a small semicircle cut out at the neck. It was fastened over the right shoulder or in the centre by means of a large round or square brooch, or it was held in place by means of a metal ring or a stuff loop through which the cloak was pushed; or it was tied by two cords sewn on to the right side of the cloak, which cords took a bunch of the stuff into a knot

and so held it, the ends of the cords having tags
of metal or plain ornaments.

One may see the very same make and fashion of
tunic as the Normans wore under their armour
being worn to-day by the Dervishes in Lower Egypt
—a coarse wool tunic, well padded, made in the

form of tunic and short drawers
in one piece, the wide sleeves
reaching just below the elbow.

The hats and caps of these
men were of the most simple
form—plain round-topped skull-
caps, flat caps close to the head
without a brim, and a hat with
a peak like the helmet.

Hoods, of course, were worn
during the winter, made very
close to the head, and they were
also worn under the helmets.

Thus in such a guise may we picture the Norman
lord at home, eating his meat with his fingers, his
feet in loose skin shoes tied with thongs, his legs in
loose trousers bound with crossed garters, his tunic
open at the neck showing the white edge of his shirt,
his face clean-shaven, and his hair neatly cropped.

THE WOMEN

Nothing could be plainer or more homely than the dress of a Norman lady. Her loose gown was made with ample skirts reaching well on to the ground, and it was gathered in at the waist by a belt of wool, cloth, silk, or cloth of gold web.

The gown fitted easily across the shoulders, but fell from there in loose folds. The neck opening was cut as the man's, about five inches down the front, and the border ornamented with some fine needlework, as also were the borders of the wide sleeves, which came just below the elbows.

Often the gown was made short, so that when it was girded up the border of it fell only to the knees, and showed the long chemise below.

The girdle was, perhaps, the richest portion of their attire, and was sometimes of silk diapered with gold thread, but such a girdle would be very costly. More often it would be plain wool, and be tied simply round the waist with short ends, which did not show.

The chemise was a plain white garment, with tight sleeves which wrinkled at the wrists; that is to say, they were really too long for the arm, and so were caught in small folds at the wrist.

The gown, opening at the neck in the same way as did the men's tunics, showed the white of the

chemise, the opening being held together sometimes by a brooch.

Towards the end of the reign the upper part of the gown—that is, from the neck to the waist—was worn close and fitted more closely to the figure, but not over-tightly— much as a tight jersey would fit.

Over all was a cloak of the semicircular shape, very voluminous—about three feet in diameter—which was brooched in the centre or on the shoulder.

On the head, where the hair was closely coiled with a few curls at the forehead, a wimple was worn, which was wound about the head and thrown

over the shoulder, not allowing the hair to show.
These wimples were sometimes very broad, and
were almost like a mantle, so that they fell over
the shoulders below the breast.

Tied round the wimple they sometimes had a
snood, or band of silk.

The shoes were like those worn by the men.

These ladies were all housewives, cooking, pre-
paring simples, doing embroidery and weaving.
They were their own milliners and dressmakers,
and generally made their husbands' clothes, although
some garments might be made by the town tailors;
but, as a rule, they weaved, cut, sewed, and fitted
for their families, and then, after the garments were
finished to satisfaction, they would begin upon
strips of embroidery to decorate them.

In such occupation we may picture them, and
imagine them sitting by the windows with their
ladies, busily sewing, looking up from their work
to see hedged fields in lambing-time, while shepherds
in rough sheepskin clothes drove the sheep into a
neat enclosure, and saw to it that they lay on warm
straw against the cold February night.

WILLIAM THE SECOND

Reigned thirteen years: 1087—1100.
Born c. 1060.

THE MEN

ABOUT this time there came to England a Norman, who settled near by the Abbey of Battle — Baldwin the Tailor by name, whom one might call the father of English tailoring.

Baldwin the Tailor sat contentedly cross-legged on his bench and plied his needle and thread, and snipped, and cut, and sewed, watching the birds pick worms and insects from the turf of the battle-ground.

10

England is getting a little more settled.

The reign opens picturesquely enough with William Rufus hastening to England with his father's ring, and ends with the tragedy of the New Forest and a blood-stained tunic.

Clothes begin to play an important part. Rich fur-lined cloaks and gowns trail on the ground, and sweep the daisies so lately pressed by mailed feet and sopped with blood where the Saxons fell.

Times have changed since Baldwin was at the coronation at Westminster on Christmas Day twenty years ago. Flemish weavers and farmers arrive from overseas, and are established by William II. in the North to teach the people pacific arts,

The Cloak pushed through a Ring.

causing in time a stream of Flemish merchandise to flow into the country, chiefly of rich fabrics and fine cloths.

The men adopt longer tunics, made after the same pattern as before—split up either side and loose in the sleeve—but in many cases the skirts reach to the ground in heavy folds, and the sleeves hang over the hands by quite a yard.

The necks of these tunics are ornamented as before, with coloured bands or stiff embroidery.

The cuffs have the embroidery both inside and out, so that when the long sleeve is turned back over the hand the embroidery will show.

The fashion in cloaks is still the same—of a semicircular pattern.

The shoes are the same as in the previous reign—that is, of the shape of the foot, except in rare cases of dandyism, when the shoes were made with long, narrow toes, and these, being stuffed with moss or wool, were so stiffened and curled up at the ends that they presented what was supposed to be a delightfully extravagant appearance.

They wore a sort of ankle garter of soft leather or cloth, which came over the top of the boot and just above the ankle.

The hair, beard, and moustaches were worn long and carefully combed—in fact, the length of the beard caused the priests to rail at them under such

A MAN OF THE TIME OF WILLIAM II.   1087-1100

A WOMAN OF THE TIME OF WILLIAM II. 1087-1100

terms as 'filthy goats.' But they had hardly the
right to censorship, since they themselves had to
be severely reprimanded by their Bishops for their
extravagance in dress.

Many gentlemen, and especially the Welsh, wore
long loose trousers as far as the ankle, leaving these
garments free from
any cross gartering.
These were secured
about the waist by a
girdle of stuff or
leather.

The ultra-fashion-
able dress was an
elongation of every
part of the simple
dress of the previous
reign. Given these
few details, it is easy
for anyone who wishes to go further to do so,
in which case he must keep to the main outline very carefully; but as to the actual length
of sleeve or shoe, or the very measurements of
a cloak, they varied with the individual folly of
the owner. So a man might have long sleeves

and a short tunic, or a tunic which trailed upon the ground, the sleeves of which reached only to the elbow.

I have noticed that it is the general custom of writers upon the dress of this early time to dwell lovingly upon the colours of the various parts of the dress as they were painted in the illuminated manuscripts. This is a foolish waste of time, insomuch as the colours were made the means of displays of pure design on the part of the very early illuminators ; and if one were to go upon such evidence as this, by the exactness of such drawings alone, then every Norman had a face the colour of which nearly resembled wet biscuit, and hair picked out in brown lines round each wave and curl.

These woollen clothes—cap, tunic, semicircular cloak, and leg coverings — have all been actually found in the tomb of a Briton of the Bronze Age. So little did the clothes alter in shape, that the early Briton and the late Norman were dressed nearly exactly alike.

When the tomb of William II. was opened in 1868, it was found, as had been suspected, that the grave had been opened and looted of what valuables it might have contained ; but there were found among the dust which filled the bottom of the tomb fragments of red cloth, of gold cloth, a turquoise, a serpent's head in ivory, and a wooden spear shaft, perhaps the very spear that William carried on that fatal day in the New Forest.

Also with the dust and bones of the dead King some nutshells were discovered, and examination showed that mice had been able to get into the tomb. So, if you please, you may hit upon a pretty moral.

THE WOMEN

And so the lady began to lace. . . .

A moralist, a denouncer of the fair sex, a satirist, would have his fling at this. What thundering epithets and avalanche of words should burst out at such a momentous point in English history!

However, the lady pleased herself.

Not that the lacing was very tight, but it commenced the habit, and the habit begat the harm, and the thing grew until it arrived finally at that buckram, square-built, cardboard-and-tissue figure which titters and totters through the Elizabethan era.

Our male eyes, trained from infancy upwards to avoid gazing into certain shop windows, nevertheless retain a vivid impression of an awesome affair therein, which we understood by hints and signs confined our mothers' figures in its deadly grip.

That the lady did not lace herself overtight is proved by the many informations we have of her household duties; that she laced tight enough for unkind comment is shown by the fact that some old monk pictured the devil in a neat-laced gown.

It was, at any rate, a distinct departure from the loosely-clothed lady of 1066 towards the neater figure of 1135.

The lacing was more to draw the wrinkles of the close-woven bodice of the gown smooth than to form a false waist and accentuated hips, the beauty of which malformation I must leave to the writers in ladies' journals and the condemnation to health faddists.

However, the lacing was not the only matter of note. A change was coming over all feminine apparel—a change towards richness, which made itself felt in this reign more in the fabric than in the actual make of the garment.

The gown was open at the neck in the usual

A MAN OF THE TIME OF HENRY I.   1100-1135

A WOMAN OF THE TIME OF HENRY I.   1100-1135

manner, was full in the skirt and longer than heretofore, was laced at the back, and was loose in the sleeve.

The sleeve as worn by the men —that is, the overlong sleeve hanging down over the hand—was also worn by the women, and hung down or was turned back, according to the freak of the wearer. Not only this, but a new idea began, which was to cut a hole in the long sleeve where the hand came, and, pushing the hand through, to let the rest of the sleeve droop down. This developed, as we shall see later.

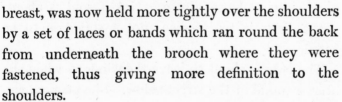

Then the cloak, which had before been fastened by a brooch on the shoulder or in the centre of the breast, was now held more tightly over the shoulders by a set of laces or bands which ran round the back from underneath the brooch where they were fastened, thus giving more definition to the shoulders.

You must remember that such fashions as the hole in the sleeve and the laced cloak were not any more universal than is any modern fashion, and that

2

the good dame in the country was about a century behind the times with her loose gown and heavy cloak.

There were still the short gowns, which, being tucked in at the waist by the girdle, showed the thick wool chemise below and the unlaced gown, fitting like a jersey.

The large wimple was still worn wrapped about the head, and the hair was still carefully hidden.

Shall we imagine that it is night, and that the lady is going to bed? She is in her long white chemise, standing at the window looking down upon the market square of a small town.

The moon picks out every detail of carving on the church, and throws the porch into a dense gloom. Not a soul is about, not a light is to be seen, not a sound is to be heard.

The lady is about to leave the window, when she hears a sound in the street below. She peers down, and sees a man running towards the church; he goes in and out of the shadows. From her open window she can hear his heavy breathing. Now he

darts into the shadow of the porch, and then out
of the gloom comes a furious knocking, and a voice
crying, ' Sanctuary !'

The lady at her window knows that cry well.
Soon the monks in the belfry will awake and ring
the Galilee-bell.

The Galilee-bell tolls, and the knocking ceases.

A few curious citizens look out. A dog barks.
Then a door opens and closes with a bang.

There is silence in the square again, but the
lady still stands at her window, and she follows
the man in her thoughts.

Now he is admitted by the monks, and goes at
once to the altar of the patron-saint of the church,
where he kneels and asks for a coroner.

The coroner, an aged monk, comes to him and
confesses him. He tells his crime, and renounces
his rights in the kingdom ; and then, in that dark
church, he strips to his shirt and offers his clothes
to the sacrist for his fee. Ragged, mud-stained
clothes, torn cloak, all fall from him in a heap upon
the floor of the church.

Now the sacrist gives him a large cloak with a
cross upon the shoulder, and, having fed him, gives
him into the charge of the under-sheriff, who will

next day pass him from constable to constable towards the coast, where he will be seen on board a ship, and so pass away, an exile for ever.

The night is cold. The lady pulls a curtain across the window, and then, stripping herself of her chemise, she gets into bed.

HENRY THE FIRST

Reigned thirty-five years: 1100—1135.

Born 1068.   Married to Matilda of Scotland, 1100; to
Adela of Louvain, 1121.

THE MEN

THE Father of Popular Literature, Gerald of Wales, says:
' It is better to be dumb than
not to be understood.   New
times require new fashions, and
so I have thrown utterly aside
the old and dry methods of
some authors, and aimed at
adopting the fashion of speech
which is actually in vogue
to-day.'

Vainly, perhaps, I have endeavoured to follow this pre-
cept laid down by Father Gerald, trying by slight
pictures of the times to make the dry bones live,

21

to make the clothes stir up and puff themselves into the shapes of men.

It is almost a necessity that one who would describe, paint, stage, or understand the costume of this reign should know the state of England at the time.

For there is in this reign a distinction without a difference in clothes; the shapes are almost identical to the shapes and patterns of the previous reigns, but everybody is a little better dressed.

The mantles worn by the few in the time of William the Red are worn now by most of the nobility, fur-lined and very full.

One may see on the sides of the west door of Rochester Cathedral Henry and his first wife, and notice that the mantle he wears is very full; one may see that he wears a supertunic, which is gathered round his waist. This tunic is the usual Norman tunic reaching to the knee, but now it is worn over an undertunic which reaches to the ground in heavy folds.

One may notice that the King's hair is long and elegantly twisted into pipes or ringlets, and that it hangs over his shoulders.

No longer is the priestly abuse of ' filthy goat '

applicable, for Henry's beard is neatly trimmed and cut round his face.

These two things are the only practical difference between the two dates—the end of the eleventh century and the beginning of the twelfth.

The undertunic was made as a perfectly plain gown with tight sleeves ending at the wrist; it hung loose and full upon the figure. Over this was worn the short tunic with wide sleeves ending at the elbow. Both tunics would have broad borders of embroidered work or bands of coloured material. The supertunic would be brooched by one of those circular Norman brooches which was an ornamental circle of open goldwork in which stones and jewels were set. The brooch was fastened by a central pin.

The extravagances of the previous reign were in some measure done away with; even the very long hair was not fashionable in the latter half of this reign, and the ultra-long sleeve was not so usual.

So we may give as a list of clothes for men in this reign:

A white linen shirt.

A long tunic, open at the neck, falling to the ground, with tight sleeves to the wrist.

A short tunic reaching only to the knees, more open at the neck than the long tunic, generally fastened by a brooch.

Tight, well-fitting drawers or loose trousers.

Bandages or garters crossed from the ankle to the knee to confine the loose trousers or ornament the tights.

Boots of soft leather which had an ornamental band at the top.

Socks with an embroidered top.

Shoes of cloth and leather with an embroidered band down the centre and round the top.

Shoes of skin tied with leather thongs.

Caps of skin or cloth of a very plain shape and without a brim.

Belts of leather or cloth or silk.

Semicircular cloaks fastened as previously described, and often lined with fur.

The clothes of every colour, but with little or no pattern; the patterns principally confined to irregular groups of dots.

And to think that in the year in which Henry died Nizami visited the grave of Omar Al Khayyám in the Hira Cemetery at Nishapur!

THE WOMEN

The greatest change in the appearance of the women was in the arrangement of the hair.

After a hundred years or more of headcloths and hidden hair suddenly appears a head of hair. Until now a lady might have been bald for all the notice she took of her hair; now she must needs borrow hair to add to her own, so that her plaits shall be thick and long.

It is easy to see how this came about. The hair, for convenience, had always been plaited in two plaits and coiled round the head, where it lay concealed by the wimple. One day some fine lady decides to discard her close and uncomfortable head-covering. She lets her plaits hang over her shoulders, and so appears in public. Contempt of other ladies who have fine heads of hair for the thinness of her plaits; competition in thick and long hair; anger of ladies whose hair is not thick and long; enormous demand for artificial hair; failure of the supply to meet the ever-increasing demand; invention of silken cases filled with a substitute for hair, these cases attached to the end of the plaits to elongate them—in this manner do many fashions arrive and flourish, until such time as the common people find means of copying them, and then my lady wonders how she could ever have worn such a common affair.

The gowns of these ladies remained much the same, except that the loose gown, without any show of the figure, was in great favour; this gown was confined by a long girdle.

The girdle was a long rope of silk or wool, which was placed simply round the waist and loosely knotted; or it was wound round above the waist once, crossed behind, and then knotted in front, and the ends allowed to hang down. The ends of the girdle had tassels and knots depending from them.

The silk cases into which the hair was placed were often made of silk of variegated colours, and these cases had metal ends or tassels.

The girdles sometimes were broad bands of silk diapered with gold thread, of which manufacture specimens remain to us.

The sleeves of the gowns had now altered in shape, and had acquired a sort of pendulent cuff, which hung down about two hands' breadth from the wrist. The border was, as usual, richly ornamented.

Then we have a new invention, the pelisse. It is a loose silk coat, which is brooched at the waist, or buttoned into a silk loop.  The sleeves are long—that is, they gradually increase in size from the underarm to the wrist, and sometimes are knotted at the ends, and so are unlike the other gown sleeves, which grow suddenly long near to the wrist.

This pelisse reaches to the knees, and is well open in front. The idea was evidently brought back from the East after the knights arrived back from the First Crusade, as it is in shape exactly like the coats worn by Persian ladies.

We may conceive a nice picture of Countess Constance, the wife of Hugh Lufus, Earl of

Chester, as she appeared in her dairy fresh from milking the cows, which were her pride. No doubt she did help to milk them; and in her long under-gown, with her plaits once more confined in the folds of her wimple, she made cheeses—such good cheeses that Anselm, Archbishop of Canterbury, rejoiced in a present of some of them.

What a change it must have been to Matilda, free of the veil that she hated, from the Black Nuns of Romsey, and the taunts and blows of her aunt Christina, to become the wife of King Henry, and to disport herself in fine garments and long plaited hair—Matilda the very royal, the daughter of a King, the sister to three Kings, the wife of a King, the mother of an Empress!

STEPHEN

Reigned nineteen years: 1135—1154.
Born 1094.   Married, 1124, to Matilda of Boulogne.

THE MEN

WHEN one regards the mass of material in existence showing costume of the tenth and eleventh centuries, it appears curious that so little fabric remains of this particular period.

The few pieces of fabric in existence are so worn and bare that they tell little, whereas pieces of earlier date of English or Norman material are perfect, although thin and delicate.

There are few illuminated manuscripts of the twelfth century, or of the first half of it, and to the

few there are all previous historians of costume
have gone, so that one is left without choice but to
go also to these same books. The possibilities,
however, of the manuscripts referred to have not
been exhausted, and too much attention has been
paid to the queer drawing of the illuminators ; so
that where they utilized to the full the artistic
license, others have sought to pin it down as
accurate delineation of the costume of the time.
In this I have left out all the supereccentric
costumes, fearing that such existed merely in the
imagination of the artist, and I have applied myself to the more ordinary and understandable.
As there are such excellent works on armour, I
have not touched at all upon the subject, so that we
are left but the few simple garments that men wore
when they put off their armour, or that the peasant
and the merchant habitually wore.

Ladies occupied their leisure in embroidery and
other fine sewing, in consequence of which the
borders of tunics, of cloaks, the edgings of sleeves,
and bands upon the shoes, were elegantly patterned.
The more important the man, the finer his shoes.

As will be seen from the drawings, the man
wore his hair long, smoothly parted in the centre,

with a lock drawn down the parting from the back
of his head.   As a rule, the hair curled back naturally, and hung on the shoulders, but sometimes the
older fashion of the past reign remained, and the
hair was carefully curled
in locks and tied with
coloured ribbon.

Besides the hood as
covering for the head,
men wore one or other
of the simple caps
shown, made of cloth or
of fur, or of cloth fur-
lined.

Next to his skin the
man of every class wore
a shirt of the pattern
shown—the selfsame
shirt that we wear to day, excepting that the
sleeves were made very long and tight-fitting, and
were pushed back over the wrist, giving those
wrinkles which we notice on all the Bayeux
tapestry sleeves, and which we see for many
centuries in drawings of the undergarment.   The
shape has always remained the same; the modes

of fastening the shirt differ very slightly — so
little, in fact, that a shirt of the fourth century
which still remains in existence shows the same
button and loop that we notice of the shirts of
the twelfth century. The richer man had his
shirt embroidered round the neck and sometimes
at the cuffs. Over this garment the man wore

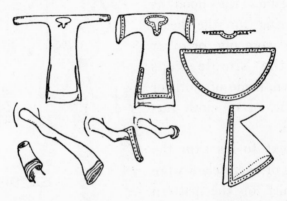

his tunic—of wool, or cloth, or (rarely) of silk;
the drawing explains the exact making of it. The
tunic, as will be seen, was embroidered at the
neck, the cuffs, and round the border. One drawing shows the most usual of these tunics, while the
other drawings will explain the variations from it—
either a tight sleeve made long and rolled back, a
sleeve made very wide at the cuff and allowed to

A MAN OF THE TIME OF STEPHEN   1135-1154

A WOMAN OF THE TIME OF STEPHEN   1135-1154

hang, or a sleeve made so that it fell some way over the hand. It was embroidered inside and out at the cuff, and was turned back to allow free use of the hand.

Over the tunic was worn the cloak. a very simple garment, being a piece of cloth cut in the shape of a semicircle, embroidered on the border or not, according to the purse and position of the owner. Sometimes a piece was cut out to fit the neck.

Another form of cloak was worn with a hood. This was generally used for travelling, or worn by such people as shepherds. It was made for the richer folk of fine cloth, fur-lined, or entirely of fur, and for the poorer people of skin or wool.

The cloak was fastened by a brooch, and was pinned in the centre or on either shoulder, most generally on the right ; or it was pushed through a ring sewn on to the right side of the neck of the cloak.

The brooches were practically the same as those worn in the earlier reigns, or were occasionally of a pure Roman design.

As will be seen in the small diagrams of men wearing the clothes of the day, the tunic, the shirt.

3

and the cloak were worn according to the season, and many drawings in the MSS. of the date show men wearing the shirt alone.

On their legs men wore trousers of leather for riding, bound round with leather thongs, and  trousers of wool also, bound with coloured straps of wool or cloth.

Stockings of wool were worn, and cloth stockings also, and socks. There was a sock without a foot, jewelled or embroidered round the top, which was worn over the stocking and over the top of the boot in the manner of ankle gaiters.

The country man wore twists of straw round his calf and ankle.

For the feet there were several varieties of boots and shoes made of leather and stout cloth, now and again with wooden soles. As has been said before, the important people rejoiced in elegant footgear of all colours. All the shoes buttoned with one button above the outside ankle. The boots were sometimes tall, reaching to the bottom of the calf of the leg, and were rolled over, showing a coloured lining. Sometimes they were loose and wrinkled over the ankle. They were both, boot and shoe, made to fit the foot; for in this reign nearly all the extravagances of the previous reign had died out, and it is rare to find drawings or mention of long shoes stuffed with tow or wool.

During the reign of Stephen the nation was too occupied in wars and battles to indulge in excessive finery, and few arts flourished, although useful improvements occurred in the crafts.

There is in the British Museum a fine enamelled plate of this date which is a representation of Henry of Blois, Stephen's brother, who was the Bishop of Winchester. Part of the inscription, translated by Mr. Franks, says that 'Art is above gold and gems,' and that 'Henry, while living, gives gifts of brass to God.'

Champlevé enamel was very finely made in the twelfth century, and many beautiful examples remain, notably a plaque which was placed on the column at the foot of which Geoffrey Plantagenet was buried. It is a portrait of him, and shows the Byzantine influence still over the French style.

This may appear to be rather apart from costume, but it leads one to suppose that the ornaments of the time may have been frequently executed in enamel or in brass—such ornaments as rings and brooches.

It is hard to say anything definite about the colours of the dresses at this time. All that we can say is that the poorer classes were clothed principally in self-coloured garments, and that the dyes used for the clothes of the nobles were of very brilliant hues. But a street scene would be more occupied by the colour of armour. One would have seen a knight and men-at-arms—the knight in his plain armour and the men in leather and steel; a few merchants in coloured cloaks, and the common crowd in brownish-yellow clothes with occasional bands of colour encircling their waists.

The more simply the people are represented, the more truthful will be the picture or presentation. Few pictures of this exact time are painted, and few stories are written about it, but this will give all the information necessary to produce any picture or stage-play, or to illustrate any story.

The garments are perfectly easy to cut out and make. In order to prove this I have had them made from the bare outlines given here, without any trouble.

THE WOMEN

Though many parts of England were at this time being harassed by wars, still the domestic element grew and flourished.

The homes of the English from being bare and rude began to know the delights of embroidery and weaving. The workroom of the ladies was the most civilized part of the castle, and the effect of the Norman invasion of foreign fashions was beginning to be felt.

As the knights were away to their fighting, so were the knights' ladies engaged in sewing sleeve embroideries, placing of pearls upon shoes, making

silk cases for their hair, and otherwise stitching,
cutting, and contriving against the return of their
lords.

It is recorded that Matilda escaped from Oxford
by a postern in a white dress, and no doubt her
women sympathizers made much
of white for dresses.

The ladies wore a simple
undergarment of thin material
called a sherte or camise; this
was bordered with some slight
embroidery, and had tightish
long sleeves pushed back over
the wrist. The garment fell
well on to the ground. This
camise was worn by all classes.

The upper garment was one
of three kinds: made from the neck to below the
breast, including the sleeves of soft material; from
the breast to the hips it was made of some elastic
material, as knitted wool or thin cloth, stiffened by
criss-cross bands of cloth, and was fitted to the
figure and laced up the back; the lower part was
made of the same material as the sleeves and bust.

The second was made tight-fitting in the body

and bust, all of one elastic material, and the skirt of loose thin stuff.

The third was a loose tunic reaching half-way between the knees and feet, showing the camise, and tied about the waist and hips by a long girdle.

The sleeves of these garments showed as many variations as those of the men, but with the poor folk they were short and useful, and with the rich they went to extreme length, and were often knotted to prevent them from trailing on the ground.

The collar and the borders of the sleeves were enriched with embroidery in simple designs.

In the case of the loose upper garment the border was also embroidered.

In winter a cloak of the same shape as was worn by the men was used—*i.e.*, cut exactly semicircular, with embroidered edges.

The shoes of the ladies were fitted to the foot in no extravagant shape, and were sewn with bands of pearls or embroidery. The poorer folk went about barefoot.

The hair was a matter of great moment and most carefully treated; it was parted in the centre and then plaited, sometimes intertwined with coloured ribbands or twists of thin coloured material; it was added to in length by artificial hair, and was tied up in a number of ways. Either it was placed in a tight silk case, like an umbrella case, which came about half-way up the plait from the bottom, and had little tassels depending from it, or the hair was added to till it reached nearly to the feet, and was bound round with ribbands, the ends having little gold or silver pendants. The hair hung, as a rule, down the front on either side of the face, or occasionally behind down the back, as was the case when the wimple was worn.

When the ladies went travelling or out riding they rode astride like men, and wore the ordinary common-hooded cloak.

Brooches for the tunic and rings for the fingers were common among the wealthy.

The plait was introduced into the architecture of the time, as is shown by a Norman moulding at Durham.

Compared with the Saxon ladies, these ladies of Stephen's time were elegantly attired; compared with the Plantagenet ladies, they were dressed in the simplest of costumes. No doubt there were, as in all ages, women who gave all their body and soul to clothes, who wore sleeves twice the length of anyone else, who had more elaborate plaits and more highly ornamented shoes; but, taking the period as a whole, the clothes of both sexes were plainer than in any other period of English history.

One must remember that when the Normans came into the country the gentlemen among the Saxons had already borrowed the fashions prevalent in France, but that the ladies still kept in the main to simple clothes; indeed, it was the man who strutted to woo clad in all the fopperies of his time —to win the simple woman who toiled and span to deck her lord in extravagant embroideries.

The learning of the country was shared by the ladies and the clergy, and the influence of Osburgha, the mother of Alfred, and Editha, the wife of Edward the Confessor, was paramount among the noble ladies of the country.

The energy of the clergy in this reign was more

directed to building and the branches of architecture than to the more studious and sedentary works of illumination and writing, so that the sources from which we gather information with regard to the costume in England are few, and also peculiar, as the drawing of this date was, although careful, extremely archaic.

Picture the market-town on a market day when the serfs were waiting to buy at the stalls until the buyers from the abbey and the castle had had their pick of the fish and the meat. The lady's steward and the Father-Procurator bought carefully for their establishments, talking meanwhile of the annual catch of eels for the abbey.

Picture Robese, the mother of Thomas, the son of Gilbert Becket, weighing the boy Thomas each year on his birthday, and giving his weight in money, clothes, and provisions to the poor. She was a type of the devout housewife of her day, and the wife of a wealthy trader.

The barons were fortifying their castles, and the duties of their ladies were homely and domestic. They provided the food for men-at-arms, the followers, and for their husbands; saw that simples were ready with bandages against wounds and sick-

ness; looked, no doubt, to provisions in case of
siege; sewed with their maidens in a vestiary or
workroom, and dressed as best they could for their
position. What they must have heard and seen
was enough to turn them from the altar of fashion
to works of compassion. Their houses contained
dreadful prisons and dungeons, where men were
put upon rachentegs, and fastened to these beams
so that they were unable to sit, lie, or sleep, but
must starve. From their windows in the towers
the ladies could see men dragged, prisoners, up to
the castle walls, through the hall, up the staircase,
and cast, perhaps past their very eyes, from the
tower to the moat below. Such times and sights
were not likely to foster proud millinery or dainty
ways, despite of which innate vanity ran to ribbands
in the hair, monstrous sleeves, jewelled shoes, and
tight waists. The tiring women were not over-
worked until a later period, when the hair would
take hours to dress, and the dresses months to
embroider.

In the town about the castle the merchants'
wives wore simple homespun clothes of the same
form as their ladies. The serfs wore plain smocks
loose over the camise and tied about the waist, and

in the bitter cold weather skins of sheep and wolves unlined and but roughly dressed.

In 1154 the Treaty of Wallingford brought many of the evils to an end, and Stephen was officially recognised as King, making Henry his heir. Before the year was out Stephen died.

I have not touched on ecclesiastical costume because there are so many excellent and complete works upon such dress, but I may say that it was above all civil dress most rich and magnificent.

I have given this slight picture of the time in order to show a reason for the simplicity of the dress, and to show how, enclosed in their walls, the clergy were increasing in riches

Cases for the Hair.

and in learning; how, despite the disorders of war, the internal peace of the towns and hamlets was growing, with craft gilds and merchant gilds. The lords and barons fighting their battles knew little of the bond of strength that was growing up in these primitive labour unions; but the lady in her bower, in closer touch with the people, receiving visits from foreign merchants and pedlars with rare goods to sell

or barter, saw how, underlying the miseries of
bloodshed and disaster, the land began to bloom
and prosper, to grow out of the rough place it
had been into the fair place of market-town and
garden it was to be.

Meanwhile London's thirteen conventual establishments were added to by another, the Priory
of St. Bartholomew, raised by Rahere, the King's
minstrel.

HENRY THE SECOND

Reigned thirty-five years : 1154—1189.
Born 1133. Married, 1152, to Eleanor of Guienne.

THE MEN

THE King himself is described
as being careless of dress,
chatty, outspoken.   His hair
was close-cropped, his neck
was thick, and his eyes were
prominent; his cheek-bones
were high, and his lips coarse.

The costume of this reign
was very plain in design, but
rich in stuffs. Gilt spurs were
attached to the boots by red
leather straps, gloves were
worn with jewels in the backs of them, and the
mantles seem to have been ornamented with
designs.

The time of patterns upon clothes began. The patterns were simple, as crescents, lozenges, stars.

William de Magna Villa had come back from the Holy Land with a new fabric, a precious silk called 'imperial,' which was made in a workshop patronized by the Byzantine Emperors.

The long tunic and the short supertunic were still worn, but these were not so frequently split up at the side.

High boots reaching to the calf of the leg were in common use.

That part of the hood which fell upon the shoulders was now cut in a neat pattern round the edge.

Silks, into which gold thread was sewn or woven, made fine clothes, and cloth cloaks lined with expensive furs, even to the cost of a thousand pounds of our money, were worn.

The loose trouser was going out altogether, and in its stead the hose were made to fit more closely to the leg, and were all of gay colours ; they were gartered with gold bands crossed, the ends of which had tassels, which hung down when the garter was crossed and tied about the knee.

Henry, despite his own careless appearance, was

nicknamed Court Manteau, or Short Mantle, on account of a short cloak or mantle he is supposed to have brought into fashion.

The shirts of the men, which showed at the opening of the tunic, were buttoned with small gold buttons or studs of gold sewn into the linen.

The initial difference in this reign was the more usual occurrence of patterns in diaper upon the clothes.

The length of a yard was fixed by the length of the King's arm.

With the few exceptions mentioned, the costume is the same as in the time of Stephen.

It is curious to note what scraps of pleasant gossip come to us from these early times: St. Thomas à Becket dining off a pheasant the day before his martyrdom; the angry King calling to his knights, " How a fellow that hath eaten my bread, a beggar that first came to my Court on a lame horse, dares to insult his King and the Royal Family, and tread upon my whole kingdom, and not one of the cowards I nourish at my table, not one will deliver me of this turbulent priest !'—the veins no doubt swelling on his bull-like neck, the prominent eyes bloodshot with temper, the result of that angry speech, to end in the King's public penance before the martyr's tomb.

Picture the scene at Canterbury on August 23, 1179, when Louis VII., King of France, dressed in the manner and habit of a pilgrim, came to the shrine and offered there his cup of gold and a royal precious stone, and vowed a gift of a hundred hogsheads of wine as a yearly rental to the convent.

A common sight in London streets at this time was a tin medal of St. Thomas hung about the necks of the pilgrims.

And here I cannot help but give another picture. Henry II., passing through Wales on his way to Ireland in 1172, hears the exploits of King Arthur which are sung to him by the Welsh bards. In this song the bards mention the place of King Arthur's burial, at Glastonbury Abbey in the churchyard. When Henry comes back from Ireland he visits the Abbot of Glastonbury, and repeats to him the story of King Arthur's tomb.

One can picture the search : the King talking eagerly to the Abbot ; the monks or lay-brothers digging in the place indicated by the words of the song ; the knights in armour, their mantles wrapped about them, standing by.

4

Then, as the monks search 7 feet below the surface, a spade rings upon stone. Picture the interest, the excitement of these antiquarians. It is a broad stone which is uncovered, and upon it is a thin leaden plate in the form of a corpse, bearing the inscription :

'HIC JACET SEPULTUS INCLYTUS REX ARTURIUS IN INSULA AVALONIA.'

They draw up this great stone, and with greedy eyes read the inscription. The monks continue to dig. Presently, at the depth of 16 feet, they find the trunk of a tree, and in its hollowed shape lie Arthur and his Queen—Arthur and Guinevere, two names which to us now are part of England, part of ourselves, as much as our patron St. George.

Here they lie upon the turf, and all the party gaze on their remains. The skull of Arthur is covered with wounds; his bones are enormous. The Queen's body is in a good state of preservation, and her hair is neatly plaited, and is of the colour of gold. Suddenly she falls to dust.

They bury them again with great care. So lay our national hero since he died at the Battle of

Camlan in Cornwall in the year 542, and after
death was conveyed by sea to Glastonbury, and all
traces of his burial-place lost except in the songs of
the people until such day as Henry found him and
his Queen.

THE WOMEN

About this time came the
fashion of the chin-band, and
again the glory of the hair
was hidden under the wimple.

To dress a lady's hair for
this time the hair must be
brushed out, and then divided
into two parts: these are to
be plaited, and then brought
round the crown of the head
and fastened in front above
the forehead. The front pieces
of hair are to be neatly pushed back from the
forehead, to show a high brow. Now a cloth of
linen is taken, folded under the chin, and brought
over the top of the head, and there pinned. Then
another thin band of linen is placed round the
head and fastened neatly at the back; and over

all a piece of fine linen is draped, and so arranged
that it shall just cover the forehead-band and fall
on to the shoulders. This last piece of linen is
fastened to the chin-band and the forehead-strap
by pins.

This fashion gave rise in later times to a linen
cap; the forehead-strap was increased in height and

stiffened so that it rose slightly
above the crown of the head,
and the wimple, instead of hanging over it, was sewn down inside
it, and fell over the top of the
cap. Later the cap was sewn
in pleats.

The gown of this time was
quite loose, with a deep band
round the neck and round the hem of the skirts,
which were very full. So far as one can tell, it
was put on over the head, having no other opening but at the neck, and was held at the waist
by an ornamental girdle.

The chemise showed above the neck of the gown,
which was fastened by the usual round brooch.

The sleeves were well fitting, rather loose at the
elbow, and fell shaped over the wrist, where there

A MAN OF THE TIME OF HENRY II.   1154-1189

A WOMAN OF THE TIME OF HENRY II. 1154-1189

was a deep border of embroidery. It is quite possible that the cuffs and hem may have been made of fur.

The shoes were, as usual to the last two reigns, rather blunt at the toe, and generally fitting without buckle, button, or strap round the ankle, where they were rolled back.

Above the waist the tied girdle was still worn, but this was being supplanted by a broad belt of silk or ornamented leather, which fastened by means of a buckle. The tongue of the belt was made very long, and when buckled hung down below the knee.

The cloaks, from the light way in which they are held, appear to have been made of silk or some such fine material as fine cloth. They are held on to the shoulders by a running band of stuff or a silk cord, the ends of which pass through two fasteners sewn on to the cloak, and these are knotted or have some projecting ornament which prevents the cord from slipping out of the fastener.

In this way one sees the cloak hanging from the shoulders behind, and the cord stretched tight across the breast, or the cord knotted in a second place, and so bringing the cloak more over the shoulders.

The effigy of the Queen at Fontevfaud shows her dress covered with diagonal bars of gold, in the triangles of which there are gold crescents placed from point to point, and no doubt other ladies of her time had their emblems or badges embroidered into their gowns.

RICHARD THE FIRST

Reigned ten years : 1189—1199.
Born 1157. Married, 1191, to Berengaria of Navarre.

THE MEN

THE King had but little influence over dress in his time, seeing that he left England as soon as he was made King, and only came back for two months in 1194 to raise money and to be crowned again.

The general costume was then as plain as it had ever been, with long tunics and broad belts fastened by a big buckle.

The difference in costume between this short reign and that of Henry II. is almost imperceptible; if any difference may be noted, it is in the tinge of Orientalism in the garments.

There is more of the long and flowing robe, more of the capacious mantle, the wider sleeve.

No doubt the many who came from the Crusades made a good deal of difference to English homes, and actual dresses and tunics from the East, of gorgeous colours and Eastern designs, were, one must suppose, to be seen in England.

Cloth of gold and cloth of gold and silks—that is, warf of silk and weft of gold—were much prized, and were called by various names from the Persian, as 'ciclatoun,' 'siglaton.'

Such stuff, when of great thickness and value— so thick that six threads of silk or hemp were in the warf—was called 'samite.'

Later, when the cloth of gold was more in use, and the name had changed from 'ciclatoun' to 'bundekin,' and from that to 'tissue,' to keep such fine cloth from fraying or tarnishing, they put very thin sheets of paper away between the folds of the garments; so to this day we call such paper tissue-paper.

Leaf-gold was used sometimes over silk to give pattern and richness to it.

A curious survival of this time, which has a connection with costume, was the case of Abraham Thornton in 1818. Abraham Thornton was accused of having drowned Mary Ashford, but he was acquitted by the jury. This acquittal did not satisfy popular feeling, and the brother of Mary Ashford appealed. Now Thornton was well advised as to his next proceeding, and, following the still existent law of this early time of which I write, he went to Westminster Hall, where he threw down, as a gage of battle, an antique gauntlet without fingers or thumb, of white tanned skin ornamented with silk fringes and sewn work, crossed by a narrow band of leather, the fastenings of leather tags and thongs.

This done, he declared himself ready to defend himself in a fight, and so to uphold his innocence, saying that he was within his rights, and that no judge could compel him to come before a jury.

This was held to be good and within the law, so Abraham Thornton won his case, as the brother refused to pick up the gauntlet. The scandal of this procedure caused the abolishment of the trial by battle, which had remained in the country's laws from the time of Henry II. until 1819.

It was a time of foreign war and improvement in military armour and arms. Richard I. favoured the cross-bow, and brought it into general use in England to be used in conjunction with the old 4-foot bow and the great bow 6 feet long with the cloth-yard arrow—a bow which could send a shaft through a 4-inch door.

For some time this military movement, together with the influence of the East, kept England from any advance or great change in costume; indeed, the Orientalism reached a pitch in the age of Henry III. which, so far as costume is concerned, may be called the Age of Draperies.

To recall such a time in pictures, one must then see visions of loose-tuniced men, with heavy cloaks; of men in short tunics with sleeves tight or loose at the wrists; of hoods with capes to them, the cape-edge sometimes cut in a round design; of soft leather boots and shoes, the boots reaching to the calf of the leg. To see in the streets bright Oriental colours and cloaks edged with broad bands of pattern; to see hooded heads and bared heads on which the hair was long; to see many long-bearded men; to see old men leaning on tan-handled sticks; the sailor in a cap or coif tied

under his chin ; the builder, stonemason, and skilled
workman in the same coif; to see, as a whole, a
brilliant shifting colour scheme in which armour
gleamed and leather tunics supplied a dull, fine
background.   Among these one might see, at a
town, by the shore, a thief of a sailor being carried
through the streets with his head shaven, tarred
and feathered.

THE WOMEN

It is difficult to describe an
influence in clothes.

It is difficult nowadays to
say in millinery where Paris
begins and London accepts.
The hint of Paris in a gown
suggests taste; the whole of
Paris in a gown savours of
servile imitation.

No well - dressed Englishwoman should, or does, look
French, but she may have
a subtle cachet of France if she choose.

The perfection of art is to conceal the means to

the end; the perfection of dress is to hide the milliner in the millinery.

The ladies of Richard I.'s time did not wear Oriental clothes, but they had a flavour of Orientalism pervading their dress—rather masculine Orientalism than feminine.

The long cloak with the cord that held it over the shoulders; the long, loose gown of fine colours and simple designs; the soft, low, heelless shoes; the long, unbound hair, or the hair held up and concealed under an untied wimple—these gave a touch of something foreign to the dress.

Away in the country there was little to dress for, and what clothes they had were made in the house. Stuffs brought home from Cyprus, from Palestine, from Asia Minor, were laboriously conveyed to the house, and there made up into gowns. Local smiths and silver-workers made them buckles and brooches and ornamental studs for their long belts, or clasps for their purses.

A wreck would break up on the shore near by, and the news would arrive, perhaps, that some bales of stuff were washed ashore and were to be sold.

The female anchorites of these days were busy gossips, and from their hermitage or shelter by a

A MAN OF THE TIME OF RICHARD I.   1189-1199

A WOMAN OF THE TIME OF RICHARD I.   1189-1199

bridge on the road would see the world go by, and pick up friends by means of gifts of bandages or purses made by them, despite the fact that this traffic was forbidden to them.

So the lady in the country might get news of her lord abroad, and hear that certain silks and stuffs were on their way home.

The gowns they wore were long, flowing and loose; they were girded about the middle with leathern or silk belts, which drew the gown loosely together. The end of the belt, after being buckled, hung down to about the knee.   These gowns were close at the neck, and there fastened by a brooch; the sleeves were wide until they came to the wrist, over which they fitted closely.

The cloaks were ample, and were held on by brooches or laces across the bosom.

The shoes were the shape of the foot, sewn, embroidered, elaborate.

The wimples were pieces of silk or white linen held to the hair in front by pins, and allowed to flow over the head at the back.

There were still remaining at this date women who wore the tight-fitting gown laced at the back, and who tied their chins up in gorgets.

JOHN

Reigned seventeen years : 1199—1216.
Born 1167. Married, in 1189, to Hadwisa, of Gloucester,
whom he divorced ; married, in 1200, to Isabella
of Angoulême.

THE MEN

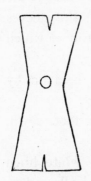 THERE was a garment in this reign which was the keynote of costume at the time, and this was the surcoat. It had been worn over the armour for some time, but in this reign it began to be an initial part of dress.

Take a piece of stuff about 9 or 10 yards in length and about 22 inches wide ; cut a hole in the centre of this wide enough to admit of a man's head passing through, and you have a surcoat.

Under this garment the men wore a flowing gown, the sleeves of which were so wide that they reached at the base from the shoulder to the waist, and narrowed off to a tight band at the wrist.

These two garments were held together by a leather belt buckled about the middle, with the tongue of the belt hanging down.

Broad borders of design edged the gowns at the foot and at the neck, and heraldic devices were sewn upon the surcoats.

King John himself, the quick, social, humorous man, dressed very finely. He loved the company of ladies and their love, but in spite of his love for them, he starved and tortured them, starved and beat children, was insolent, selfish, and wholly indifferent to the truth. He laughed aloud during the Mass, but for all that was superstitious to the degree of hanging relics about his neck ; and he was buried in a monk's cowl, which was strapped under his chin.

Silk was becoming more common in England, and the cultivation of the silkworm was in some measure gaining hold. In 1213 the Abbot of Cirencester, Alexander of Neckham, wrote upon the habits of the silkworm.

Irish cloth of red colour was largely in favour, presumably for cloaks and hoods.

The general costume of this reign was very much
the same as that of Henry II. and Richard I.—the
long loose gown, the heavy cloak, the long hair cut
at the neck, the fashion of beards, the shoes, belts,
hoods, and heavy fur cloaks, all much the same as

before, the only real difference
being in the general use of
the surcoat and the very convenient looseness of the sleeves
under the arms.

There is an inclination in
writing of a costume one can
visualize mentally to leave out
much that might be useful to
the student who knows little or
nothing of the period of dress
in which one is writing; so
perhaps it will be better to now dress a man
completely.

First, long hair and a neatly-trimmed beard; over
this a hood and cape or a circular cap, with a slight
projection on the top of it.

Second, a shirt of white, like a modern soft shirt.

Third, tights of cloth or wool.

Fourth, shoes strapped over the instep or tied

with thongs, or fitting at the ankle like a slipper, or boots of soft leather turned over a little at the top, at the base of the calf of the leg.

Fifth, a gown, loosely fitting, buckled at the neck, with sleeves wide at the top and tight at the wrist, or quite loose and coming to just below the elbow, or a tunic reaching only to the knees, both gown and tunic fastened with a belt.

Sixth, a surcoat sometimes, at others a cloak held together by a brooch, or made for travelling with a hood.

This completes an ordinary wardrobe of the time.

THE WOMEN

As may be seen from the plate, no change in costume took place.

The hair plaited and bound round the head or allowed to flow loose upon the shoulders.

Over the hair a gorget binding up the neck and chin. Over all a wimple pinned to the gorget.

A long loose gown with brooch at the neck.

5

Sleeves tight at the wrist. The whole gown held in at the waist by a belt, with one long end hanging down.

Shoes made to fit the shape of the foot, and very elaborately embroidered and sewn.

A long cloak with buckle or lace fastening.

In this reign there were thirty English towns which had carried on a trade in dyed cloths for fifty years.

HENRY THE THIRD

Reigned fifty-six years: 1216—1272.
Born 1207. Married, 1236, to Eleanor of Provence.

THE MEN

 DESPITE the fact that historians allude
to the extravagance of this reign, there
is little in the actual form of the costume to bear out the idea. Extravagant it was in a large way, and costly
for one who would appear well dressed;
but the fopperies lay more in the stuffs
than in the cut of the garments worn.

It was an age of draperies.

This age must call up pictures of
bewrapped people swathed in heavy
cloaks of cloth of Flanders dyed with
the famous Flemish madder dye; of people in silk
cloaks and gowns from Italy; of people in loose
tunics made of English cloth.

This long reign of over fifty years is a transitional period in the history of clothes, as in its course the draped man developed very slowly towards the coated man, and the loose‑hung clothes very gradually began to shape themselves to the body.

The transition from tunic and cloak and Oriental draperies is so slow and so little marked by definite change that to the ordinary observer the Edwardian cotehardie seems to have sprung from nowhere: man seems to have, on a sudden, dropped his stately wraps and mantles and discarded his chrysalis form to appear in tight lines following the figure—a form infinitely more gay and alluring to the eye than the ponderous figure that walks through the end of the thirteenth century.

Up to and through the time from the Conquest until the end of Henry III.'s reign the clothes of England appear—that is, they appear to me—to be lordly, rich, fine, but never courtier-like and elegant.

If one may take fashion as a person, one may say: Fashion arrived in 1066 in swaddling-clothes, and so remained enveloped in rich cloaks and flowing draperies until 1240, when the boy began to show a more active interest in life; this interest

A MAN OF THE TIME OF JOHN   1199-1216

A WOMAN OF THE TIME OF JOHN   1199-1216

grew until, in 1270, it developed into a distaste for heavy clothes; but the boy knew of no way as yet in which to rid himself of the trailings of his mother cloak. Then, in about 1272, he invented a cloak more like a strange, long tunic, through which he might thrust his arms for freedom; on this cloak he caused his hood to be fastened, and so made himself three garments in one, and gave himself greater ease.

Then dawned the fourteenth century—the youth of clothes—and our fashion boy shot up, dropped his mantles and heaviness, and came out from thence slim and youthful in a cotehardie.

Of such a time as this it is not easy to say the right and helpful thing, because, given a flowing gown and a capacious mantle, imagination does the rest. Cut does not enter into the arena.

Imagine a stage picture of this time: a mass of wonderful, brilliant colours—a crowd of men in long, loose gowns or surcoats; a crowd of ladies in long, loose gowns; both men and women hung with cloaks or mantles of good stuffs and gay colours. A background of humbler persons in homespun tunics with cloth or frieze hoods over their heads. Here and there a fop—out of his

date, a quarter-century before his time—in a loose
coat with pocket-holes in front and a buttoned neck
to his coat, his shoes very pointed and laced at the
sides, his hair long, curled, and bound by a fillet or
encompassed with a cap with an upturned brim.

The beginning of the coat was this: the surcoat,
which up till now was split at both sides from the

shoulder to the hem, was now
sewn up, leaving only a wide
armhole from the base of the
ribs to the shoulder. This surcoat was loose and easy, and
was held in at the waist by a
belt. In due time a surcoat appeared which was slightly shaped
to the figure, was split up in front
instead of at the sides, and in
which the armholes were smaller
and the neck tighter, and fastened
by two or three buttons. In front
of this surcoat two pocket-holes showed. This
surcoat was also fastened by a belt at the waist.

In common with the general feeling towards
more elaborate clothes, the shoes grew beyond
their normal shape, and now, no longer conforming

to the shape of the foot, they became elongated at the toes, and stuck out in a sharp point; this point was loose and soft, waiting for a future day when men should make it still longer and stuff it with tow and moss.

Of all the shapes of nature, no shape has been so marvellously maltreated as the human foot. It has suffered as no other portion of the body has suffered: it has endured exceeding length and exceeding narrowness; it has been swelled into broad, club-like shapes; it has been artificially raised from the ground, ended off square, pressed into tight points, curved under, and finally, as to-day, placed in hard, shining, tight leather boxes. All this has been done to one of the most beautiful parts of the human anatomy by the votaries of fashion, who have in turn been delighted to expose the curves of their bodies, the round swelling of their hips, the beauties of their nether limbs, the whiteness of their bosoms, the turn of their elbows and arms, and the rotundity of their shoulders, but who have, for some mysterious reasons, been for hundreds of years ashamed of the nakedness of their feet.

Let me give a wardrobe for a man of this time.

A hood with a cape to it; the peak of the hood made full, but about half a hand's breadth longer than necessary to the hood; the cape cut sometimes at the edge into a number of short slits.

A cap of soft stuff to fit the head, with or without an upturned brim. A fillet of silk or metal for the hair.

A gown made very loose and open at the neck, wide in the body, the sleeves loose or tight to the wrist. The gown long or short, on the ground or to the knee, and almost invariably belted at the waist by a long belt of leather with ornamental studs.

A surcoat split from shoulder to hem, or sewn up except for a wide armhole.

A coat shaped very slightly to the figure, having pocket-holes in front, small armholes, and a buttoned neck.

A great oblong-shaped piece of stuff for a cloak, or a heavy, round cloak with an attached hood.

Tights of cloth or sewn silk—that is, pieces of silk cut and sewn to the shape of the leg.

Shoes with long points—about 2 inches beyond the toes—fastened by a strap in front, or laced at the sides, or made to pull on and fit at the ankle, the last sometimes with a V-shaped piece cut away on either side.

There was a tendency to beads, and a universal custom of long hair.

In all such clothes as are mentioned above every rich stuff of cloth, silk, wool, and frieze may be used, and fur linings and fur hats are constant, as also are furred edges to garments.

There was a slight increase of heraldic ornament, and a certain amount of foreign diaper patterning on the clothes.

THE WOMEN

Now the lady must needs begin to repair the ravages of time and touch the cheek that no longer knows the bloom of youth with—rouge.

This in itself shows the change in the age. Since the Britons—poor, simple souls—had sought to embellish Nature by staining themselves blue with wode and yellow with ochre, no paint had touched the faces of the fashionable until this reign. Perhaps discreet historians had left that fact veiled, holding the secrets of the lady's toilet too sacred for the black of print; but now the murder came out. The fact in itself is part of the psychology of clothes. Paint the face, and you have a hint towards the condition of fashion.

Again, as in the case of the men, no determined cut shows which will point to this age as one of such and such a garment or such an innovation, but—and this I would leave to your imagination— there was a distinction that was not great enough to be a difference.

The gowns were loose and flowing, and were gathered in at the waist by a girdle, or, rather, a belt, the tongue of which hung down in front; but as the end of the reign approached, the gowns were shaped a little more to the figure.

A lady might possess such clothes as these: the gowns I have mentioned above, the sleeves of which were tight all the way from the shoulder to the wrist, or were loose and cut short just below the elbow, showing the tight sleeves of the under-gown.

Shoes very elaborately embroidered and pointed at the toes.

A rich cloak made oblong in shape and very ample in cut.

A shaped mantle with strings to hold it together over the shoulders.

For the head a wimple made of white linen or perhaps of silk ; this she would put above her head, leaving the neck bare.

A long belt for her waist, and, if she were a great lady, a pair of gloves to wear or stick into her belt.

THE COUNTRY FOLK

From the Conquest to the reign of Edward I.

UNTIL the present day the countryman has dressed in a manner most fitted to his surroundings; now the billycock hat, a devil-derived offspring from a Greek source, the Sunday suit of shiny black with purple trousers, the satin tie of Cambridge blue, and the stiff shirt, have almost robbed the peasant of his poetical appearance.

Civilization seems to have arrived at our villages with a pocketful of petty religious differences, a bagful of public-houses, a bundle of penny and halfpenny papers full of stories to show the fascination of crime, and—these Sunday clothes.

A MAN OF THE TIME OF HENRY III.   1216-1272

A WOMAN OF THE TIME OF HENRY III.   1216-1272

The week's workdays still show a sense of the picturesque in corduroys and jerseys or blue shirts, but the landscape is blotted with men wearing out old Sunday clothes, so that the painter of rural scenes with rural characters must either lie or go abroad.

As for the countrywoman, she, I am thankful to say, still retains a sense of duty and beauty, and, except on Sunday, remains more or less respectably clad. Chivalry prevents one from saying more.

In the old days—from the Conquest until the end of the thirteenth century —the peasant was dressed in perfect clothes.

The villages were self-providing; they grew by then wool and hemp for the spindles. From this was made yarn for materials to be made up into coats and shirts. The homespun frieze that the peasant wore upon his back was hung by the nobleman upon his walls. The village bootmaker made, besides skin sandals to be tied with thongs upon the feet, leather trousers and belts.

The mole-catcher provided skin for hats. Hoods

of a plain shape were made from the hides of sheep or wolves, the wool or hair being left on the hood. Cloaks lined with sheepskin served to keep away the winter cold.

To protect their legs from thorns the men wore bandages of twisted straw wrapped round their trousers, or leather thongs cross-gartered to the knee.

The fleece of the sheep was woven in the summer into clothes of wool for the winter. Gloves were made, at the beginning of the thirteenth century, of wool and soft leather; these were shaped like the modern baby's glove, a pouch for the hand and fingers and a place for the thumb.

A coarse shirt was worn, over which a tunic, very loosely made, was placed, and belted at the waist. The tunic hardly varied in shape from the Conquest to the time of Elizabeth, being but a sack-like garment with wide sleeves reaching a little below the elbow. The hood was ample and the cloak wide.

The women wore gowns of a like material to the men—loose gowns which reached to the ankles and gave scope for easy movement. They wore their hair tied up in a wimple of coarse linen.

The people of the North were more ruggedly clothed than the Southerners, and until the monks founded the sheep-farming industry in Yorkshire the people of those parts had no doubt to depend for their supply of wool upon the more cultivated peoples.

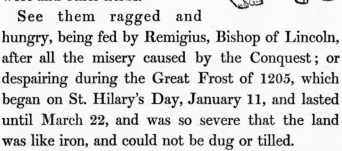

Picture these people, then, in very simple natural wool-coloured dresses going about their ordinary country life, attending their bees, their pigs, sheep, and cattle, eating their kele soup, made of cole-wort and other herbs.

See them ragged and hungry, being fed by Remigius, Bishop of Lincoln, after all the misery caused by the Conquest; or despairing during the Great Frost of 1205, which began on St. Hilary's Day, January 11, and lasted until March 22, and was so severe that the land was like iron, and could not be dug or tilled.

When better days arrived, and farming was taken more seriously by the great lords, when Grosseteste, the Bishop of Lincoln, wrote his book on farming and estate management for Margaret, the Dowager-

Countess of Lincoln, then clothes and stuffs manufactured in the towns became cheaper and more easy to obtain, and the very rough skin clothes and undressed hides began to vanish from among the clothes of the country, and the rough gartered trouser gave way before cloth cut to fit the leg.

On lord and peasant alike the sun of this early age sets, and with the sunset comes the warning bell—the *couvre-feu*—so, on their beds of straw-covered floors, let them sleep. . . .

EDWARD THE FIRST

Reigned thirty-five years : 1272—1307.
Born 1239.   Married, 1254, Eleanor of Castile ;
    1299, Margaret of France.

MEN AND WOMEN

UNTIL the performance of the Sherborne Pageant,
I had never had the opportunity of seeing a mass
of people, under proper, open-air conditions, dressed
in the peasant costume of Early England.

For once traditional stage notions of costume
were cast aside, and an attempt was made, which
was perfectly successful, to dress people in the
colours of their time.

The mass of simple colours—bright reds, blues,
and greens—was a perfect expression of the date,
giving, as nothing else could give, an appearance of
an illuminated book come to life.

One might imagine that such a primary-coloured
crowd would have appeared un-English, and too

Oriental or Italian ; but with the background of
trees and stone walls, the English summer sky
distressed with clouds, the moving cloud shadows
and the velvet grass, these fierce hard colours
looked distinctly English, undoubtedly of their
date, and gave the spirit of the ages, from a clothes
point of view, as no other colours could have done.
In doing this they attested to the historical truth
of the play.

It seemed natural to see an English crowd
one blazing jewel-work of colour, and, by the
excellent taste and knowledge of the designer,
the jewel-like hardness of colour was consistently
kept.

It was interesting to see the difference made to
this crowd by the advent of a number of monks
in uniform black or brown, and to see the setting
in which these jewel-like peasants shone — the
play of brilliant hues amid the more sombre
browns and blacks, the shifting of the blues
and reds, the strong notes of emerald green
— all, like the symmetrical accidents of the
kaleidscope, settling into their places in perfect
narmony.

The entire scene bore the impress of the spirit

of historical truth, and it is by such pageants that we can imagine coloured pictures of an England of the past.

Again, we could observe the effect of the light-reflecting armour, cold, shimmering steel, coming in a play of colour against the background of peasants, and thereby one could note the exact appearance of an ordinary English day of such a date as this of which I now write, the end of the thirteenth century.

The mournful procession bearing the body of Queen Eleanor of Castile, resting at Waltham, would show a picture in the same colours as the early part of the Sherborne Pageant.

Colour in England changed very little from the Conquest to the end of the reign of Edward I.; the predominant steel and leather, the gay, simple colours of the crowds, the groups of one colour, as of monks and men-at-arms, gave an effect of constantly changing but ever uniform colours and designs of colour, exactly, as I said before, like the shifting patterns of the kaleidoscope.

It was not until the reign of Edward II. that the effect of colour changed and became pied, and later, with the advent of stamped velvets, heavily

designed brocades, and the shining of satins, we
get that general effect best recalled to us by
memories of Italian pictures ; we get, as it were,
a varnish of golden-brown over the crude beauties
of the earlier times.

It is intensely important to a knowledge of
costume to remember the larger changes in the
aspect of crowds from the colour point of view.
A knowledge of history—by which I do not mean
a parrot-like acquirement of dates and Acts of
Parliament, but an insight into history as a living
thing—is largely transmitted to us by pictures ;
and, as pictures practically begin for us with the
Tudors, we must judge of coloured England from
illuminated books. In these you will go from
white, green, red, and purple, to such colours as
I have just described : more vivid blues, reds, and
greens, varied with brown, black, and the colour of
steel, into the chequered pages of pied people and
striped dresses, into rich-coloured people, people
in black ; and as you close the book and arrive at
the wall-picture, back to the rich-coloured people
again.

The men of this time, it must be remembered,
were more adapted to the arts of war than to those

of peace; and the knight who was up betimes and
into his armour, and to bed early, was not a man
of so much leisure that he could stroll about in
gay clothes of an inconvenient make. His principal
care was to relieve himself of his steel burden and
get into a loose gown, belted at the waist, over

which, if the weather was inclement, he would
wear a loose coat. This coat was made with a
hood attached to it, very loose and easy about the
neck and very wide about the body; its length
was a matter of choice, but it was usual to wear
it not much below the knees. The sleeves were
also wide and long, having at a convenient place

a hole cut, through which the arms could be placed.

The men wore their hair long and brushed out about the ears—long, that is, to the nape of the neck. They also were most commonly bearded, with or without a moustache.

Upon their heads they wore soft, small hats, with a slight projection at the top, the brim of the hat turned up, and scooped away in front.

Fillets of metal were worn about the hair with some gold-work upon them to represent flowers; or they wore, now and again, real chaplets of flowers.

There was an increase of heraldic ornament in this age, and the surcoats were often covered with a large device.

These surcoats, as in the previous reign, were split from shoulder to bottom hem, or were sewn up below the waist; for these, thin silk, thick silk (called samite), and sendal, or thick stuff, was used, as also for the gowns.

The shoes were peaked, and had long toes, but nothing extravagant, and they were laced on the outside of the foot. The boots came in a peak up to the knee.

The peasant was still very Norman in appearance, hooded, cloaked, with ill-fitting tights and clumsy shoes; his dress was often of bright colours on festivals, as was the gown and head-hankerchief of his wife.

Thus you see that, for ordinary purposes, a man dressed in some gown which was long, loose, and comfortable, the sleeves of it generally tight for freedom, so that they did not hang about his arm, and his shoes, hat, cloak, everything, was as soft and free as he could get them.

The woman also followed in the lines of comfort: her under-gown was full and slack at the waist, the sleeves were tight, and were made to unbutton from wrist to elbow; they stopped short at the wrist with a cuff.

Her upper gown had short, wide sleeves, was fastened at the back, and was cut but roughly to the figure. The train of this gown was very long.

They sought for comfort in every particular but one: for though I think the gorget very becoming, I think that it must have been most distressing to wear. This gorget was a piece of white linen wrapped about the throat, and pinned into its place; the ends were brought up to meet a wad of hair over the ears and there fastened, in this way half framing the face.

The hair was parted in the middle, and rolled over pads by the ears, so as to make a cushion

on which to pin the gorget. This was the general fashion.

Now, the earlier form of head-dress gave rise to another fashion. The band which had been tied round the head to keep the wimple in place was enlarged and stif-

fened with more material, and so became a round linen cap, wider at the top than at the bottom. Sometimes this cap was hollow-crowned, so that it was possible to bring the wimple under the chin, fasten it into place with the cap, and allow it to fall over the top of the cap in folds; sometimes the cap was solidly crowned, and was pleated; sometimes the cap met the gorget, and no hair showed between them.

What we know as 'the true lovers' knot' was

sometimes used as an ornament sewn on to dresses
or gowns.

You may know the effigy of Queen Eleanor
in Westminster Abbey, and if you do, you will
see an example of the very plainest dress of the
time. She has a shaped mantle over her shoulders,
which she is holding together by a strap; the long
mantle or robe
is over a plain,
loosely - pleated
gown, which fits
only at the shoul-
ders; her hair is
unbound, and she
wears a trefoil
crown upon her
head.

The changes in
England can best be seen by such monuments
as Edward caused to be erected in memory of his
beloved wife. The arts of peace were indeed magnificent, and though the knight was the man of war,
he knew how to choose his servant in the great arts.

Picture such a man as Alexander de Abyngdon,
'le Imaginator,' who with William de Ireland

carved the statues of the Queen for five marks each—such a man, with his gown hitched up into his belt, his hood back on his shoulders, watching his statue put into place on the cross at Charing. He is standing by Roger de Crundale, the architect of that cross, and he is directing the workmen who are fixing the statue. . . . A little apart you may picture Master William Tousell, goldsmith, of London, a very important person, who is making a metal statue of the Queen and one of her father-in-law, Henry III., for Westminster Abbey. At the back men and women in hoods and wimples, in short tunics and loose gowns. A very brightly-coloured picture, though the dyes of the dresses be faded by rain and sun—they are the finer colours for that: Master Tousell, no doubt, in a short tunic for riding, with his loose coat on him, the heavy hood back, a little cap on his head; the workmen with their tunics off, a twist of coloured stuff about their waists, their heads bare.

It is a beautiful love-story this, of fierce Edward, the terror of Scotland, for Eleanor, whom he 'cherished tenderly,' and 'whom dead we do not cease to love.'

A MAN AND WOMAN OF THE TIME OF EDWARD I.   1272-1307

A MAN AND WOMAN OF THE TIME OF EDWARD II. 1307-1327

The same man, who could love so tenderly and well, who found a fantastic order of chivalry in the Round Table of Kenilworth, could there swear on the body of a swan the death of Comyn, Regent of Scotland, and could place the Countess of Buchan, who set the crown upon the head of Bruce, in a cage outside one of the towers of Berwick.

Despite the plain cut of the garments of this time, and the absence of superficial trimmings, it must have been a fine sight to witness one hundred lords and ladies, all clothed in silk, seated about the Round Table of Kenilworth.

EDWARD THE SECOND

Reigned twenty years : 1307—1327.
Born 1284.   Married, 1308, Isabella of France.

MEN AND WOMEN

WHETHER the changes in costume that took place
in this reign were due to enterprising tailors, or to
an exceptionally hot summer, or to the fancy of
the King, or to the sprightliness of Piers Gaveston,
it is not possible to say.   Each theory is arguable,
and, no doubt, in some measure each theory is
right, for, although men followed the new new
mode, ladies adhered to their earlier fashions.

Take the enterprising tailor—call him an artist.
The old loose robe was easy of cut; it afforded no
outlet for his craft; it cut into a lot of material,
was easily made at home—it was, in fact, a baggy
affair that fitted nowhere.   Now, is it not possible
that some tailor-artist, working upon the vanity of
a lordling who was proud of his figure, showed how

he could present this figure to its best advantage
in a body-tight garment which should reach only
to his hips?

Take the hot summer. You may or may not
know that a hot summer some years ago suddenly
transformed the City of London from a place of
top-hats and black coats into
a place of flannel jackets and
hats of straw, so that it is now
possible for a man to arrive at
his City office clad according
to the thermometer, without
incurring the severe dis-
pleasure of the Fathers of the
City.

It seems that somewhere
midway between 1307 and
1327 men suddenly dropped
their long robes, loosely tied at the waist, and
appeared in what looked uncommonly like vests,
and went by the name of 'cotehardies.'

It must have been surprising to men who
remembered England clothed in long and decorous
robes to see in their stead these gay, debonair,
tight vests of pied cloth or parti-coloured silk.

Piers Gaveston, the gay, the graceless but graceful favourite, clever at the tournament, warlike and vain, may have instituted this complete revolution in clothes with the aid of the weak King.

Sufficient, perhaps, to say that, although long

robes continued to be worn, cotehardies were all the fashion.

There was a general tendency to exaggeration. The hood was attacked by the dandies, and, instead of its modest peak, they caused to be added a long pipe of the material, which they called a ' liripipe.'

Every quaint thought and invention for tieing up this liripipe was used: they wound it about their heads, and tucked the end into the coil; they put it about their necks, and left the end dangling ; they rolled it on to the top of their heads.

The countryman, not behindhand in quaint ideas, copied the form of a Bishop's hood, and appeared with his cloth hood divided into two peaks, one on either side of his head.

This new cotehardie was cut in several ways. Strictly speaking, it was a cloth or silk vest, tight to the body, and close over the hips ; the length was determined by the fancy of the wearer. It also had influence on the long robes still worn, which, although full below the waist to the feet, now more closely fitted the body and shoulders.

The fashionable sleeves were tight to the elbow, and from there hanging and narrow, showing a sleeve belonging to an undergarment.

The cloak also varied in shape. The heavy travelling-cloak, with the hood attached, was of the old pattern, long, shapeless, with or without hanging sleeves, loose at the neck, or tightly buttoned.

Then there was a hooded cloak, with short sleeves, or with the sleeves cut right away, a sort of hooded surcoat. Then there were tow distinct

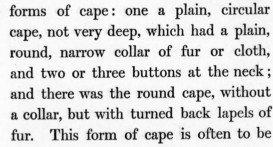

 forms of cape: one a plain, circular cape, not very deep, which had a plain, round, narrow collar of fur or cloth, and two or three buttons at the neck; and there was the round cape, without a collar, but with turned back lapels of fur. This form of cape is often to be seen.

The boots and shoes were longer at the toes, and were sometimes buttoned at the sides.

The same form of hats remain, but these were now treated with fur brims.

Round the waist there was always a belt, generally of plain black leather; from it depended a triangular pouch, through which a dagger was sometimes stuck.

The time of parti-coloured clothes was just beginning, and the cotehardie was often made from two coloured materials, dividing the body in

two parts by the colour difference ; it
was the commencement of the age
which ran its course during the next
reign, when men were striped diagonally, vertically, and in angular bars ;
when one leg was blue and the other
red.

You will note that all work was
improving in this reign when you hear
that the King paid the wife of John
de Bureford 100 marks for an embroidered cope, and that a great green
hanging was procured for King's Hall,
London, for solemn feasts—a hanging

of wool, worked with figures of kings
and beasts. The ladies made little
practical change in their dress, except
to wear an excess of clothes against the
lack of draperies indulged in by the
men.

It is possible to see three garments,
or portions of them, in many dresses.

First, there was a stuff gown, with tight
sleeves buttoned to the elbow from the wrist ;
this sometimes showed one or two buttons under

7

the gorget in front, and was fitted, but not tightly,
to the figure. It fell in pleated folds to the feet,
and had a long train; this was worn alone, we
may suppose, in summer. Second, there was a
gown to go over this other, which had short, wide
sleeves, and was full in the skirts. One or other

of these gowns
had a train, but if
the upper gown
had a train the
under one had
not, and *vice
versâ*. Third,
there was a surcoat like to a man's, not over-long
or full, with the sleeve-holes cut out wide; this
went over both or either of the other gowns.

Upon the head they wore the wimple, the fillet,
and about the throat the gorget.

The arrangement of the wimple and fillet were
new, for the hair was now plaited in two tails, and

these brought down straight on either side of the face; the fillet was bound over the wimple in order to show the plait, and the gorget met the wimple behind the plait instead of over it.

The older fashion of hair-dressing remained, and the gorget was pinned to the wads of hair over the ears, without the covering of the wimple.

Sometimes the fillet was very wide, and placed low on the head over a wimple tied like a gorget; in this way the two side-plaits showed only in front and appeared covered at side-face, while the wimple and broad fillet hid all the top hair of the head.

Very rarely a tall, steeple head-dress was worn over the wimple, with a hanging veil; but this was not common, and, indeed, it is not a mark of the time, but belongs more properly to a later date. However, I have seen such a head-dress drawn at or about this time, so must include it.

The semicircular mantle was still in use, held over the breast by means of a silk cord.

It may seem that I describe these garments in too simple a way, and the rigid antiquarian would have made comment on courtepys, on gamboised garments, on cloth of Gaunt, or cloth of Dunster.

7—2

I may tell you that a gambeson was the quilted tunic worn under armour, and, for the sake of those whose tastes run into the arid fields of such research, that you may call it wambasium, gobison, wambeys, gambiex, gaubeson, or half a dozen other names; but, to my mind, you will get no further with such knowledge.

Falding is an Irish frieze; cyclas is a gown; courtepy is a short gown; kirtle—again, if we know too much we cannot be accurate—kirtle may be a loose gown, or an apron, or a jacket, or a riding-cloak.

The tabard was an embroidered surcoat—that is, a surcoat on which was displayed the heraldic device of the owner.

Let us close this reign with its mournful end, when Piers Gaveston feels the teeth of the Black Dog of Warwick, and is beheaded on Blacklow Hill; when Hugh le Despenser is hanged on a gibbet; when the Queen lands at Orwell, conspiring against her husband, and the King is a prisoner at Kenilworth.

Here at Kenilworth the King hears himself deposed.

'Edward, once King of England,' is hereafter

accounted 'a private person, without any manner of royal dignity.'

Here Edward, in a plain black gown, sees the steward of his household, Sir Thomas Blount, break his staff of office, done only when a King is dead, and discharge all persons engaged in the royal service.

Parliament decided to take this strong measure in January ; in the following September Edward was murdered in cold blood at Berkeley Castle.

EDWARD THE THIRD

Reigned fifty years: 1327—1377.
Born 1312.   Married, 1328, Philippa of Hainault.

THE MEN

KINGS were Kings in those days; they managed England as a nobleman managed his estates.

Edward I., during the year 1299, changed his abode on an average three times a fortnight, visiting in one year seventy-five towns and castles.

Edward II. increased his travelling retinue until, in the fourth year of the reign of Edward III., the crowd who accompanied that King had grown to such proportions that he was forced to introduce a law forbidding knights and soldiers to bring their wives and families with them.

Edward III., with his gay company, would not be stopped as he rode out of one of the gates of London to pay toll of a penny a cart and a farthing a horse, nor would any of his train.

This toll, which included threepence a week on gravel and sand carts going in or out of the City, was raised to help pay for street repairs, the streets and roads of that time being in a continual state of slush, mud, and pits of water.

Let us imagine Edward III. and his retinue passing over Wakefield Bridge before he reduced his enormous company.

The two priests, William Kaye and William Bull, stand waiting for the King outside the new Saint Mary's Chapel. First come the guard of four-and-twenty archers in the King's livery; then a Marshal and his servants (the other King's Marshal has ridden by some twenty-four hours ago); then comes the Chancellor and his clerks, and with them a good horse carrying the Rolls (this was stopped in the fourth year of Edward's reign); then they see the Chamberlain, who will look to it that the King's rooms are decent and in order, furnished with benches and carpets; next comes the Wardrobe Master, who keeps the King's accounts; and, riding beside the King, the first personal officer of the kingdom, the Seneschal; after that a gay company of knights and their ladies, merchants, monks dressed as ordinary laymen for travelling, soldiers of fortune, women, beggars, minstrels—a motley gang of brightly-clothed people, splashed with the mud and dust of the cavalcade.

Remembering the condition of the day, the rough travelling, the estates far apart, the dirty

inns, one must not imagine this company spick and span.

The ladies are riding astride, the gentlemen are in civil garments or half armour.

Let us suppose that it is summer, and but an hour or so after a heavy shower. The heat is oppressive: the men have slung their hats at their belts, and have pushed their hoods from their heads; their heavy cloaks, which they donned hastily against the rain, are off now, and hanging across their saddles.

These cloaks vary considerably in shape. Here we may see a circular cloak, split down the right

side from the neck, it buttons on the shoulder. Here is another circular cloak, jagged at the edge; this buttons at the neck. One man is riding in a cloak, parti-coloured, which is more like a gown, as it has a hood attached to it, and reaches down to his feet.

Nearly every man is alike in one respect—clean-shaven, with long hair to his neck, curled at the ears and on the forehead.

Most men wear the cotehardie, the well-fitting garment buttoned down the front, and ending over the hips. There is every variety of cotehardie—the long one, coming nearly to the knees; the short one, half-way up the thigh. Some are buttoned all the way down the front,

and others only with two or three buttons at the neck.

Round the hips of every man is a leather belt, from which hangs a pouch or purse.

Some of these purses are beautiful with stitched arabesque designs; some have silver and enamel clasps; some are plain black cloth or natural-coloured leather; nearly all, however, are black.

The hoods over the men's heads vary in a number of ways: some are very full in the cape, which is jagged at the hem; some are close about the neck and are plain; some have long liripipes falling from the peak of the hood, and others have a liripipe of medium length.

There are two or three kinds of hat worn, and felt and fur caps of the usual shape—round, with a rolled-up brim and a little peak on the top. Some of the hats are tall-crowned, round hats with a close, thick brim—these have strings through the brim so that the hat may be strung on the belt when it is not in use; other hats are of the long, peaked shape, and now and again one may see a feather stuck into them; a third variety shows the brim of a high-crowned hat, castellated.

Among the knights you will notice the general tendency to parti-coloured clothes, not only divided completely into halves of two colours, but striped diagonally, vertically, and horizontally, so giving a very diverse appearance to the mass of colour.

Here and there a man is riding in his silk surcoat, which is embroidered with his coat of arms or powdered with his badge.

Here are cloth, velvet, silk, and woollen stuffs, all of fine dyes, and here is some fine silk cotehardie with patterns upon it gilt in gold leaf, and there is a magnificent piece of stuff, rich in design, from the looms of Palermo.

Among the merchants we shall see some more sober colours and quieter cut of clothes; the archers in front are in leather tunics, and these quiet colours in front, and the respectable merchants behind, enclose the brilliant blaze of colour round the King.

Behind all come the peasants, minstrels, mummers, and wandering troupes of acrobats; here is a bearward in worn leather cloak and hood, his legs strapped at the ankle, his shoes tied on with thongs; here is a woman in a hood, open at the neck and short at the back: she wears a smocked apron; here is a beggar with a hood of black stuff over his head—a hood with two peaks, one on either side of his head; and again, here is a minstrel with a patched round cloak, and a mummer with a two-peaked hood, the peaks stuffed out stiff, with bells jangling on the points of them.

Again, among this last group, we must notice the old-fashioned loose tunics, the coif over the head, tied under the chin, wooden-soled shoes and pouch-gloves.

There are some Norfolk merchants and some

merchants from Flanders among the crowd, and they talk as best they can in a sort of French-Latin-English jargon among themselves; they speak of England as the great wool-producing country, the tax on which produced £30,000 in one year; they talk of the tax, its uses and abuses, and how

Norfolk was proved the richest county in wool by
the tax of 1341.

The people of England little thought to hear
artillery used in a field of battle so soon as 1346,
when on August 26 it was used for the first time,
nor did they realize the horrors that were to come
in 1349, when the Great Plague was to
sweep over England and kill half the
population.

There is one man in this crowd who
has been marked by everybody. He is
a courtier, dressed in the height of
fashion. His cotehardie fits him very
well: the sleeves are tight from elbow
to wrist, as are the sleeves of most of
his fellows—some, however, still wear
the hanging sleeve and show an under-
sleeve—and his sleeve is buttoned from wrist to
elbow. He wears the newest fashion upon his arm,
the tippet, a piece of silk which is made like a
detachable cuff with a long streamer hanging from
it: his cotehardie is of medium length, jagged
at the bottom, and it is of the finest Sicilian
silk, figured with a fine pattern; round his hips
he wears a jewelled belt. His hood is parti-

coloured and jagged at the edge and round his face, and his liripipe is very long. His tights are parti-coloured, and his shoes, buttoned up the front, are long-toed and are made of red-and-white chequered leather. By him rides a knight, also in the height of fashion, but less noticeable: he has his cotehardie skirt split up in front and

turned back; he has not any buttons on his sleeves, and his belt about his waist holds a large square pouch; his shoes are a little above his ankles, and are buckled over the instep. His hair is shorter than is usual, and it is not curled.

As we observe these knights, a party of armed knights come riding down the road towards the cavalcade; they have come to greet the King.

These men have ridden through the rain, and

now, as they come closer, one can see that their armour is already red with rust.

So the picture should remain on your mind, as I have imagined it for you: the knights in armour and surcoats covered with their heraldic device; the archers; the gay crowd of knights in parti-coloured clothes; the King, in his cotehardie of plain black velvet and his black beaver hat, just as he looked after Calais in later years; the merchants; the servants in parti-coloured liveries of their masters' colours; the tattered crowd behind; and, with the aid of the drawings, you should be able to visualize the picture.

Meanwhile Edward will arrive at his destination, and to soothe him before sleep, he will read out of the book of romances, illustrated by Isabella, the nun of Aumbresbury, for which he had paid £66 13s. 4d., which sum was heavy for those days, when £6 would buy twenty-four swans. £66 13s. 4d. is about £800 of our money to-day.

THE WOMEN

'I looked on my left half as the lady taught me,
And was aware of a woman worthily clothed,
Trimmed with fur, the finest on earth,
Crowned with a crown, the King had none better.
Handsomely her fingers were fretted with gold wire,
And thereon red rubies, as red as any hot coal,
And diamonds of dearest price, and double manner of
    sapphires,
Orientals and green beryls. . . .
Her robe was full rich, of red scarlet fast dyed,
With bands of red gold and of rich stones;
Her array ravished me, such richness saw I never'

Piers the Plowman.

There are two manuscripts in existence the illuminations in which give the most wonderfully pictorial idea of this time; they are the manuscript marked MS. Bodl., Misc. 264, in the Bodleian Library at Oxford, and the Loutrell Psalter in the British Museum.

The Loutrell Psalter is, indeed, one of the most notable books in the world; it is an example of illumination at the height of that art; it has for illustrator a person, not only of a high order of intelligence, but a person possessed of the very

A MAN OF THE TIME OF EDWARD III. 1327-1377

A WOMAN OF THE TIME OF EDWARD III.   1327-1377

spirit of Gothic humour, who saw rural England, not only with the eyes of an artist, but with the eyes of a gossiping philosopher.

Both this book and the book in the Bodleian Library were illustrated by persons who were charged to the brim with the spirit of their age; they were Chaucerian in their gay good-humour and in their quaint observation, and they have that moral knowledge and outspoken manner which characterize William Langland, whose 'Piers the Plowman' I have quoted above.

With Chaucer, Langland, and these illuminators we have a complete exhibition of English life of these times. The pulse of rural England is felt by them in a most remarkable way; the religion, language, thought, politics, the whole trend of rural, provincial, and Court life may be gathered from their books.

The drawings in the Loutrell Psalter were completed before the year 1340, and they give us all that wonderful charm, that intimate knowledge, which we enjoy in the 'Canterbury Pilgrims' and the 'Vision of Piers Plowman.'

There seems to be something in road-travelling which levels all humanity: there is no road in

England which does not throb with history ; there
is no poem or story written about roads in England
which does not in some way move the Englishness
in us.   Chaucer and Langland make comrades of
us as they move along the highway, and with them
we meet, on terms of intimacy, all the characters of
the fourteenth century.   With these illuminators
of the Loutrell Psalter and the Bodleian MS. we
see actually the stream of English life along a
crowded thoroughfare.

In these books we may see drawings of every
form of agricultural life and manorial existence : we
see the country sports, the bear-baiting, and the
cock-fighting ; we see the harvesters with straw
hats, scythes, and reaping-hooks ; we see carters,
carriers, and great carriages, all depicted in a manner
which we can only compare, in later years, to the
broad humour of Hogarth ; and, as we turn the
priceless pages over, the whole fourteenth-century
world passes before our eyes—japers and jugglers ;
disours and jesters ; monk, priest, pilgrim, and
pardoner ; spendthrift and wench ; hermits, good
and evil ; lords, ladies, and Kings.

I have written of the men and their dress—how
they were often—very often—dirty, dusty, and

travel-stained—of the red-rusted armour and the striped and chequered clothes, and now I must write of the women and the manner of their dress.

Of the time, you must remember that it was the time of chivalry, when there was a Round Table of Knights at Windsor, founded in 1345; when the Order of the Garter was founded; when tiltings and all manner of tournaments were at their height; and you listen to the minstrels of King Edward's household playing upon the trumpet, the cytole, the pipe, the taberet, the clarion, and the fiddle.

St. George, the Primate of Egypt in the fourth century, had now risen to public esteem and notice, so that he became in this time not only the patron saint of chivalry, but the tutelar saint of England.

Boys were taken from the care of the ladies of the household at the age of seven, when they became pages to knights, and were sworn to devote themselves to the graces and favours of some girl. At fourteen the boy became a squire, and at twenty-one, if he were possessed of a rental of £20 a year in land, he made his fast and vigil, and was afterward dubbed knight and given his spurs.

8—2

The noteworthy point about a woman of this reign was her hair. The Queen herself wore an elaborate mode of coiffure for that time ; she wore **a**

metal fillet round her head, to which was attached two cases, circular in shape, of gold fretwork, ornamented with precious stones. She wore her hair unplaited, and brought in two parts from the back of her head, and as far as one can see, pushed into the jewelled cases.

The most general form of hair-dressing was an excess on the mode of the previous reign, a richness of jewel-work, an abundance of gold wire. It was usual to divide the hair into two plaits, and arrange these on either side of the face, holding them in their place by means of a fillet; they might be worn folded straight up by the face, or at an angle, but they were never left hanging; if hair was left loose it was not plaited, but flowing.

The gorget, or throat cloth, was still in general use, and it was attached to the hair by very elaborate-headed pins. Sometimes the hair, dressed with the gorget, was divided into four plaits, two on either side of the face, and fastened horizontally.

The wimple of silk or linen was very generally worn. A caul of gold net came into fashion, but not until the end of the reign. The ladies were great upon hunting and hawking, and this must have been a convenient fashion to keep the hair in order. Some wore a white silk or linen cap, so shaped as to include and cover the two side-plaits and combine a gorget and wimple in one. Pointed frontals of pearls were worn across the forehead,

and fillets of silk or linen were so tied that long ends hung down the back.

Yellow hair was much esteemed, and ladies who were not favoured by Nature, brought saffron to their aid, and by such efforts brought Nature into line with Art.

There was the general custom of wearing the surcoat in imitation of the men, a garment I have

described frequently—a slightly-fitting garment
without sleeves—you will see how this grew later
into a gorgeous affair. These surcoats
were sometimes of fine cloth of gold
covered with an intricate, delicate pattern in which beasts, birds, and foliage
mingled in arabesque. Under this surcoat was a plainer, better-fitting
garment, made sometimes of the barred
and rayed material so common to the
men, or of velvet, cloth, or silk, in
plain colours, green and red being then
very favourite ; ermines and many other furs were
used to border these gowns. Sometimes you may
see that this gown had sleeves short at the elbow,
exposing a different coloured under-sleeve, buttoned
from elbow to wrist ; at other times—in fact, among
all fashionable persons—the curious fashion of the
tippet, or long streamer, was worn. I have carefully described this fashion in the previous chapter.

The plain gown with tight sleeves was most in
use, and the skirts of this gown were very voluminous, and had either pockets or holes in the front of
them ; the holes enabled the wearer to reach the
purse hanging from a girdle which encircled the

waist of the under-dress. These gowns were generally buttoned in front, from neck to waist, or they were laced.

They also wore a heavier gown which reached just below the knee, showing the skirts of the under-gown; the heavy gowns were often fur-lined, and had loose wide sleeves to the elbow.

There was at this time a curious fur or cloth cape in use, longer behind than in front—in fact, it varied with the taste of the owner. It was cut in even scallops all round; I say even to show that they were sewn-edged, not jagged and rough-edged. Any pair of these scallops might be longer than any other pair. Ladies wore these capes for hunting, and ornamented the ends with bells.

The shoes of the women were not very exaggerated in length, but, as a rule, fitted well to the foot and came out in a slight point. You may use for this reign shoes buckled across the instep, laced at the side, or buttoned up the front.

For riding and sport the ladies wore the hood, and sometimes a broad round hat over it, or the peaked hat. The countrywoman wore an ill-fitting gown with tight sleeves, an apron, and an open hood.

Imagine London in the year of the third great pestilence, 1369. It is October, and the worst of the pestilence is over; John Chichester, the Mayor, is riding through the streets about some great affairs; many knights and ladies pass by. It is raining hard after the long drought of the summer, but, despite the rain, many citizens are abroad to see the doings in the City, and one may see the bright parti-coloured clothes of the lords and ladies, and here and there, as a cloak is blown back, a glimpse of rich-patterned cloth of gold.

Perhaps Will Langland—Long Will—a gaunt man of thirty-seven, is brushing past a young man of twenty-nine, Chaucer, going to his work.

Silk dresses and frieze gowns, velvet and home-spun, hurry along as the rain falls more heavily, and after a while the street becomes quite deserted. Then nothing but the dreary monotony of the rain falling from the gables will come to the room of the knight's lady as she lies sick of small-pox. John de Gaddesden, the King's doctor, has prescribed for her that she must lie clothed in scarlet red in a room of that colour, with bed-hangings of that same colour, and so she must lie, without much comfort, while the raindrops, falling down the wide chimney, drip on the logs in the fire and make them hiss.

RICHARD THE SECOND

Reigned twenty-two years: 1377—1399.
Born 1366.   Married, 1381, Anne of Bohemia;
1395, Isabella of France.

THE MEN

THE King himself was a leader of fashion; he had
by grace of Nature the form, face, and manner
which go to make a dandy.   The nobles followed
the King; the merchants followed the nobles after
their kind; the peasants were still clothed in the
simplest of garments, having retained the Norman
tunic with the sleeves pushed back over the wrist,
kept the loose boots and straw gaiters, and showed
the improvement in their class by the innovation
of gloves made as a thumb with a pouch for the
fingers, and pouches for money of cloth and leather
hung on a leather belt.   This proved the peasant
to be a man of some substance by need of his
wallet.   Everyone wore the chaperon—a cap and
cape combined.

We have now arrived at the reign which made
such a difference to the labourer and workman—
such as the blacksmith and miller—and in consequence altered and improved the character of
his clothes. The poll-tax of 1380 brought the
labourer into individual notice for the first time,
and thus arose the free labourer in England and
the first labour pamphlets.

We have two word-pictures of the times of the
greatest value, for they show both sides of the
coin: the one by the courtly and comfortable
Chaucer, the other by Long Will—William Langland, or Piers the Ploughman. Picture the two
along the Strand—Long Will singing his dirges
for hire, and Chaucer, his hand full of parchments,
bustling past.

One must remember that, as always, many
people dressed out of the fashion; that many men
still wore the cotehardie, a well-fitting garment
reaching half-way down the thigh, with tight
sleeves coming over the hand, decorated with
buttons under the sleeve from the elbow to the
little finger. This garment had a belt, which was
placed round the hips; and this was adorned in
many ways: principally it was composed of square

pieces of metal joined together, either of silver, or
enamel in copper, or of gold set with precious
stones.

The cotehardie was generally made of a pied
cloth in horizontal or diagonal bars, in silk or other
rich fabric. With this garment the
chaperon (to be more fully described)
was worn as a hood; the legs were in
tights, and the feet in pointed shoes a
little longer than the foot. A pouch or
wallet depended from the belt, and a
sheath containing two daggers, an anelace,
and a misericorde. The pouch was a
very rich affair, often of stamped gilded
leather or sewn velvet—ornamented, in
fact, according to the purse of the wearer. In winter
such a man as he of the cotehardie would wear an

overcoat with an attached
hood. This coat was
made in various forms:
one form with wide sleeves
the same width all the
way down, under which
were slits in the coat to enable the wearer to place
his hands inside, as in the modern Raglan coat-

pocket.   Another form was made very loose and
without sleeves, but with the same slits at the
side; it was buckled round the waist on occasion
by a broad leather belt, very
plain.   The common heavy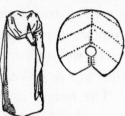
travelling-coat was made in
this way, and it was only the
very fashionable who wore
the houppelande for riding or
travelling.   Sometimes such a man would wear
in winter about the town a cloak fastened over
the right shoulder with three or four buttons,
leaving the right arm free; such a cloak is seen in
the brass of Robert Attelathe, Mayor of Lynn.

In travelling, our gentleman would wear, often
in addition to his chaperon, a peaked hat of cloth,
high in the crown, with a brim turned up all round,
ending in a long peak in front—the same hat that
we always associate with Dick Whittington.

His gloves would be of leather, often ornamented
with designs on the back, or, if he were a knight,
with his badge.

On this occasion he would wear his sword in a
baldric, a long belt over his right shoulder and
under his left arm, from which hung also his

daggers. Although I am not dealing even with personal arms, one must remember, in representing these people, that daggers were almost as necessary a part of dress as boots or shoes, and that personal comfort often depended upon a skilful use of that natty weapon ; the misericorde was used to give the *coup de grâce.*

The farmer in harvest-time wore, if he did not wear a hood, a peaked hat or a round, large-brimmed straw hat.

We may now arrive at the fashionable man, whose eccentricities in clothes were the object of

The Houppelande or Pelicon.

much comment. How the houppelande or peliçon actually was originated I do not know, but it came about that men suddenly began to clothe themselves in this voluminous and awkward garment. It was a long loose-fitting robe, made to fit on the shoulders only, having very long loose sleeves, varying according to the whim of the owner. These sleeves were

cut at the edges into the forms of leaves or
other designs, and were lined, as the houppelande,
with fur or silk. It will be seen that such a
garment to suit all weathers and temperatures
must be made of various materials and lined
accordingly. These materials were almost invariably powdered with badges or some other device,
sometimes with a flowing pattern embracing an
heraldic design or motto. The sleeves turned back
disclosed the sleeve of a cotehardie underneath,
with the little buttons running from the elbow to
the first knuckle of the little finger. The houppelande had a very high collar, coming well up to the
middle of the back of the head; it was buttoned up
to the chin in front, and the collar was often turned
down half-way, the two top buttons being left
undone. It was fastened about the middle by a
thin leather belt, very long; this was buckled, and
the long end turned under and brought over to
hang down; the end was ornamented with many
devices—figures of saints, heraldic figures, or other
ornaments. Sometimes the entire belt was sewn
with small devices in precious metal or enamels.

Now, to be in the height of fashion, one either
wore the houppelande extremely long in the skirt

or extremely short—so short, in fact, as to leave
but a frill of it remaining below the waist—leaving
the sleeves still their abnormal length.   Pretty
fads, as tying a dagger round the neck, or allowing
it to hang low between the legs, or placing it in
the small of the back, were much in vogue.

Every form of beard or moustache was used, and
the hair was worn long to the nape of the neck.
By the dandy it was elaborately pressed and curled
at the ends.   Bands of real or artificial flowers
encircled the heads of the dandies, the artificial
flowers made in enamels or gold.   Rings were
worn of great size on thumb and finger ; long staffs
with elaborate heads were carried.

Under the houppelande was the skirt and the
cotehardie of thin material, and on the legs hose,

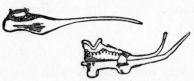

pied or powdered,
made of silk or cloth
cut to the form and
sewn.

The shoes were of great length, with long
points ; rarely we find examples of the absurd
fashion of wearing the points so long that they
were tied back to the knees, but often they were
so long that the points came out 6 inches beyond

A MAN OF THE TIME OF RICHARD II.   1377-1399

A WOMAN OF THE TIME OF RICHARD II.   1377-1399

the toe.   They were made of every material, sewn
with pearls on cloth or velvet, stamped with gold
on leather, or the leather raised.   The toes were
sometimes stuffed hard, sometimes allowed to hang
limp.

For walking in the streets high clogs of wood
were used, made with long pointed ends to support
the shoes.

I may add that the hose were gartered below the
knee to hold them taut with rich garters, but if a

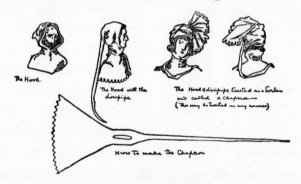

The Hood.

The Hood with the
dirigipe

The Hood & dirigipe Twisted as a Turban
and called   A Chaperon —
(This may be Twisted in any manner)

How to make The Chaperon

man were a Garter Knight he wore but the garter
of his Order.

Much in favour with this court of gallants were
rich chains about the neck, having for pendant
their badge or some saint's figure in gold or silver.

Now we come to the most interesting and

9

universal fashion of wearing the chaperon, which I am anxious to show in its various stages. It began with a cape and a hood worn separately; these were joined for convenience so that a man might put on both at once. This fashion held for many years, and then the fashionable man in search of novelty caused the peak of the hood to be lengthened until it grew to reach to his feet. Then he cast about for a fresh mode for his head-wear,

and so he twisted the whole affair about his head, leaving the end of the cape, which was jagged at the edge, protruding like a cockscomb. Time went on, and he avoided the trouble of tying this himself, so he had the hat made up all ready tied, much in the manner of a turban. Finally, the chaperon grew into disuse, and it remains to-day a curious reminder in the cockade worn by coachmen (it is almost a replica in miniature, with the round twist and the jagged edge sticking up above the hat) and on the cloaks of the Knights of the Garter, where it is carefully made, and forms a cape on the right shoulder, and in the present head - dress of the French lawyer, a relic of the Middle Ages.

The chains worn about the neck remain as badges of office in Mayors and Judges and in various Orders.

The button worn by the members of the Legion of Honour and other foreign Orders is, I believe, an idea resulting from the cockade, which, of course, was at the beginning the chaperon in the colours of the servant's lord.

When one knows a custom so well, one is apt to leave out many things in describing it. For example, the houppelande was open from the bottom of the skirt to the knee in front or at the side, and this opening was often cut or jagged into shapes ; also it was open all the way up the side of the leg, and from the neck to the breast, and buttoned over.

I have not remarked on the jester, a member of many households, who wore an exaggeration of the prevalent costume, to which bells were attached at all points.

9—2

So was much good cloth wasted in vanity, and much excellent time spent upon superfluities, to the harm of the people ; perhaps useful enough to please the eye, which must have been regaled with all these  men in wonderful colours, strutting peacockwise.

The poor peasant, who found cloth becoming very dear, cared not one jot or tittle for the feast of the eye, feeling a certain unreasonable hunger elsewhere.

And so over the wardrobe of Dandy Richard stepped Henry, backed by the people

THE WOMEN

If ever women were led by the nose by the demon of fashion it was at this time. Not only were their clothes ill-suited to them, but they abused that crowning glory, their hair.

No doubt a charming woman is always charming,

be she dressed by woad or worth; but to be
captivating with your eyebrows plucked out, and
with the hair that grows so prettily low on the
back of the neck
shaved away—was
it possible? I ex-
pect it was.

The days of high
hennins was yet to come; the day of simple hair-
dressing was nearly dead, and in the interval were
all the arts of the cunning devoted to the guimpe,

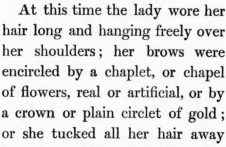 the gorgières, the mentonnières,
the voluminous escoffions.

At this time the lady wore her
hair long and hanging freely over
her shoulders; her brows were
encircled by a chaplet, or chapel
of flowers, real or artificial, or by
a crown or plain circlet of gold;
or she tucked all her hair away
under a tight caul, a bag of gold net enriched with
precious stones. To dress hair in this manner it
was first necessary to plait it in tight plaits and
bind them round the head, then to cover this with
a wimple, which fell over the back of the neck, and

over this to place the caul, or, as it was sometimes called, the dorelet. Now and again the caul
was worn without the wimple, and this left the

back of the neck ex-
posed; from this all the
hair was plucked.

For outdoor exercises
the lady would wear the chaperon (explained in the
previous chapter), and upon this the peaked hat.

The poorer woman wore always the hood, the
wimple tied under the chin, or plain plaited hair.

One must remember always
that the advance of costume
only affected the upper classes
in the towns, and that the
knight's lady in the country
was often fifty years behind
the times in her gowns. As an
instance of this I give the fur
tippet hung with bells, used
when hawking.

In the early part of the reign
the cotehardie was the universal woman's garment.
It was made in two ways: the one a simple, well-
fitting garment, skirts and bodice in one, buttoned

in front, with neck well open, the skirts ample and long, the sleeves over the hands to the first joints of the fingers, and ornamented with buttons from the elbow to the little finger—this was the general form of the garment for all degrees of rank. The lady enriched this with a belt like a man's, narrow in width round the waist with hanging end, or broad round the hips and richly ornamented. The other form of cotehardie was exactly as the man's, ending short below the hips, under which was worn the petticoat.

The winter addition to these was the surcoat (as usually worn by a knight over his armour); this was often lined with fur. The surcoat was a long garment without sleeves, and with a split down the sides from the shoulder to the top of the thigh; through this split was seen the cotehardie and the hip-belt. The edges were trimmed with fur, and very frequently ornamental buttons were worn down the front.

Over the shoulders was the cloak, left open in front, and fastened by means of a cord of rich substance passing through two loops in the backs of large ornamental studs ; this cord was, as a rule,

knotted at the waist, the ends hanging down as tassels.

Later in the reign, when the second Queen of Richard had brought over many rich fashions, the ladies adopted the houppe-lande, with its heavy collar and wide, hanging sleeves.

Every lady and most women carried a purse in the hand or on the girdle, ornamented according to their station.

The merchant's wife wore, in common with her maids, a white apron. The child who was spinning a peg-top in the street was simply dressed in a short-skirted cotehardie.

For riding and sport the woman was dressed almost exactly as a man—with houppelande or heavy cloak buttoned on the right shoulder, hawking-glove on her left hand with a bell or metal ball depending from it. She wore boots laced up at the side, or long boots of soft leather fastened with hook and eye; shoes like a man's, but not so pointed and extreme. Sometimes for riding a big round hat was worn over a hood.

In many cases the dresses were powdered with the monogram of the Blessed Virgin, with badges of the family or some small device, or they were ornamented with a simple flowing pattern, or were plain.

All the fripperies of fashion lay in pins for the wimple, the head made as a figure of a patron saint; or girdles rich with precious stones; or mirror-cases on whose ivory fronts were carved the Castle of Love, or hunting scenes, or Calvary. The clasps of purses were rich in design, and rings of every kind were worn on every finger and upon the thumb. Charms against evil were hung about the neck or sewn into the clothes. No matter who wrote, passed, and practised the many sumptuary laws, still, one may know it to have been frequent for persons owning less than £20 a year to wear gold and silver ornaments, although expressly forbidden, and ladies of a lower estate than wives of knights-banneret wore cloth of gold and velvet, and gowns that reached and trailed upon the ground, while their husbands braved it in ermine and marten-lined sleeves which swept the road.

The custom of wearing crowns was common to all people of rank, as heraldic distinction of crowns did not commence until the sixteenth century.

What a magnificent time for colour was this reign !—the rich houppelandes, the furs, the long-piked shoes with pearls and gold upon them, the massive chains about men's necks ; ladies whose heads shone with rich caps and cauls of pearl-embroidered gold, the rich-sheathed baselard stuck in the girdle or hanging from it on a silver chain. Even the poor begging friar was touched by all this finery, and, forgetful of the rules of Saint Francis, he made great haste to convert his alms into a furred cote 'cutted to the knee and quaintly buttoned, hose in hard weather fastened at the ankle, and buckled shoes.'

Imagine that amazing woman the Wife of Bath, in her great hat and pound-weight kerchief ; the carpenter's wife in her gored apron, at her girdle a purse of leather hanging, decorated with silk tassels and buttons of metal.

It is almost impossible to describe clearly the head-dresses—the great gold net bags which encased the hair—for they were ornamented in such different ways, always, or nearly always, following some pattern in diaper in contrast to the patterns which came later when the design followed such lines as are formed by wire-netting, while later still the connecting-thread of the patterns was done away with and the inside decoration alone remained.

Well, Richard the King no longer can whistle to Matthew, his favourite greyhound, and Anne the Queen lies stately in the Abbey at Westminster without solace of her little lap-dog; but we are not all modern in our ways, and ladies hang charms about them, from scarabs to queer evil eye coral hands, from silver shoes to month-stones. Crowns of flowers have been worn and crowns of jewels too, just as men and women wore them then, except on Fridays and the eves of fêtes.

These things we do, and other ancient things beside, but let us hope that Fashion has lost her cruel mood, and deems it wise to leave our ladies' eyebrows where they be, nor schemes to inspire her faithful devotees with mad desires to hide their hair and shave their napes.

The crinoline is threatened—let it come; sandals are here, with short hair and the simple life, but leave me, I pray thee, royal dame, an eyebrow on my lady, if only to give occupation to the love-lorn sonneteer.

THE END OF THE FOURTEENTH CENTURY

Chaucer.

IN the last year of the fourteenth century there were still living two men whose voices have made the century live for us. One of them —Chaucer—remains to-day the father of English poetry, the forerunner of Shakespeare ; the other —Gower—less known to most of us, was the author of three long poems—'Speculum Meditantis,' in French; 'Vox Clamantis,' in Latin 'Confessio Amantis,' in English. Boccaccio had written his ' Decameron,' and it was this method of writing a series of poems or stories by means of connecting-links of narrative that should run through the series, that inspired the form of the ' Confessio Amantis ' and the ' Canterbury Tales '; indeed, many stories in both of these works are retold out of the ' Decameron.'

Gower wrote of his age as a man giving advice, philosophically; he did not attempt character studies, but framed his poems as narratives with morals fit for application to his times.

Chaucer drew his characters clearly—so clearly that they have become as living as have Uncle Toby or Mrs. Gamp—symbolic people, embracing a type of national character.

A third writer—Langland—pictured his age from the poor man's point of view, and the three writers, together with the artist of the Louttrell Psalter, bring the age most vividly to our eyes.

Of course, in these days of hasty work, it seems hardly feasible to suggest that artists who would illustrate these times should read the works of these three men, and go to the British Museum to look at the Psalter; but any writer must do this, and can do this, considering that the works of the poets are cheap to obtain and the British British Museum is free to all.

Anyone wishing to picture these times will find that Chaucer has written very carefully of the costume of his Pilgrims. They will find the pith of the costume in this book of mine; but since no book is complete in every sense, they should see for themselves how men of the day drew the costume they saw about them. It will give them a sense of the spirit of the age which so many modern drawings lack.

I give you Gower's picture of an exquisite; no words of mine could show so well the manner of the man :

> ' And therof thenketh he but a lite,
> For all his lust is to delite
> In newé thingés, proude and veine,
> Als ferforth as he may atteine.
> I trowe, if that he mighté make
> His body newe, he woldé take
> A newé form and leve his olde.
> For what thing that he may behold
> The which to common use is straunge,
> Anone his oldé guisé chaunge
> He woll, and fallé therupon
> Lich unto the camelion,
> Whiche upon every sondry hewe
> That he beholt he moté newe
> His coloun ; and thus unavised
> Full ofté time he stand desguised.
> More jolif than the brid in Maie,
> He maketh him ever fressh and gaie
> And doth all his array desguise,
> So that of him the newé guise
> Of lusty folke all other take.'

Now, if I have described the costume of these times clearly—and I think I have done so—these lines should conjure up a gay fellow, with his many changes of dress. If the vision fails, then allow me to say that you are at fault, and have taken no pains with the description. Because the coloured drawing to the chapter of Richard II. shows a long houppelande and a chaperon tied in a certain way, you will very possibly forget that this dandy would have also a short houppelande, differently jagged sleeves, more ruffle about the twisting of his chaperon, more curve to the points of his shoes.

You may see the image of Gower for yourself in St. Mary Overies Church, now called St. Saviour's, on the Southwark side of London Bridge. He is dressed in his sober black, his head resting upon his three books.

In 1397 Gower retired from active life, and re-signed his Rectory of Great Braxted, Essex ; he was seventy years of age, and at that age he married Agnes Groundolf in a chapel of his own under the rooms where he lived in the Priory of St. Mary Overies.

In 1400 his friend Chaucer died and Gower went blind. He died in 1408.

Chaucer, whose eyes saw England in her great-

ness after the Battle of Crecy in 1346, and in her
pitiful state at the downfall of Richard II., saw
such a pageant of clothes pass before him that,
in describing those wonderful national types,
his Canterbury Pilgrims, he marks each one with
some hint of array that we may know what
manner of habit was proper to
them. Here, then, is a list of
the clothes he pictured them as
wearing:

THE KNIGHT

wears a fustian doublet, all rust-
stained by his coat of mail. It is
interesting to note
how old-fashioned is
the character of this
'verray parfit gentil knight,' for he
belongs more rightly to the chival-
rous time of the first half of
Edward III.'s reign rather than to
the less gentle time of Richard.

THE SQUIRE.

His locks were curled, 'as they
were leyed in presse.' His short gown with

10

wide sleeves was covered with embroidery of red and white flowers.

THE YEOMAN

is in a coat and hood of green. He has a sheaf of peacock arrows in his belt; across his shoulder is a green baldrick to carry a horn. There is a figure of St. Christopher in silver hanging on his breast.

THE PRIORESS

is in a handsome cloak; she wears coral beads gauded with green, and a brooch of gold—

> ' On which was first write a-crowned A,
> And after, " Amor vincit omnia." '

THE MONK

wears his gown, but has his sleeves trimmed with gray squirrel. To fasten his hood he has a curious gold pin, wrought at the greater end with a love-knot.

THE FRIAR

has his cape stuck full of knives and pins ' for to yeven faire wyves.'

THE MERCHANT

is in a motley of colours—-parti-coloured. His beard is forked; upon his head is a Flaunderish beaver hat. His boots are elegantly clasped.

THE CLERK

wears a threadbare tunic.

THE MAN OF LAW

is in a coat of parti-colours, his belt of silk with small metal bars on it.

THE FRANKELEYN OR COUNTRY GENTLEMAN

has a white silk purse and a two-edged dagger, or akelace, at his girdle.

'Then come the HABERDASHER, the CARPENTER, the WEAVER, the DYER, and the TAPESTRY WORKER, all in the livery of their companies. They all carry pouches, girdles, and knives, mounted in silver.'

THE SHIPMAN

is in a gown of falding (a coarse cloth), reaching to his knees. A dagger is under his arm, on a lace hanging round his neck.

The Doctor

wears a gown of red and blue (pers was a blue cloth) lined with taffeta and sendal.

The Wife of Bath.

Her wimples of fine linen—

> 'I dorste swere they weyeden ten pound
> That on a Sonday were upon hir heed.'

Her hose was of fine scarlet red; her shoes were moist and new. Her hat was as broad as a buckler, and she wore a foot-mantle about her hips.

The Ploughman

wears a tabard, a loose smock without sleeves.

The Reve or Steward

wears a long surcoat of blue cloth (pers).

The Somnour

(an officer who summoned persons before the ecclesiastical courts) wears on his head a garland—'as greet as it were for an ale-stake.'

THE PARDONER

has long yellow hair falling about his shoulders; his hood is turned back, and he wears a tall cap, on which is sewn a Vernicle. This is the handkerchief of St. Veronica on which there was an impression of our Lord's face.

This completes the list of Pilgrims, but it will be useful to give a few more descriptions of dress as described by Chaucer. The Carpenter's wife in the Miller's Tale is described :

'Fair was this yonge wyf, and ther-with-al
As any wesele hir body gent (slim) and small.
A ceynt (belt) she werede barred al of silk,
A barneclooth (apron) eek as whyt as morne milk
Upon hir lendes (loins), ful of many a gore.
Whyt was hir smok and brouded al before
And eek behinde, on hir coler aboute,
Of col-blak silk, within and eek withoute.
The tapes of his whyte voluper (a cap)
Were of the same suyte—of hir coler ;
Hir filet broad of silk, and set ful hye.

  *   *   *   *   *

And by hir girdel heeng a purs of lether
Tasseld with silk and perked with latoun (a compound of copper and zinc).

  *   *   *   *   *

A brooch she bare upon hir lowe coler,
As broad as is the bos of a buckler.
Her shoes were laced on hir legges hye.'

Here also, from the Parson's Tale, is a sermon
against the vain clothing of his time, that will
serve to show how you may best paint this age,
and to what excess of imagination you may run.
I have reduced the wording into more modern
English :

'As to the first sin, that is in superfluitee of
clothing, which that maketh it so dere, to the
harm of the people ; not only the cost of embroidering, the elaborate endenting or barring, orna-
menting with waved lines, paling, winding, or
bending, and semblable waste of cloth in vanity ;
but there is also costly furring in their gowns, so
muche pounching of chisels to make holes, so
much dagging of shears ; forthwith the superfluity
in the length of the foresaid gowns, trailing in
the dung and the mire, on horse and eek on foot,
as well of man as of woman, that all this trailing
is verily as in effect wasted, consumed, threadbare,
and rotten with dung, rather than it is given to the
poor ; to great damage of the aforesaid poor folk.
'Upon the other side, to speak of the horrible
disordinate scantiness of clothing, as be this cutted

sloppes or hainselins (short jackets), that through their shortness do not cover the shameful members of man, to wicked intent.'

After this, the good Parson, rising to a magnificent torrent of wrathful words, makes use of such homely expressions that should move the hearts of his hearers—words which, in our day, are not seemly to our artificial and refined palates.

Further, Chaucer remarks upon the devices of love-knots upon clothes, which he calls 'amorettes'; on trimmed clothes, as being 'apyked'; on nearly all the fads and fashions of his time.

It is to Chaucer, and such pictures as he presents, that our minds turn when we think vaguely of the Middle Ages, and it is worth our careful study, if we wish to appreciate the times to the full, to read, no matter the hard spelling, the 'Vision of Piers the Plowman,' by Langland.

I have drawn a few of the Pilgrims, in order to show that they may be reconstructed by reading the chapters on the fourteenth century.

HENRY THE FOURTH

Reigned fourteen years: 1399—1413.
Born 1366. Married, 1380, Mary de Bohun;
1403, Joan of Navarre.

THE MEN AND WOMEN

THE reign opens sombrely enough—Richard in
prison, and twenty-five suits of cloth of gold left,
among other of his butterfly raiment, in Haverford
Castle.

We are still in the age of the houppelande,
the time of cut edges, jagging, big sleeves and
trailing gowns. Our fine gentlemen take the air
in the long loose gown, or the short edition of
the same with the skirts cut from it. They have
invented, or the tailor has invented, or necessity
has contrived, a new sleeve. It is a bag sleeve,
very full and fine, enormous at the elbow, tight
at the wrist, where it may fall over the hand in
a wide cuff with dagged edges, or it may end in
a plain band.

152

Let us take six gentlemen met together to learn the old thirteenth-century part-song, the round entitled 'Sumer is icumen in.'

The first, maybe, is in the high-collared houppe-lande with the long skirts; his sleeves are of a different colour to his gown, and are fastened to it under cut epaulettes at his shoulders; he wears

a baldrick, hung with bells, over his shoulder; his houppelande is split on one side to show his parti-coloured hose beyond his knee; his shoes are long and very pointed; his hair is cut short, and he wears a twisted roll of stuff round his head.

The second is in the latest mode; he wears the

voluminous sleeves which end in a plain band at his wrist, and these sleeves are of a different colour to his houppelande, the skirts of which are cut short at the knee, and then are cut into neat dags. This garment is not so full as that of the first gentle-man, which is gathered in at the waist by a long-tongued belt, but is buttoned down the front to the waist and is full in the skirt; also it has no collar. This man wears his hair long and curled at the nape of his neck.

A third of these gentlemen, a big burly man, is in a very short tunic with wide sleeves; his tights are of two colours, his left leg red, his right blue. Over his tunic he wears a quilted waistcoat, the collar and armholes of which are trimmed with fur.

A fourth wears a loose houppelande, one half of which is blue and the other half black; it is buttoned from throat to foot; the

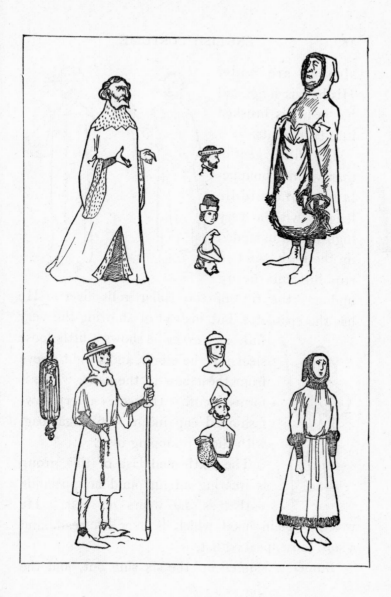

sleeves are wide. His hair is long, and his beard is brushed into two points.

The fifth gentleman wears a houppelande of middle length, with a very high collar buttoned up the neck, the two top buttons being undone; the top of the collar rolls over. He has the epaulette, but instead of showing the very

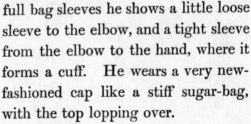

full bag sleeves he shows a little loose sleeve to the elbow, and a tight sleeve from the elbow to the hand, where it forms a cuff. He wears a very new-fashioned cap like a stiff sugar-bag, with the top lopping over.

The sixth and last of this group is wearing an unbound houppelande —that is, he wears no belt. He wears a plain hood which is over his head, and a soft, loose, peaked hat.

'Sumer is icumen in,' the six sing out, and the

shepherd, who can hear them from outside, is considering whether he can play the air upon his pipe. He is dressed in a loose tunic, a hood, and a wide-brimmed straw hat; his pipe is stuck in his belt.

Let us suppose that the wives of the six gentlemen are seated listening to the manly voices of their lords.

The first wears a dress of blue, which is laced from the opening to the waist, where the laces  are tied in a neat bow and hang down. Her dress is cut fairly low; it has tight sleeves which come over her hands to the knuckles in tight cuffs. There is a wide border, about a foot and a half, of ermine on the skirt of her dress. She wears a mantle over her shoulders. Her hair is enclosed in a stiff square caul of gold wire over cloth of gold.

The second lady is wearing a houppelande with wide, hanging sleeves all cut at the edge; the cut of this gown is loose, except that it fits across her shoulders; she also wears a caul, from the back of which emerges a linen wimple.

The third lady is in surcoat and cotehardie ; the
surcoat has a pleated skirt, and the borders of it
are edged thickly with fur ; it is cut low enough at
the sides to show a belt over the hips. The cotehardie, of a different colour to the surcoat, has
tight sleeves with buttons from elbow to little

finger. This lady has her hair cut short at the
nape of her neck, and bound about the brows with
a golden circlet.

A fourth wears a very loose houppelande, encircled about the waist with a broad belt, the
tongue of which hangs down and has an ornamented
end. This houppelande falls in great folds from the
neck to the feet, and is gathered into the neck ; it
has loose, but not wide, sleeves, falling just below
the elbow. The gown is worn over a cotehardie,

the sleeves of which show through the other sleeves, and the skirt of which shows when the gown skirt is gathered up.

The fifth lady also wears a cotehardie with a skirt to it; she wears over it a circular mantle, buttoned by three buttons on the right shoulder, and split from there to the edge on both sides, showing the dress; the front semicircle of the cloak is held to the waist by a belt so that the back hangs loose. Her hair is in a caul.

The sixth is in a very plain dress, tight fitting, buttoned in front, with full skirts. She wears a white linen hood which shows the shape of the caul in which her hair is imprisoned.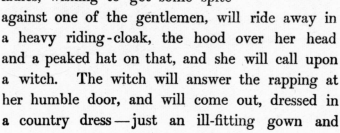

So is this queer old round sung, 'Sumer is icumen in.'

Afterwards, perhaps one of these ladies, wishing to get some spite against one of the gentlemen, will ride away in a heavy riding-cloak, the hood over her head and a peaked hat on that, and she will call upon a witch. The witch will answer the rapping at her humble door, and will come out, dressed in a country dress—just an ill-fitting gown and hood, with some attempt at classical ornament on the gown, or a cloak sewn with the sacred initials thrown over her back. These two will bargain awhile for the price of a leaden image to be made in the likeness of the ill-fated gentleman, or, rather, a rough figure, on which his name will be scratched ; then the puppet will be cast into the fire and melted while certain evil charms are spoken, and the malicious accident required to befall him will be spoken aloud for the Devil's private ear. Possibly some woman sought a witch near Evesham in the year 1410, and bought certain intentions against a tailor of that place, Badby by name; for this much is certain: that the tailor was burnt for Lollardy ten years after the first victim for Lollard heresy, William Sawtre.

A MAN AND WOMAN OF THE TIME OF HENRY IV. 1399-1413

HENRY THE FIFTH

Reigned nine years: 1413—1422.
Born 1388.   Married, 1420, Katherine of France.

THE MEN

I THINK I may call this a transitional period of clothes, for it contains the ragged ends of the time of Richard II. and the old clothes of the time of Henry IV., and it contains the germs of a definite fashion, a marked change which came out of the chrysalis stage, and showed itself in the prosperous butterflies of the sixth Henry's time.

We retain the houppelande, its curtailments, its exaggerations, its high and low collar, its plain or jagged sleeves.   We retain the long hair, which busheth pleasauntlie,' and the short hair of the previous reign. Also we see the new ideas for the priest-cropped hair and the roundlet hat.

I speak of the men only.

It was as if, in the press of French affairs, man had but time to ransack his grandfather's and his father's chests, and from thence to pull out a garment or two at a venture. If the garment was a little worn in the upper part of the sleeve, he had a slash made there, and embroidered it round. If the baldrick hung with bells was worn out in parts, he cut those pieces away and turned the baldrick into a belt. If the skirts of the houppelande were sadly frayed at the edge, enter Scissors again to cut them off short; perhaps the sleeves were good — well, leave them on; perhaps the skirts were good and the sleeves soiled—well, cut out the sleeves and pop in some of his father's bag sleeves. Mind you, my honest gentleman had trouble brewing: no sooner had he left the wars in Normandy and Guienne than the siege of Harfleur loomed to his vision, and after that Agincourt— Agincourt, where unarmoured men prevailed over mailed knights at the odds of six to one; Agincourt, where archers beat the great knights of

France on open ground! Hear them hammer on
the French armour with their steel mallets, while
the Frenchmen, weighed down with their armour,
sank knee-deep in the mud—where we lost 100 men,
against the French loss of 10,000 !

See the port of Le Havre, with the English
army landed there — Henry in his full-sleeved
gown, his hair cropped close and
shaven round his head from his
neck to an inch above his ears,
buskins on his feet, for he wore
buskins in preference to long
boots or pointed shoes. The
ships in the harbour are painted
in gay colours — red, blue, in
stripes, in squares; the sails are
sewn with armorial bearings or
some device. Some of our
gentlemen are wearing open

A Belt with Bells.

houppelandes over their armour; some wear the
stuffed turban on their heads, with a jewelled
brooch stuck in it; some wear the sugar-bag cap,
which falls to one side; some are hooded, others
wear peaked hats. One hears, 'By halidom!'
wonder if all the many, many people who have

hastily written historical novels of this age, and have peppered them with 'By halidoms,' knew that 'By halidom' means 'By the relics of the saints,' and that an 'harlote' means a man who was a buffoon who told ribald stories?

Still, among all these gentlemen, clothed, as it were, secondhand, we have the fine fellow, the  dandy—he to whom dress is a religion, to whom stuffs are sonnets, cuts are lyrical, and tailors are the poets of their age. Such a man will have his tunic neatly pleated, rejecting the chance folds of the easy-fitting houppelande, the folds of which were determined by the buckling of the belt. His folds will be regular and precise, his collar will be very stiff, with a rolled top; his

The Turban.

hose will be of two colours, one to each leg, or particoloured. His shoes will match his hose, and be of two colours; his turban hat will be cocked at a jaunty angle; his sleeves will be of a monstrous length and width. He will hang a

chain about his neck, and load his fingers with
rings. A fellow to him, one of his own kidney,
will wear the skirt of his tunic a little longer,
and will cause it to be cut up the middle; his
sleeves will not be pendant, like drooping wings,
but will be swollen like full-blown bagpipes.
An inner sleeve, very finely embroidered, will
peep under the upper cuff. His collar is done
away with, but he wears a little hood with cut
edges about his neck; his hair is cropped in the
new manner, like a priest's without a tonsure; his
hat is of the queer sugar-bag shape, and it flops in
a drowsy elegance over the stuffed brim. As for
his shoes, they are two fingers long beyond his
toes.

We shall see the fashions of the two past reigns
hopelessly garbled, cobbled, and stitched together;
a sleeve from one, a skirt from another. Men-at-
arms in short tunics of leather and quilted waistcoats to wear under their half-armour; beggars
in fashions dating from the eleventh century; a
great mass of people in undistinguishable attire,
looking mostly like voluminous cloaks on spindle
legs, or mere bundles of drapery; here and there a
sober gentleman in a houppelande of the simplest

kind, with wide skirts reaching to his feet, and the belt with the long tongue about his middle.

The patterns upon the dresses of these people are heraldry contortions — heraldic beasts intertwined in screws and twists of conventional foliage, griffins and black dogs held by floral chains to architectural branches, martlets and salamanders struggling in grotesque bushes, or very elaborate geometrical patterned stuffs.

There is a picture of the Middle Ages which was written by Langland in ' Piers the Plowman ' —a picture of an alehouse, where Peronelle of Flanders and Clarice of Cockeslane sit with the hangman of Tyburn and a dozen others. It is a picture of the fourteenth century, but it holds good until the time of Henry VIII., when Skelton, his tutor, describes just such another tavern on the highroad, where some bring wedding-rings to pay their scot of ale, and

> ' Some bryngeth her husband's hood
> Because the ale is good.'

Both accounts are gems of description, both full of that rich, happy, Gothic flavour, that sense of impressionist portraiture, of broad humour, which distinguishes the drawings in the Loutrell Psalter.

I feel now as if I might be accused of being interesting and of overlaying my history with too much side comment, and I am well aware that convention demands that such books as this shall be as dull as possible; then shall the vulgar rejoice, because they have been trained to believe that dullness and knowledge snore in each other's arms.

The Sugar-bag Cap.

However wholeheartedly you may set about writing a list of clothes attributable to certain dates, there will crop up spirits of the age, who blur the edges of the dates, and give a lifelike semblance to them which carries the facts into the sphere of fiction, and fiction was ever on the side of truth. No story

A Hood.

has ever been invented by man but it has been beaten out of time by Nature and the police-courts; no romance has been penned so intricate but fact will supply a more surprising twist to life. But, whereas facts are of necessity bald and naked things, fiction, which is the wardrobe of fact, will clothe truth in more accustomed guise.

I put before you some true facts of the clothes of this time, clothed in a little coat of facts put fictionally. I write the word 'cloak'; describe to you that such people wore circular cloaks split at one or both sides, on one side to the neck, on the other below the shoulder; of semicircular cloaks, of square cloaks, of oblong cloaks, all of which were worn (I speak of these, and you may cut them out with some thought); but I wish to do more than that—I wish to give you a gleam of the spirit in which the cloaks were worn. A cloak will partake of the very soul and conscience of its owner; become draggle-tailed, flaunting, effeminate, masterful, pompous, or dignified. Trousers, I think, of all the garments of men, fail most to show the state of his soul; they merely proclaim the qualities of his purse. Cloaks give most the true man, and after that there is much in the cock of a hat and the conduct of a cane.

In later days one might tell what manner of man had called to find you away if he chanced to leave his snuff-box behind. This reasoning is not finicky, but very profound ; accept it in the right spirit.

Now, one more picture of the age.

The rich man at home, dressed, as I say, in his father's finery, with some vague additions of his own, has acquired a sense of luxury. He prefers to dine alone, in a room with a chimney and a fire in it. He can see through a window in the wall by his side into the hall, where his more patriarchal forebears loved to take their meals. The soiled rushes are being swept away, and fresh herbs and rushes strewn in their place ; on these mattresses will in their turn be placed, on which his household presently will lay them down to sleep.

THE WOMEN

Every time I write the heading ' The Women ' to such chapters as these, I feel that such thread-bare cloak of chivalry as I may pin about my shoulders is in danger of slipping off.

Should I write ' The Ladies ' ? But although all ladies are women, not all women are ladies, and as it is far finer to be a sweet woman than a great dame, I will adhere to my original heading, ' The Women.'

However, in the remote ages of which I now write, the ladies were dressed and the women wore clothes, which is a subtle distinction. I dare not bring my reasoning up to the present day.

As I said in my last chapter, this was an age of medley—of this and that wardrobe flung open, and old fashions renovated or carried on. Fashion, that elusive goddess, changes her moods and modes with such a quiet swiftness that she leaves us breathless and far behind, with a bundle of silks and velvets in our arms.

How is a fashion born? Who mothers it? Who nurses it to fame, and in whose arms does it die? High collar, low collar, short hair, long hair, boot, buskin, shoe — who wore you first? Who last condemned you to the World's Great Rag Market of Forgotten Fads?

Now this, I have said, was a transitional age, but I cannot begin to say who was the first great dame to crown her head with horns, and who the last to forsake the jewelled caul. It is only on rare occasions that the decisive step can be traced to any one person or group of persons: Charles II. and his frock-coat, Brummell and his starched stock, are finger-posts on Fashion's highroad, but they are not quite true guides. Charles was recommended to the coat, and I think the mist of soap and warm water that enshrines Brummell as the Apostle of Cleanliness blurs also the mirror of truth. It does not much matter.

No doubt—and here there will be readers the first to correct me and the last to see my point—there are persons living full of curious knowledge who, diving yet more deeply into the dusty crevices of history, could point a finger at the man who first cut his hair in the early fifteenth-century manner, and could write you the name and the dignities of the lady who first crowned her fair head with horns.

For myself, I begin with certainty at Adam and the fig-leaf, and after that I plunge into the world's wardrobe in hopes.

Certain it is that in this reign the close caul grew out of all decent proportions, and swelled into every form of excrescence and protuberance, until in the reign of Henry VI. it towered above the heads of the ladies, and dwarfed the stature of the men.

This curious headgear, the caul, after a modest appearance, as a mere close, gold-work cap, in the time of Edward III., grew into a stiffer affair in the time of Richard II., but still was little more than a stiff sponge-bag of gold wire and stuff and a little padding; grew still more in the time of Henry IV., and took squarer shapes and stiffer padding; and in the reign of Henry V. it became like a great orange, with a hole cut in it for the face—an orange which covered the ears, was cut straight across the forehead, and bound all round with a stiff jewelled band.

Then came the idea of the horn. Whether some superstitious lady thought that the wearing of horns would keep away the evil eye, or whether it was a mere frivol of some vain Duchess, I do not know.

As this fashion came most vividly into prominence in the following reign, I shall leave a more detailed description of it until that time, letting myself give but a short notice of its more simple forms.

We see the caul grow from its circular shape into two box forms on either side of the head; the uppermost points of the boxes are arranged in horns, whose points are of any length from 4 to 14 inches. The top of this head-dress is covered with a wimple. which is sometimes stiffened with wires.

There is also a shape something like a fez or a flower-pot, over which a heavy wimple is hung, attached to this shape; outside the wimple are two horns of silk, linen, or stuff—that is, silk bags stuffed to the likeness of horns.

I should say that a true picture of this time would give but few of these very elaborate horn head-dresses, and the mass of women would be wearing the round caul.

The surcoat over the cotehardie is the general wear, but it has more fit about it than formerly; the form of the waist and bust are accentuated by means of a band of heavy gold embroidery, shaped to the figure. The edges of the surcoat are furred somewhat heavily, and the skirt often has a deep border of fur. Sometimes a band of metal ornament runs across the top of the breast and down the centre of the surcoat, coming below the fur edging. The belt over the hips of the cotehardie holds the purse, and often a ballade or a rondel.

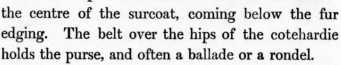

You will see a few of the old houppelandes, with

their varieties of sleeve, and in particular that long, loose double sleeve, or, rather, the very long under-sleeve, falling over the hand. This under-sleeve is part of the houppelande.

All the dresses have trains, very full trains, which sweep the ground, and those readers who wish to make such garments must remember to be very generous over the material.

The women commonly wear the semicircular mantle, which they fasten across them by cords running through ornamental brooches.

They wear very rich metal and enamel belts round their hips, the exact ornamentation of which cannot be described here ; but it was the ornament of the age, which can easily be discovered.

In the country, of course, simpler garments prevail, and plain surcoats and cotehardies are wrapped in cloaks and mantles of homespun material. The hood has not fallen out of use for women, and the peaked hat surmounts it for riding or rough weather. Ladies wear wooden clogs or sandals besides their shoes, and they have not yet taken to the horns upon their heads ; some few of them, the great dames of the counties whose lords have been to London on King's business, or returned from France with new ideas, have donned the elaborate business of head-boxes and wires and great wimples.

As one of the ladies rides in the country lanes, she may pass that Augustine convent where Dame Petronilla is spiritual Mother to so many, and may see her in Agincourt year keeping her pig-tally with Nicholas Swon, the swineherd. They may see some of the labourers she hires dressed in the blood-red cloth she has given them, for the dyeing of which she paid 7s. 8d. for 27 ells. The good dame's nuns are very neat ; they have an allowance of 6s. 8d. a year for dress.

This is in 1415. No doubt next year my lady, riding through the lanes, will meet some sturdy beggar, who will whine for alms, pleading that he is an old soldier lately from the field of Agincourt.

NOTE

As there is so little real change, for drawings of women's dress see the numerous drawings in previous chapter.

HENRY THE SIXTH

Reigned thirty-nine years : 1422-1461.
Born 1421.   Dethroned 1461.   Died 1471.
Married, 1446, Margaret of Anjou.

THE MEN

WHAT a reign! Was history ever better dressed?

I never waver between the cardboard figures of the great Elizabethan time and this reign as a monument to lavish display, but if any time should beat this for quaintness, colour, and variety, it is the time of Henry VIII.

Look at the scenes and characters to be dressed : John, Duke of Bedford, the Protector, Joan of Arc, Jack Cade, a hundred other people ; Crevant, Verneuil, Orleans, London

A MAN OF THE TIME OF HENRY V.   1413-1422

A WOMAN OF THE TIME OF HENRY V.   1413-1422

Bridge, Ludlow, St. Albans, and a hundred other historical backgrounds.

Yet, in spite of all this, in spite of the fact that Joan of Arc is one of the world's personalities, it is difficult to pick our people out of the tapestries.

Now, you may have noticed that in trying to recreate a period in your mind certain things immediately swing into your vision : it is difficult to think of the Conquest without the Bayeux tapestry ; it is difficult to think of the dawn of the sixteenth century without the dreamy, romantic landscapes which back the figures of Giorgione ; and it is not easy to think of these people of the Henry VI. period without placing them against conventional tapestry trees, yellow-white castles with red, pepper-pot roofs, grass luxuriant with needlework flowers, and all the other accessories of the art.

The early times are easily imagined in rough surroundings or in open air; knights in armour ride quite comfortably down modern English lanes. Alfred may burn his cakes realistically, and Canute rebuke his courtiers on the beach— these one may see in the round. Elizabeth rides

12

to Tilbury, Charles II. casts his horoscope, and George rings the bell, each in their proper atmosphere, but the Dark Ages are dark, not only in modes of thought, but in being ages of grotesque, of ornamentation, of anything but realism.

One has, I think, a conventional mind's eye for the times from Edward I. to Richard III., from 1272 to 1485, and it is really more easy for a Chinaman to call up a vision of 604 A.D., when Laot-sen, the Chinese philosopher, was born. Laot-sen, the child-old man, he who was born with white hair, lived till he was eighty-one, and, having had five million followers, went up to heaven on a black buffalo. In China things have changed very little: the costume is much the same, the customs are the same, the attitude towards life has not changed. But here the semicivilized, superstitious, rather dirty, fourteenth and fifteenth century person has gone. Scratch a Russian, they say, and you will see a Tartar ; do the same office by an Englishman, and you may find a hint of the Renaissance under his skin, but no more. The Middle Ages are dead and dust.

We will proceed with that congenial paradox which states that the seat of learning lies in the head, and so discuss the most distinctive costumery of this time, the roundlet.

Now, the roundlet is one of those things which delight the clothes-hunter or the costume expert.

It is the natural result of a long series of fashions for the head, and its pedigree is free from any impediment or hindrance; it is the great-grandson of the hood, which is derived from a fold in a cloak, which is the beginning of all things.

I am about to run the risk of displeasure in repeating to some extent what I have already written about the chaperon, the hood, and the other ancestors and descendants of the roundlet.

A fashion is born, not made. Necessity is the mother of Art, and Art is the father of Invention. A man must cover his head, and if he has a cloak, it is an easy thing in rain or sunshine to pull the folds of the cloak over his head. An ingenious fellow in the East has an idea: he takes his 8 feet —or more—of material; he folds it in half, and

12—2

at about a foot and a half, or some such convenient
length, he puts several neat and strong stitches
joining one point of the folded material. When
he wraps this garment about him, leaving the
sewn point in the centre of his neck at the back,
he finds that he has directed the folds of his coat
in such a manner as to form a hood, which he may
place on or off his head more conveniently than
the plain unsewn length of stuff. The morning
sun rises on the sands of Sahara and lights upon the
first burnoose. By a simple process in tailoring,
some man, who did not care that the peak of his
hood should be attached to his cloak, cut his cloth
so that the cloak had a hood, the peak of which
was separate and so looser, and yet more easy to
pull on or off. Now comes a man who was taken
by the shape of the hood, but did not require to
wear a cloak, so he cut his cloth in such a way that
he had a hood and shoulder-cape only. From this
to the man who closed the front of the hood from
the neck to the edge of the cape is but a quick
and quiet step. By now necessity was satisfied
and had given birth to art. Man, having admired
his face in the still waters of a pool, seeing how the
oval framed in the hood vastly became him, sought

to tickle his vanity and win the approbation of the other sex, so, taking some shears, cut the edge of his cape in scallops and leaves. A more dandified fellow, distressed at the success of his brother's plumage, caused the peak of his hood to be made long.

Need one say more? The long peak grew and grew into the preposterous liripipe which hung down the back from the head to the feet. The dandy spirit of another age, seeing that the liripipe can grow no more, and that the shape of the hood is common and not in the true dandiacal spirit, whips off his hood, and, placing the top of his head where his face was, he twists the liripipe about his head, imprisons part of the cape, and, after a fixing twist, slips the liripipe through part of its twined self and lets the end hang down on one side of his face, while the jagged end of the hood rises or falls like a cockscomb on the other. Cockscomb! there's food for discussion in that—fops, beaux, dandies, coxcombs—surely.

I shall not go into the matter of the hood with two peaks, which was not, I take it, a true child of fashion in the direct line, but a mere cousin—a junior branch at that.

As to the dates on this family tree, the vague, mysterious beginnings B.C.—goodness knows when —in a general way the Fall, the Flood, and the First Crusade, until the time of the First Edward ;

the end of the thirteenth century, when the liripipe budded, the time of the Second Edward; the first third of the fourteenth century, when the liripipe was in full flower, the time of the Third Edward; the middle of the fourteenth century, when the liripipe as a liripipe was dying, the time of the Second Richard ; the end of the century, when the chaperon became the twisted cockscomb turban. Then, after that, until the twenty-second year of the fifteenth century, when the roundlet was born— those are the dates.

We have arrived by now, quite naturally, at the roundlet. I left you interested at the last phase of the hood, the chaperon so called, twisted up in a fantastical shape on man's head. You must see that the mere process of tying and retying, twisting, coiling and arranging, was tedious in the extreme, especially in stirring times with the trumpets sounding in England and France. Now what more likely for the artist of the tied hood than to puzzle his brains in order to reach a means by which he could get at the effect without so much labour? Enter invention—enter invention and exit art. With invention, the made-up chaperon sewn so as to look as if it had been tied. There was the twist round the head, the cockscomb, the hanging piece of liripipe. Again this was to be simplified: the twist made into a smooth roll, the skull to be covered by an ordinary cap attached to the roll, the cockscomb converted into a plain piece of cloth or silk, the liripipe to become broader. And the end of this, a little round hat with a heavily-rolled and stuffed brim, pleated drapery hanging over one side and streamer of broad stuff over the other; just such a hat did these people wear, on their heads or slung over their shoulder, being held in the left hand by means of the streamer. There the honourable family of hood came to a green old age, and was, at the end of the fifteenth century, allowed to retire from the world of fashion, and was given a pension and a home, in which home you may still see it—on the shoulders of the Garter robe. Also it has two

more places of honourable distinction—the roundlet
is on the Garter robe; the chaperon, with the cut
edge, rests as a cockade in the hats of liveried
servants, and the minutest member of the family
remains in the foreign buttons of honourable
Orders.

We have the roundlet, then, for principal head-
gear in this reign, but we must not forget that

the hood is not dead; it is out
of the strict realms of fashion,
but it is now a practical country
garment, or is used for riding
in towns. There are also other
forms of headwear—tall, conical
hats with tall brims of fur, some
brims cut or scooped out in
places; again, the hood may
have a furred edge showing
round the face opening; then
we see a cap which fits the
head, has a long, loose back falling over the
neck, and over this is worn a roll or hoop
of twisted stuff. Then there is the sugar-loaf
hat, like a circus clown's, and there is a
broad, flat-brimmed hat with a round top, like

Noah's hat in the popular representations of the Ark.

Besides these, we have the jester's three-peaked hood and one-peaked hood, the cape of which

came, divided into points, to the knees, and had arms with bell sleeves.

Let us see what manner of man we have under such hats : almost without exception among the gentlemen we have the priestly hair—that queer, shaved, tonsure-like cut, but without the circular piece cut away from the crown of the head.

The cut of the tunic in the body has little variation; it may be longer or shorter, an inch above or an inch below the knee, but it is on one main principle. It is a loose tunic with a wide neck open in front about a couple or three inches; the skirt is full, and may be cut up on one or both sides; it may be edged with fur or some stuff different to the body of the garment, or it may be jagged, either

in regular small scoops or in long fringe-like
jags. The tunic is always belted very low, giving
an odd appearance to the men of this time, as it
made them look very short in the leg.

The great desire for variety is displayed in the
forms of sleeve for this tunic: you may have the
ordinary balloon sleeve ending in a stuff roll or
fur edge for cuff, or you may have a half-sleeve,
very wide indeed, like shoulder-capes, and termi-
nated in the same manner as the bottom of the
tunics—that is, fur-edged tunic, fur-edged sleeve,
and so on, as described; under this shows the tight
sleeve of an undergarment, the collar of which
shows above the tunic collar at the neck. The
length of these shoulder-cape sleeves varies according to the owner's taste, from small epaulettes
to heavy capes below the elbow. There is also a
sleeve tight from wrist to below the elbow, and at
that point very big and wide, tapering gradually
to the shoulder. You will still see one or two
high collars rolled over, and there is a distinct
continuance of the fashion for long-pointed shoes.

There is an almost new form of overcoat which
is really a tunic of the time, unbelted, and with
the sleeves cut out; also one with short, but very

full, sleeves, the body very loose; and besides the
ordinary forms of square, oblong, and round cloak,
there is a circular cloak split up the right side to
the base of the biceps, with a
round hole in the centre, edged
with fur, for the passage of the
head.

Velvet was in common use for
gowns, tunics, and even for bed-
clothes, in the place of blankets.
It was made in all kinds of
beautiful designs, diapered, and raised over a
ground of gold or silk, or double-piled, one pile
on another of the same colour making the pattern
known by the relief.

The massed effect of well-dressed crowds must
have been fine and rich in colour—here and there
a very rich lady or a magnificent gentleman in
pall (the beautiful gold or crimson web, known
also as bandekin), the velvets, the silks of marvellous
colours, and none too fresh or new. I think that
such a gathering differed most strongly from a
gathering of to-day by the fact that one is impressed
to-day with the new, almost tinny newness, of the
people's clothes, and that these other people were

not so extravagant in the number of their dresses
as in the quality, so that then one would have seen
many old and beautifully-faded velvets and sun-
licked silks and rain-improved cloths.

Among all this crowd would pass, in a plain
tunic and short shoes, Henry, the ascetic King.

THE WOMEN

One is almost disappointed
to find nothing upon the
curious subject of horns in
'Sartor Resartus.' Such a
flaunting, Jovian spirit, and
poetry of abuse as might
have been expected from the
illustrious and iconoclastic
author would have suited me, at this present date,
most admirably.

I feel the need of a few thundering German
words, or a brass band at the end of my pen, or
purple ink in my inkwell, or some fantastic and
wholly arresting piece of sensationalism by which
to convey to you that you have now stepped into
the same world as the Duchess out of 'Alice in
Wonderland.'

Look out of your window and see upon the flower-enamelled turf a hundred bundles of vanity taking the air. The heads of these ladies are carried very erect, as are all heads bearing weights. The waists of these ladies are apparently under their bosoms; their feet seem to be an ell long. An assembly hour is,  after the manner of Lydgate's poem, a dream of delicious faces surmounted by minarets, towers, horns, excresences of every shape — enormous, fat, heart-shaped erections, covered with rich, falling drapery, or snow-white linen, or gold tissue; gold-wire boxes sewn with pearls and blazing with colours; round, flat-topped caps, from under which girls' hair escapes in a river of colour; crown shapes, circular shapes, mitre shapes, turbans, and shovel-shaped linen erections, wired into place.

Oh, my lady, my lady! how did you ever hear the soft speeches of gallantry? How did the gentle whispers of love ever penetrate those bosses of millinery?

And the moralists, among whom Heaven forbid that I should be found, painted lurid pictures for you of hell and purgatory, in which such head-dresses turned into instruments of torture; you lifted your long-fingered, medieval hand and shook the finger with the toad-stone upon it, as if to dispel the poison of their words.

I think it is beyond me to describe in understandable terms the proper contortions of your towered heads, for I have little use for archaic words, for crespine, henk, and jacque, for herygouds with honginde sleeves, for all the blank cartridges of antiquarianism. I cannot convey the triple-curved crown, the ear buttress, the magnet-shaped roll in adequate language, but I can draw them for you.

I will attempt the most popular of the roll head-dresses and the simpler of the stiff-wired box. Take a roll, stuffed with hemp or tow, of some rich material and twist it into the form of a heart in front and a V shape behind, where join the ends, or, better, make a circle or hoop of your rolled stuff and bend it in this way. Then make a cap that will fit the head and come

over the ears, and make it so that this cap shall join
the heart-shaped roll at all points and cause it to
appear without any open spaces between the head
and the roll; the point of the heart in front will be
round, and will come over the centre of the face.
By joining cap and roll you will have one complete
affair; over this you may brooch a linen wimple
or a fine piece of jagged silk. In fact, you may.
twist your circle of stuff in any manner, providing
you keep a vague U shape in front and completely
cover the hair behind.

For the box pattern it is necessary to make a
box, let us say of octagonal shape, flat before and
behind, or slightly curved; cut away the side under
the face, or leave but a thin strip of it to go under
the chin.   Now stuff your box on either side of the
face and cut away the central square, except for
3 inches at the top, on the forehead; here, in
this cut-away piece, the face shows. You will
have made your box of buckram and stuffed the
wings of it with tow; now you must fit your box
to a head and sew linen between the sides of the
head and the tow to hold it firm and make it good
to wear. You have now finished the rough shape,
and you must ornament it. Take a piece of thin

gold web and cover your box, then get some gold
braid and make a diaper or criss-cross pattern all
over the box, leaving fair sized lozenges; in these
put, at regular intervals as a plain check, small
squares of crimson silk so that they fit across the
lozenge and so make a double pattern. Now take
some gold wire or brass wire and knot it at neat
intervals, and then stitch it on to the edges of the
gold braid, after which pearl beads may be arranged
on the crimson squares and at the cross of the
braid; then you will have your box-patterned head-
dress complete.

It remains for you to enlarge upon this, if you
wish, in the following manner: take a stiff piece
of wire and curve it into the segment of a circle,
so that you may bend the horns as much or as
little as you will, fasten the centre of this to the
band across the forehead, or on to the side-boxes,
and over it place a large wimple with the front
edge cut. Again, for further enhancement of
this delectable piece of goods, you may fix a
low gold crown above all—a crown of an ellip-
tical shape—and there you will have as much
magnificence as ever graced lady of the fifteenth
century.

A MAN OF THE TIME OF HENRY VI. 1422-1461

A WOMAN OF THE TIME OF HENRY VI.   1422-1461

September 28, 1443, Margaret Paston writes to
her husband in London

' I would ye were at home, if it were your ease,
and your sore might be as well looked to here as
it is where ye be now, liefer than a gown though
it were of scarlet.'

My dear diplomatist, I have forgotten if you
got both your husband and the gown, or the gown
only, but it was a sweetly pretty
letter, and worded in such a way
as must have caused your good
knight to smile, despite his sore.
And what had you in your mind's
eye when you wrote ' liefer than a
gown though it were of scarlet ?
It was one of those new gowns
with the high waist and the bodice opening very
low, the collar quite over your shoulders, and the
thick fur edge on your shoulders and tapering
into a point at your bosom. You wanted sleeves
like wings, and a fur edge to the bottom of
the gown, besides the fur upon the edges of the
sleeves—those quaint sleeves, thin to your elbows,
and then great and wide, like a foresail. I sup-

13

pose you had an under-gown of some wonderful diapered silk which you thought would go well with scarlet, because, as you knew, the under-gown would show at your neck, and its long train would trail behind you, and its skirt would fall about your feet and show very bravely when you bunched up the short upper gown — all the môde—and so you hinted at scarlet.

Now I come to think of it, the sleeve must have been hard to arrive at, the fashions were so many.

To have had them tight would have minimized the use of your under-garment; to have had them of the same width from elbow to wrist would not have given you the newest of the new ideas to show in Norfolk; then, for some reason, you rejected the bag sleeve, which was also in the fashion.

No doubt you had a cotehardie with well-fitting sleeves and good full skirts, and a surcoat with a wide fur edge, or perhaps, in the latest fashion of these garments, with an entire fur bodice to it. You may have had also one of those rather ugly little jackets, very full, with very full sleeves which

came tight at the wrist, long-waisted, with a little
skirt an inch or so below the belt. A mantle, with
cords to keep it on, I know you had.
Possibly—I have just thought of it—
the sleeves of your under-gown, the
tight sleeves, were laced together from
elbow to wrist, in place of the old-
fashioned buttons.

I wonder if you ever saw the great
metal-worker, William Austin, one of
the first among English artists to leave
a great name behind him—I mean the

Austin who modelled the effigy of
Earl Richard Beauchamp, at Warwick.
You must have heard the leper
use his rattle to warn you of his
proximity. You, too, may have
thought that Joan of Arc was a sor-
ceress and Friar Bungay a magician.
You may have—I have not your
wonderful letter here for reference—
heard all about Eleanor of Cobham,
and how she did penance in a shift
in the London streets for magic against the
King's person.

Some ladies, I notice, wore the long-tongued belt—buckled it in front, and then pushed it  round until the buckle came into the centre of the back and the tongue hung down like a tail; but these ladies were not wearing the high-waisted gown, but a gown with a normal waist, and with no train, but a skirt of evenfulness and of the same length all the way round.

There were striped stuffs, piled velvet, rich-patterned silks, and homespun cloths and wool to choose from.   Long - peaked shoes, of course, and wooden clogs out of doors.

The town and country maids, the merchants' wives, and the poor generally, each and all according to purse and pride, dressed in humbler imitation of the cut of the clothes of the high-born, in quite simple dresses, with purse, girdle, and apron, with heads in hoods, or twisted wimples of coarse linen.

Well, there you lie, ladies, on the tops of cold tombs, stiff and sedate, your hands up-lifted in prayer, your noses as often as not

knocked off by later-day school-boys, crop-headed
Puritans, or Henry VIII.'s sacrilegious hire-
lings. Lie still in your huge head-dresses and
your neat-folded gowns—a moral, in marble or
bronze, of the pomps and vanities of this wicked
world.

EDWARD THE FOURTH

Reigned twenty-two years: 1461—1483.
Born 1441.   Married, 1464, Elizabeth Woodville.

THE MEN

I INVITE you to call up this reign by a picture of Caxton's shop: you may imagine yourself in the almonry at Westminster, where, in a small enclosure by the west front of the church, there is a chapel and some almshouses. You will be able to see the rich come to look at Mr. Caxton's wares and the poor slinking in to receive alms.

'If it please any man, spiritual or temporal, to buy any pyes of two or three commemorations of Salisbury use emprynted after the form of this present letter, which be well and truly correct, let him come to Westminster into the Almonry at the red pale, and he shall have them good cheap.'

This was Caxton's advertisement.

198

As you watch the people going and coming about the small enclosure, you will notice that the tonsured hair has gone out of fashion, and that whereas the merchants, citizens, and such people wear the roundlet hat, the nobles and fine gentlemen are in black velvet caps, or tall hats with long-peaked brims, or in round high hats with fur brim close to the crown of the hat, or in caps with little rolled brims with a button at the top, over which two laces pass from back to front, and from under the brim there falls the last sign, the dying gasp of the liripipe, now jagged and now with tasselled ends.

We have arrived at the generally accepted vague idea of 'medieval costume,' which means really a nazy notion of the dress of this date: a steeple head-dress for ladies, a short waist, and a train; a tall, sugar-loaf hat with a flat top for the men, long hair, very short and very long tunics, long-pointed shoes, and wide sleeves—this, I think, is the amateur's idea of 'costume in the Middle Ages.'

You will notice that all, or nearly all, the passers-by Caxton's have long hair; that the dandies have extra-long hair brushed out in a cloud at the back; that the older men wear long, very simple gowns, which they belt in at the waist with a stuff or leather belt, on which is hung a bag-purse; that these plain gowns are laced across the front to the

waist over a vest of some coloured stuff other than the gown.

You will see that the poor are in very simple tunics—just a loose, stuff shirt with sleeves about 8 inches wide, and with the skirts reaching to the knees, a belt about their middle — rough, shapeless leather shoes, and woollen tights.

You will remember in the early part of the reign, before the heraldic shield with the red pale, Caxton's sign, caught your eye, that the fashionable wore very wide sleeves, great swollen bags fitting only at shoulder and wrist, and you may recall the fact that a tailor was fined twenty shillings in 1463 for making such wide sleeves. Poulaines, the very long shoes, are now forbidden, except that an esquire and anyone over that rank might wear them 2 inches beyond the toes; but I think the

dandies wore the shoes and paid the fine if it were
enforced.

See Caxton, in a sober-coloured gown, long, and
laced in the front, showing a plain vest under the
lacing, talking to some of his great customers.
The Duchess of Somerset has just lent him
'Blanchardine and Eglantine'; Earl Rivers, the
Queen's brother, talks over his own translation of
'The Sayings of the Philosophers'; and Caxton
is extolling that worshipful man Geoffrey Chaucer,
and singing praises in reverence 'for that noble
poet and great clerke, Vergyl.'

Edward himself has been to the shop and has
consented to become patron of an edition of
Tully—Edward, with his very subtle face, his
tall, handsome appearance, his cold, elegant
manners. He is dressed in a velvet gown edged
with fur; the neck of the gown is low, and the
silk vest shows above it. Across his chest are
gold laces tapering to his waist; these are straight
across the front of his gown-opening. His hair is
straight, and falls to the nape of his neck; he wears
a black velvet cap upon his head. The skirts of
his gown reach to his knees, and are fur-edged; his
sleeves are full at the elbows and tight over his

wrists; he is wearing red Spanish leather, tall
boots, turned over at the top.

As he stands talking to Caxton, one or two
gentlemen, who have also dismounted, stand about

him. Three of them are in the
height of the fashion. The first
wears a velvet tunic, with fur
edges. The tunic is pleated
before and behind, and is full
and slightly pursed in front;
the sleeves are long, and are
cut from shoulder to wrist,
where they are sewn together
again; cuff and border of the
cut or opening are both edged with fur. The neck
is high, but there is no collar. The length of the
tunic is quite short; it comes well above the knees.
His under-sleeves are full, and are of rich silk;
his shoes are certainly over the allowed length; his
tights are well cut. His peaked hat has gold bands
round the crown.

The second gentleman is also in a very short
tunic, with very wide sleeves; this tunic is pleated
into large even folds, and has a belt of its own
material. His hair is long, and bushed behind;

his tights are in two colours, and he wears an eighteen-penny pair of black leather slops or shoes. His hat is black, tall, but without a peak ; a long feather is brooched into one side of it.

The third man is wearing a low black cap, with a little close brim ; a jagged piece of stuff, about 3 feet long, hangs from under the brim of his hat. He is wearing long, straight hair.   This man is wearing a little short tunic, which is loose at the waist, and comes but an inch or two below it ; the sleeves are very loose and wide, and are not fastened at the wrist ; the tunic has a little collar.   The shortness of his tunic shows  the whole of his tights, and also the ribbon-fastened cod-piece in front.   His shoes are split at the sides, and come into a peak before and behind.

Now, our gentlemen of this time, having cut open their baggy sleeves, and made them to hang down and expose all the under-sleeve, must now needs lace them up again very loosely.   Then, by way of change, the tight sleeve was split at the elbow to show a white shirt. Then came the broad shoulders, when the sleeves were swelled out  at the top to give an air of great breadth to the shoulders and a more elegant taper to the waist. Some men had patterns sewn on one leg of their tights. The gown, or whatever top garment was being worn, was sometimes cut into a low, V shape behind at the neck to show the undergarment, above which showed a piece of white shirt.

A long gown, in shape like a monk's habit, wide sleeves, the same width all the way down, a loose neck—a garment indeed to put on over the head, to slip on for comfort and warmth—was quite a marked fashion in the streets —as marked as the little tunic.

If you are remembering Caxton's shop and a crowd of gentlemen, notice one in a big fur hat, which comes over his eyes; and see also a man who has wound a strip of cloth about his neck and over his head, then, letting one end hang down, has clapped his round, steeple-crowned hat over it.

You will see high collars, low collars, and
absence of collar, long gown open to the waist,
long gown without opening, short-skirted tunic,
tunic without any skirt, long, short, and medium
shoes, and, at the end of the reign, one or two
broad-toed shoes. Many of these men would be
carrying sticks ; most of them would have their
fingers covered with rings.

Among the group of gentlemen about Edward
some merchants have pressed closer to see the
King, and a girl or two has stolen into the front
row. The King, turning to make a laughing
remark to one of his courtiers, will see a roguish,
pretty face behind him—the face of a merchant's
wife ; he will smile at her in a meaning way.

THE WOMEN

France, at this date, shows
us a sartorial Savonarola, by
name Thomas Conecte, a preaching friar, who held an Anti-
Hennin Crusade, which ended in
a bonfire of these steeple head-
dresses. The flames of these peculiar hats lit
up the inspired devotees, and showed their heads

wrapped in plain linen wimples or some little unaffected caps. But the ashes were hardly cold before the gray light of the next day showed the figure of the dreaded preacher small upon the horizon, and lit upon the sewing-maids as they sat making fresh steeples for the adornment of their ladies' heads.

Joan of Arc is dead, and another very different apparition of womankind looms out of the mists of history. Whilst Joan of Arc is hymned and numbered among the happy company of saints triumphant, Jane Shore is roared in drinking-songs and ballads of a disreputable order, and is held up as an awful example. She has for years been represented upon the boards of West End and Surrey-side theatres—in her prime as the mistress of Edward IV., in her penance before the church door, and in her poverty and starvation, hounded from house to house in a Christian country where bread was denied to her. I myself have seen her through the person of a stout, melancholy, and h-less lady, who, dressed in a sort of burlesque fish-wife costume, has lain dying on the prompt-side of the stage, in a whirl of paper snow, while, to the edification of the twopenny gallery, she has bewailed her evil life, and has been allowed, by a munificent management, to die in the arms of white-clad angels.   There is a gleam of truth in the representation, and you may see the real Jane Shore in a high steeple head-dress, with a thin veil thrown over it, with a frontlet or little loop of black velvet over her forehead ; in a high-waisted dress, open in a V shape from shoulder to waist, the opening laced over the square-cut under-gown, the upper gown having a collar of fur or silk, a long train, broad cuffs, perhaps 7 inches long from the base of her fingers, with a broad, coloured band about her waist, a broader trimming of the same colour round the hem of her shirt, and in long peaked shoes.   In person of mean stature, her hair dark yellow, her face round and full, her eyes gray, and her countenance as cheerful as herself.   The second real picture of her shows you a haggard woman, with her hair unbound and falling about her shoulders, shivering in a shift, which she clutches about her with one hand, while the other holds a dripping candle ; and the third picture shows an old woman in dirty wimple and untidy rags.

There are many ways of making the steeple

head-dress.   For the most part they are long,
black-covered steeples, resting at an angle of forty-
five degrees to the head, the broad end having a
deep velvet band round it, with hanging sides,
which come to the level of the chin ; the point end
has a long veil attached to it, which floats lightly
down, or is carried on to one shoulder.   Sometimes this steeple hat is worn over a hood, the cape

of which is tucked into the dress.
Some of these hats have a jutting,
upturned piece in front, and they
are also covered with all manner
of coloured stuffs, but not commonly so.   All persons having an
income of £10 a year and over
will have that black velvet loop,
the frontlet, sewn into their hats.
There is another new shape for hats, varying in
height from 8 to 18 inches.   It is a cylinder,
broader at the top than the bottom, the crown
sometimes flat and sometimes rounded into the hat
itself ; this hat is generally jewelled, and covered
with rich material.   The veils are attached to these
hats in several ways ; either they float down behind
from the centre of the crown of the hat, or they

A MAN OF THE TIME OF EDWARD IV.   1461-1483

A WOMAN OF THE TIME OF EDWARD IV.   1461-1483

are sewn on to the base of the hat, and are supported on wires, so as to shade the face, making a roof over it, pointed in front and behind, or flat across the front and bent into a point behind, or circular. Take two circles of wire, one the size of the base of your hat and the other larger, and dress your linen or thin silk upon them ; then you may pinch the wire into any variations of squares and circles you please.

The veil was sometimes worn all over the steeple hat, coming down over the face, but stiff enough to stand away from it. Towards the end of the reign the hats were not so high or so erect.

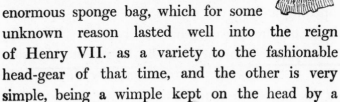

Remember, also, that the horned head-dress of the previous reign is not by any means extinct.

There remain two more forms of making the human face hideous: one is the head-dress closely resembling an enormous sponge bag, which for some unknown reason lasted well into the reign of Henry VII. as a variety to the fashionable head-gear of that time, and the other is very simple, being a wimple kept on the head by a

14

circular stuffed hoop of material, which showed plain and severe across the forehead. The simple folk wore a hood of linen, with a liripipe and wide ear-flaps.

The dresses are plain in cut; they are all short-waisted if at all fashionable. The most of them have a broad waist-belt, and very deep borders to their skirts; they have broad, turned-back cuffs, often of black. These cuffs, on being turned down over the hand, show the same colour as the dress; they are, in fact, the old long cuff over the fingers turned back for comfort.

It is by the variety of openings at the necks of the gowns that you may get change. First, let me take the most ordinary—that is, an opening of a V shape from shoulders to waist, the foot of the V at the waist, the points on the top of the shoulders at the join of the arm. Across this opening is seen, cut square and coming up to the base of the bosom, the under-gown. You may now proceed to vary this by lacing the V across, but not drawing it together, by having the V fur-edged, or made to turn over in a collar of

black upon light material, or its opposite, by showing a vest of stuff other than that of the under-
gown, which will then make a variety of colour
when the skirt is held up over the arm. Or you
may have your dress so cut that it is high in front
and square cut, and over this you may sew a false
V collar wither to or above the waist. I have said
that the whole neck-opening may be
covered by a gorget of cloth, which
was pinned up to the steeple hat, or by
a hood of thin stuff or silk, the cape
of which was tucked into the dress.

The lady, I think, is now complete
down to her long-pointed shoes, her
necklet of stones or gold chain, with
cross or heraldic pendant, and it
remains to show that the countrywoman dressed very plainly, in a
decent-fitting dress, with her waist in its proper
place, her skirt full, the sleeves of her dress turned
back like my lady's, her head wrapped in a wimple
or warmed in a hood, her feet in plain, foot-
shaped shoes, and wooden clogs strapped on to
them for outdoor use or kitchen work ; in fact,
she looked much like any old body to-day who has

14—2

lived in a village, except that the wimple and the hood then worn are out of place to-day, more's the pity!

No doubt ladies were just human in those days, and fussed and frittered over an inch or so of hennin, or a yard or two of train. One cut her dress too low to please the others, and another wore her horned head-dress despite the dictates of Fashion, which said, ' Away with horns, and into steeples.' No doubt the tall hennins, with their floating veils, looked like black masts with silken sails, and the ladies like a crowd of shipping, with velvet trains for waves about their feet; no doubt the steeples swayed and the silks rustled when the heads turned to look at the fine men in the days when hump-shouldered Richard was a dandy.

A MAN OF THE TIME OF RICHARD III.   1483-1485

A WOMAN OF THE TIME OF RICHARD III. 1483-1485

EDWARD THE FIFTH

Reigned two months: April and June, 1487.

RICHARD THE THIRD

Reigned two years: 1483—1485.
Born 1450.   Married, 1473, Anne Neville.

THE MEN

 FASHION's pulse beat very weak in the spring of 1483. More attune to the pipes of Fate were the black cloaks of conspirators and a measured tread of soft-shoed feet than lute and dance of airy millinery.   The axe of the executioner soiled many white shirts, and dreadful forebodings fluttered the dovecots of high-hennined ladies.

The old order was dying; Medievalism, which made a last spluttering flame in the next reign, was now burnt low, and was saving for that last effort. When Richard married Anne Neville, in the same year was Raphael born in Italy ; literature was beginning, thought was beginning ; many of the great spirits of the Renaissance were alive and working in Italy ; the very trend of clothes showed something vaguely different, something which shows, however, that the foundations of the world were being shaken—so shaken that men and women, coming out of the gloom of the fourteenth century through the half-light of the fifteenth, saw the first signs of a new day, the first show of spring, and, with a perversity or an eagerness to meet the coming day, they began to change their clothes.

It is in this reign of Richard III. that we get, for the men, a hint of the peculiar magnificence of the first years of the sixteenth century ; we get the first flush of those wonderful patterns which are used by Memlinc and Holbein, those variations of the pine-apple pattern, and of that peculiar convention which is traceable in the outline of the Tudor rose.

The men, at first sight, do not appear very
different to the men of Edward IV.'s time; they
have the long hair, the general clean-shaven faces,
open-breasted tunics, and full-pleated skirts.   But,
as a rule, the man, peculiar to his time, the clothes-
post of his age, has discarded the tall peaked hat,
and is almost always dressed in the black velvet,
stiff-brimmed hat.   The pleated skirt to his tunic
has grown longer, and his purse has grown larger ;
the sleeves are tighter, and the old tunic with the
split, hanging sleeves has grown fuller, longer, and
has become an overcoat, being now open all the
way down.   You will see that the neck of the
tunic is cut very low, and that you may see above
it, above the black velvet with which it is so often
bound, the rich colour or fine material of an undergarment, a sort of waistcoat, and yet again above
that the straight top of a finely-pleated white
shirt.   Sometimes the sleeves of the tunic will be
wide, and when the arm is flung up in gesticulation,
the baggy white shirt, tight-buttoned at the wrist,
will show.   Instead of the overcoat with the hanging sleeves, you will find a very plain-cut overcoat,
with sleeves comfortably wide, and with little plain
lapels to the collar.   It is cut wide enough in the

back to allow for the spread of the tunic. Black velvet is becoming a very fashionable trimming, and will be seen as a border or as under-vest to show between the shirt and the tunic. No clothes of the last reign will be incongruous in this; the very short tunics which expose the cod-piece, the split-sleeve tunic, all the variations, I have described. Judges walk about, looking like gentlemen of the time of Richard II.: a judge wears a long loose gown, with wide sleeves, from out of which appear the sleeves of his under-tunic, buttoned from elbow to wrist; he wears a cloak with a hood, the cloak split up the right side, and fastened by three buttons upon the right shoulder. A doctor is in very plain, ample gown, with a cape over his shoulders and a small round cap on his head. His gown is not bound at the waist.

The blunt shoes have come into fashion, and with this the old long-peaked shoe dies for ever. Common-sense will show you that the gentlemen who had leisure to hunt in these times did not wear their most foppish garments, that the tunics were plain, the boots high, the cloaks of strong material. They wore a hunting-hat, with a long

peak over the eyes and a little peak over the neck
at the back; a broad band passed under the chin,
and, buttoning on to either side of the hat, kept it
in place. The peasant wore a loose tunic, often
open-breasted and laced across; he had a belt
about his waist, a hood over his head, and often
a broad-brimmed Noah's Ark hat over the hood;
his slops, or loose trousers, were tied below the
knee and at the ankles. A shep-
herd would stick his pipe in his
belt, so that he might march before his flock, piping them into the
fold.

To sum up, you must picture a
man in a dress of Edward IV.'s time, modified,
or, rather, expanded or expanding into the costume
of Henry VII.'s time—a reign, in fact, which
hardly has a distinct costume to itself—that is, for
the men—but has a hand stretched out to two
centuries, the fifteenth and the sixteenth; yet, if
I have shown the man to you as I myself can see
him, he is different from his father in 1461, and
will change a great deal before 1500.

THE WOMEN

Here we are at the end of an epoch, at the close of a costume period, at one of those curious final dates in a history of clothes which says that within a year or so the women of one time will look hopelessly old-fashioned and queer to the modern woman. Except for the peculiar sponge-bag turban, which had a few years of life in it, the woman in Henry VII.'s reign would look back at this time and smile, and the young woman would laugh at the old ideas of beauty. The River of Time runs under many bridges, and it would seem that the arches were low to the Bridge of Fashion in 1483, and the steeple hat was lowered to prevent contact with them. The correct angle of forty-five degrees changed into a right angle, the steeple hat, the hennin, came toppling down, and an embroidered bonnet, perched right on the back of the head, came into vogue. It is this bonnet which gives, from our point of view, distinction to the reign. It was a definite fashion, a distinct halt.

It had travelled along the years of the fourteenth century, from the wimple and the horns, and the stiff turbans, and the boxes of stiffened cloth of gold ; it had languished in the caul and blossomed in the huge wimple-covered horns ; it had shot up in the hennin ; and now it gave, as its last transformation, this bonnet at the back of the head, with the stiff wimple stretched upon wires. Soon was to come the diamond-shaped head-dress, and after that the birth of hair as a beauty.

In this case the hair was drawn as tightly as possible away from the forehead, and at the forehead the smaller hairs were plucked away ; even eyebrows were a little out of fashion. Then this cylindrical bonnet was placed at the back of the head, with its wings of thin linen stiffly sewn or propped on wires. These wires were generally of a V shape, the V point at the forehead. On some occasions two straight wires came out on either side of the face in addition to the V, and so made two wings on either side of the face and two wings over the back of the head. It is more easy to describe through means of the drawings, and the reader will soon see what bend to give to the wires in order that the wings may be properly held out.

Beyond this head-dress there was very little alteration in the lady's dress since the previous reign. The skirts were full; the waist was high, but not absurdly so; the band round the dress was broad; the sleeves were tight; and the cuffs, often of fur, were folded back to a good depth.

The neck opening of the dress varied, as did that of the previous reign, but whereas the most fashionable opening was then from neck to waist, this reign gave more liking to a higher corsage, over the top of which a narrow piece of stuff showed, often of black velvet. We may safely assume that the ladies followed the men in the matter of broad shoes. For a time the old fashion of the long-tongued belt came in, and we see instances of such belts being worn with the tongue reaching nearly to the feet, tipped with a metal ornament.

Not until night did these ladies discard their winged head erections; not until the streets were dark, and the brass basins swinging from the

A MAN OF THE TIME OF HENRY VII.　1485-1509

A WOMAN OF THE TIME OF HENRY VII.   1485-1509

barbers' poles shone but dimly, and the tailors no
longer sat, cross-legged, on the benches in their
shop-fronts—then might my lady uncover her head
and talk, in company with my lord, over the
strange new stories of Prester John and of the
Wandering Jew ; then, at her proper time, she will
go to her rest and sleep soundly beneath her
embroidered quilt, under the protection of the
saints whose pictures she has sewn into the corners
of it.   Matthew, Mark, Luke, and John, bless the
bed that she lies on.

So we come to an end of a second series of
dates, from the First Edward to the Third Richard,
and we leave them to come to the Tudors and
their follies and fantastics ; we leave an age that is
quaint, rich, and yet fairly simple, to come to an
age of padded hips and farthingales, monstrous
ruffs, knee-breeks, rag-stuffed trunks, and high-
heeled shoes.

With the drawings and text you should be able
to people a vast world of figures, dating from the
middle of the thirteenth century, 1272, to nearly
the end of the fifteenth, 1485, and if you allow
ordinary horse-sense to have play, you will be able
to people your world with correctly-dressed figures

in the true inspiration of their time. You cannot disassociate the man from his tailor; his clothes must appeal to you, historically and soulfully, as an outward and visible sign to the graces and vices of his age and times.

HENRY THE SEVENTH

Reigned 24 years: 1485—1509.
Born, 1456.   Married, 1486, Elizabeth of York.

THE MEN

EVERYONE has felt that curious faint aroma, that sensation of lifting, which proclaims the first day of Spring and the burial of Winter. Although nothing tangible has taken place, there is in the atmosphere a full-charged suggestion of promise, of green-sickness; there is a quickening of the pulse, a thrumming of the heart, and many an eager, quick glance around for the first buds of the new order of things.

England's winter was buried on Bosworth Field :
England's spring, as if by magic, commenced with
Henry's entry into London.

The first picture of the reign shows the mayor,
the sheriffs, and the aldermen, clothed in violet,
waiting at Shoreditch for the coming of the victor.
The same day shows Henry in St. Paul's, hearing
a *Te Deum ;* in the Cathedral church, packed to
its limit, three new banners waved, one bearing a
figure of St. George, another a dragon of red on
white and green sarcenet, and the third showed a
dun cow on yellow tarterne.

Spring, of course, does not, except in a poetic
sense, burst forth in a day, there are long months
of preparation, hints, signs in the air, new notes
from the throats of birds.

The springtime of a country takes more than
the preparation of months. Nine years before
Henry came to the throne Caxton was learning
to print in the little room of Collard Mansion—
he was to print his ' Facts of Arms,' joyous tales
and pleasant histories of chivalry, by especial desire
of Henry himself.

Later still, towards the end of the reign, the
first book of travel in the West began to go from

hand to hand—it was written by Amerigo Ves-
pucci, cousin to La Bella Simonetta.

Great thoughts were abroad, new ideas were
constantly under discussion, the Arts rose to the
occasion and put forth flowers of beauty on many
stems long supposed to be dead or dormant and
incapable of improvement. It was the great age
of individual English expression in every form
but that of literature and painting, both these
arts being but in their cradles; Chaucer and
Gower and Langland had written, but they lay
in their graves long before new great minds arose.

The clouds of the Middle Ages were dispersed,
and the sun shone.

The costume was at once dignified and magnificent—not that one can call the little coats great
ideals of dignity, but even they, by their richness
and by the splendour of the persons they adorned,
come into the category.

The long gowns of both men and women were
rich beyond words in colour, texture, and design.
they were imposing, exact, and gorgeous. Upon
a fine day the streets must have glittered when a
gentleman or lady passed by.

The fashions of the time have survived for us

15

in the Court cards: take the jacks, knaves, valets
—call them as you will, and you will see the
costume of this reign but slightly modified into
a design, the cards of to-day and the cards of that
day are almost identical. Some years ago the
modification was less noticeable; I can remember

playing Pope Joan with cards printed
with full-length figures, just as the
illustrations to 'Alice in Wonderland' are drawn. In the knave you
will see the peculiar square hat which
came in at this time, and the petti-
cote, the long coat, the big sleeve,
and the broad-toed shoes. You will
see the long hair, undressed and
flowing over the shoulders (the pro-
fessional classes, as the lawyer, cut
their hair close, so also did the peasant). Over
this flowing hair a dandy would wear a little cap
with a narrow, rolled-up brim, and over this, on
occasions, an enormous hat of felt, ornamented
with a prodigious quantity of feathers.

There was, indeed, quite a choice of hats: the
berretino—a square hat pinched in at the corners;
many round hats, some with a high, tight brim,

some with the least brim possible; into these
brims, or into a band round the hat, one might
stick feathers or pin a brooch.

The chaperon, before described, was still worn
by Garter Knights at times, and by official, legal,
civic, and college persons.

What a choice of coats the gentlemen had, and
still might be in the fashion! Most common
among these was the long coat like a dressing-
gown, hanging upon the ground all round, with
a wide collar, square behind, and turning back in
the front down to the waist—this was the general
shape of the collar, and you may vary it on this
idea in every way: turn it back and show the
stuff to the feet, close it up nearly to the neck,
cut it off completely. Now for the sleeves of such
a coat. I have shown in the illustrations many
varieties, the most common was the wide sleeve,
narrow at the shoulder, and hanging over the hand
in folds. The slashes, which show the white shirt,
are usual, and of every order. The shirt itself
was often ornamented with fine gathers and fancy
stitching, and was gathered about the neck by a
ribbon. As the years went on it is easy to see
that the shirt was worn nearer to the neck, the

15—2

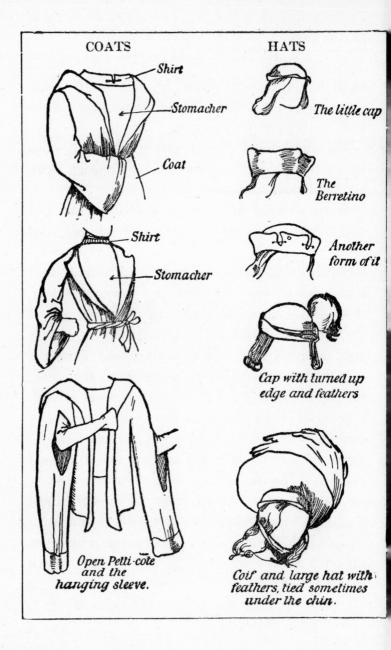

COATS

Shirt

Stomacher

Coat

Shirt

Stomacher

Open Petti-cote
and the
hanging sleeve.

HATS

The little cap

The
Berretino

Another
form of it

Cap with turned up
edge and feathers

Coif and large hat with
feathers, tied sometimes
under the chin.

gathers became higher and higher, became more ornamented, and finally rose, in all extravagant finery, to behind the ears—and we have the Elizabethan ruff.

Next to the shirt a waistcoat, or stomacher, of the most gorgeous patterned stuff, laced across the breast sometimes, more often fastened behind. This reached to the waist where it met long hose of every scheme of colour—striped, dotted, divided in bands—everything—displaying the indelicate but universal pouch in front, tied with coloured ribbons.

On the feet, shoes of all materials, from cloth and velvet to leather beautifully worked, and of the most absurd length ; these also were slashed with puffs of white stuff. Many of these shoes were but a sole and a toe, and were tied on by thongs passing through the sole.

Of course the long coat would not alone satisfy the dandy, but he must needs cut it off into a short jacket, or petti-cote, and leave it open to better display his marvellous vest. Here we have the origin of the use of the word 'petticoat'— now wrongly applied; in Scotland, to this day, a woman's skirts are called her 'coats.'

About the waists of these coats was a short sash, or a girdle, from which hung a very elaborate purse, or a dagger.

Stick in hand, jewel in your hat, dandy—extravagant, exquisite dandy ! All ages know you, from the day you choose your covering of leaves with care, to the hour of your white duck motoring-suit: a very bird of a man, rejoicing in your plumage, a very human ass, a very narrow individual, you stride, strut, simper through the story of the universe, a perfect monument of the Fall of Man, a gorgeous symbol of the decay of manhood. In this our Henry's reign, your hair busheth pleasantly, and is kembed prettily over the ear, where it glimmers as gold i' the sun—pretty fellow—Lord ! how your feathered bonnet becomes you, and your satin stomacher is brave over a padded chest. Your white hands, freed from any nasty brawls and clean of any form of work, lie in their embroidered gloves. Your pride forbids the carriage of a sword, which is borne behind you—much use may it be !—by a mincing fellow in your dainty livery. And if—oh, rare disguise !—your coiffure hides a noble brow, or your little, neat-rimmed coif a clever head, less

SLEEVES

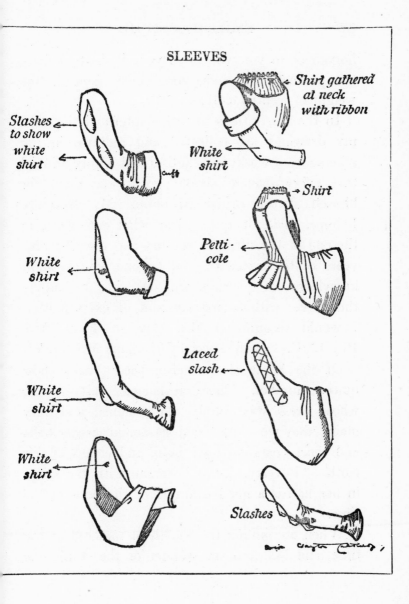

Slashes to show white shirt

Shirt gathered at neck with ribbon

White shirt

Cuff

Shirt

Petti-cote

White shirt

White shirt

Laced slash

White shirt

Slashes

honour be to you who dress your limbs to imitate the peacock, and hide your mind beneath the weight of scented clothes.

In the illustrations to this chapter and the next, my drawings are collected and redrawn in my scheme from works so beautiful and highly finished that every student should go to see them for himself at the British Museum. My drawings, I hope, make it quite clear what was worn in the end of the fifteenth century and the first nine years of the sixteenth, and anyone with a slight knowledge of pictures will be able to supply themselves with a large amount of extra matter. I would recommend MS. Roy 16, F. 2; MS. Roy 19, C. 8; and especially Harleian MS. 4425.

Of the lower classes, also, these books show quite a number. There are beggars and peasants, whose dress was simply old-fashioned and very plain; they wore the broad shoes and leather belts and short coats, worsted hose, and cloaks of fair cloth. 'Poverty,' the old woman with the spoon in her hat, is a good example of the poor of the time.

When one knows the wealth of material of the time, and has seen the wonder of the stuffs, one

knows that within certain lines imagination may
have full scope. Stuffs of silk, embroidered with
coupled birds and branches, and flowers following
out a prescribed line, the embroideries edged and
sewn with gold thread; velvet on velvet, short-
napped fustian, damasked stuffs and diapered stuffs
—what pictures on canvas, or on the stage, may
be made; what marvels of colour
walked about the streets in those
days! It was to the eye an age of
elaborate patterns—mostly large—and
all this broken colour and glitter of
gold thread must have made the
streets gay indeed.

Imagine, shall we say, Corfe Castle
on a day when a party of ladies and
gentlemen assembled to 'course a
stagge,' when the huntsmen, in green,
gathered in the outer ward, and the grooms, in
fine coloured liveries, held the gaily-decked
horses; then, from the walls lined with archers,
would come the blast of the horn, and out
would walk my lord and my lady, with knights,
and squires, and ladies, and gallants, over the
bridge across the castle ditch, between the round

towers.   Behind them the dungeon tower, and
the great gray mass of the keep—all a fitting and
impressive background to their bravery.

The gentlemen, in long coats of all wonderful
colours and devices, with little hats, jewelled and
feathered, with boots to the knee of soft leather,

turned back in colours at the top;
on their left hands the thick hawking glove on which, jessed and
hooded, sits the hawk—for some
who will not go with the hounds
will fly the hawk on the Isle of
Purbeck.

Below, in the town over the moat,
a crowd is gathered to see them off
—merchants in grave colours, and
coats turned back with fur, their
ink-horns slung at their waists, with
pens and dagger and purse; beggars; pilgrims,
from over seas, landed at Poole Harbour, in long
gowns, worn with penitence and dusty travels,
shells in their hats, staffs in their hands; wide-
eyed children in smocks; butchers in blue; men
of all guilds and women of all classes.

The drawbridge is down, the portcullis up, and

the party, gleaming like a bed of flowers in their multi-coloured robes, pass over the bridge, through the town, and into the valley.

The sun goes in and leaves the grim castle, gray and solemn, standing out against the green of the hills. . . .

And of Henry himself, the great Tudor, greater, more farseeing than the eighth Henry, a man who so dominates the age, and fills it with his spirit, that no mental picture is complete without him. His fine, humorous face, the quizzical eye, the firm mouth, showing his character. The great lover of art, of English art, soon to be pulverized by pseudo-classic influences; the man who pulled down the chapel at the west end of Westminster Abbey with the house by it—Chaucer's house— to make way for that superb triumph of ornate building, his chapel, beside which the mathematical squares and angles of classic buildings show as would boxes of bricks by a gorgeous flower.

The stories against him are, in reality, stories for him, invented by those whom he kept to their work, and whom he despoiled of their ill-gotten gains. He borrowed, but he paid back in full;

he came into a disordered, distressed kingdom,
ruled it by fear—as had to be done in those days—
and left it a kingdom ready for the fruits of his
ordered works—to the fleshy beast who so nearly
ruined the country.   What remained, indeed, was
the result of his father's genius.

THE WOMEN

Take up a pack of cards and look at the queen.
You may see the extraordinary head-gear as worn
by ladies at the end of the fifteenth century and
in the first years of the sixteenth, worn in a
modified form all through the next reign, after
which that description of head-dress vanished for
ever, its place to be taken by caps, hats, and
bonnets.

The richest of these head-dresses were made of
a black silk or some such black material, the top
stiffened to the shape of a sloping house-roof, the
edges falling by the face on either side—made
stiff, so as to stand parallel—these were sewn
with gold and pearls on colour or white.   The
end of the hood hung over the shoulders and
down the back; this was surmounted by a stole

of stiffened material, also richly sewn with jewels, and the whole pinned on to a close-fitting cap of

The ordinary Hood of Cloth

The Pointed Hood of silk stiffened & edged with frais & jewel work

The Hood a couple of Linen

Hood over white Coif

Shoes

Hood over hair in two plaits.

The Barbe of Pleated Linen

The Hood folded up & pinned.

a different colour, the edge of which showed above the forehead.

The more moderate head-dress was of black again, but in shape nearly square, and slit at the sides to enable it to hang more easily over the shoulders. It was placed over a coif, often of white linen or of black material, was turned over from the forehead, folded, and pinned back; often it was edged with gold.

On either side of the hood were hanging ornamental metal-tipped tags to tie back the hood from the shoulders, and this became, in time— that is, at the end of the reign—the ordinary manner of wearing them, till they were finally made up so.

The ordinary head-dress was of white linen, crimped or embroidered in white, made in a piece to hang over the shoulders and down the back, folded back and stiffened in front to that peculiar triangular shape in fashion; this was worn by the older women over a white hood.

The plain coif, or close-fitting linen cap, was the most general wear for the poor and middle classes.

The hair was worn long and naturally over the shoulders by young girls, and plainly parted in the centre and dressed close to the head by women wearing the large head-dress.

Another form of head-dress, less common, was the turban—a loose bag of silk, gold and pearl embroidered, fitting over the hair and forehead tightly, and loose above.

The gowns of the women were very simply cut, having either a long train or no train at all, these last cut to show the underskirt of some fine material, the bodice of which showed above the over gown at the shoulders. The ladies who wore the long gown generally had it lined with some fine fur, and to prevent this dragging in the mud, as also to show

the elegance of their furs, they fastened the train to a button or brooch placed at the back of the waistband. This, in time, developed into the looped skirts of Elizabethan times.

The bodice of the gown was square cut and not very low, having an ornamental border of fur, embroidery, or other rich coloured material sewn on

to it. This border went sometimes round the
shoulders and down the front of the dress to below
the knees. Above the bodice was nearly always
seen the V-shaped opening of the under petticoat
bodice, and across and above that, the white
embroidered or crimped chemise.

The sleeves were as the men's—tight all the
way down from the shoulder to the wrist, the
cuffs coming well over the first
joints of the fingers (sometimes
these cuffs are turned back to show
elaborate linings), or they were made
tight at the shoulder and gradually
looser until they became very full
over the lower arm, edged or lined
with fur or soft silk, or loose and
baggy all the way from shoulder to
hand.

At this time Bruges became
world-famed for her silken texture ; her satins were
used in England for church garments and other
clothes. The damask silks were greatly in use,
and were nearly always covered with the peculiar
semi-Spanish pattern, the base of which was some
contortion of the pomegranate. Some of these

patterns were small and wonderfully fine, depending on their wealth of detail for their magnificent appearance, others were huge, so that but few repeats of the design appeared on the dress. Block-printed linens were also in use, and the samples in South Kensington will show how beautiful and artistic they were, for all their simple design. As Bruges supplied us with silks, satins, and velvets, the last also beautifully damasked, Yprès sent her linen to us, and the whole of Flanders sent us painters and illuminators who worked in England at the last of the great illuminated books, but this art died as printing and illustrating by wood-blocks came in to take its place.

Nearly every lady had her own common linen, and often other stuffs, woven in her own house, and the long winter evenings were great times for the sewing chambers, where the lady and her maids sat at the looms. To-day one may see in Bruges the women at the cottage doors busy over their lace-making, and the English women by the sea making nets—so in those times was every woman at her cottage door making coarse linens and other stuffs to earn her daily bread, while my lady was sitting in her chamber weaving, or

embroidering a bearing cloth for her child against
her time.

However, the years of the Wars of the Roses
had had their effect on every kind of English
work, and as the most elegant books were painted
and written by Flemings, as the finest linen came
from Yprès, the best silks and velvets from Bruges,
the great masters of painting from Florence,
Germany, and Belgium, so also the elaborate and
wonderful embroidery, for which we had been so
famous, died away, and English work was but
coarse at the best, until, in the early sixteen
hundreds, the new style came into use of raising
figures some height above the ground-work of
the design, and the rich embroidery of the Stuart
times revived this art.

I have shown that this age was the age of fine
patterns, as some ages are ages of quaint cut, and
some of jewel-laden dresses, and some of dainty
needlework.

A few ladies wore their gowns open to the
waist to show the stomacher, as the men did,
and open behind to the waist, laced across,
the waist being embraced by a girdle of the
shape so long in use, with long ends and metal

ornaments; the girdle held the purse of the lady.

The illustrations given with this chapter show very completely the costume of this time, and, except in cases of royal persons or very gorgeously apparelled ladies, they are complete enough to need no description.

The shoes, it will be seen, are very broad at the toes, with thick soles, sometimes made much in the manner of sandals—that is, with only a toecap, the rest flat, to be tied on by strings.

As this work is entirely for use, it may be said, that artists who have costumes made for them, and costumiers who make for the stage, hardly ever allow enough material for the gowns worn by men and women in this and other reigns, where the heaviness and richness of the folds was the great keynote. To make a gown, of such a kind as these good ladies wore, one needs, at least, twelve yards of material, fifty-two inches wide, to give the right appearance. It is possible to acquire at many of the best shops nowadays actual copies of embroidered stuffs, velvets, and damask silks of this time, and of stuffs up to Early Victorian patterns, and this makes it easy for

16—2

painters to procure what, in other days, they were forced to invent.

Many artists have their costumes made of Bolton sheeting, on to which they stencil the patterns they wish to use—this is not a bad thing to do, as sheeting is not dear and it falls into beautiful folds.

The older ladies and widows of this time nearly all dressed in very simple, almost conventual garments, many of them wearing the ' barbe' of pleated linen, which covered the lower part of the face and the chin—a sort of linen beard —it reached to the breast, and is still worn by some religious orders of women.

Badges were still much in use, and the servants always wore some form of badge on their left sleeve—either merely the colours of their masters, or a small silver, or other metal, shield. Thus, the badge worn by the servants of Henry VII. would be either a greyhound, a crowned hawthorn bush, a red dragon, a portcullis, or the red and white roses joined together. The last two were used by all the Tudors, and the red rose and the portcullis are still used. From these badges we get the signs of many of our inns, either started

by servants, who used their master's badge for a
device, or because the inn lay on a certain property
the lord of which carried chequers, or a red dragon,
or a tiger's head.

I mentioned the silks of Bruges and her velvets
without giving enough prominence to the fine
velvets of Florence, a sample of which, a cope,
once used in Westminster Abbey, is preserved at
Stonyhurst College; it was left by Henry VII.
to 'Our Monastery of Westminster,' and is of
beautiful design—a gold ground, covered with
boughs and leaves raised in soft velvet pile of
ruby colour, through which little loops of gold
thread appear.

I imagine Elizabeth ot York, Queen to
Henry VII., of the subtle countenance—gentle
Elizabeth, who died in child-birth—proceeding
through London, from the Tower to Westminster, to her coronation; the streets cleansed
and the houses hung with tapestry, arras and
gold cloth, the fine-coloured dresses of the
crowd, the armoured soldiers, all the rich estate
of the company about her, and the fine trappings
of the horses. Our Queen went to her coronation
with some Italian masts, paper flowers, and some

hundreds of thousands of yards of bunting and cheap flags; the people mostly in sombre clothes; the soldiers in ugly red, stiff coats, were the only colour of note passing down Whitehall, past the hideous green stuck with frozen Members of Parliament, to the grand, wonderful Abbey, which has seen so many Queens crowned.

HENRY THE EIGHTH

Reigned thirty-eight years : 1509—1547.
Born, 1491. Married, 1509, Katharine of Aragon ;
  1532, Anne Boleyn ; 1536, Jane Seymour ; 1540,
  Anne of Cleves ; 1540, Katharine Howard ; 1543,
  Katherine Parr.

THE MEN

VERSES BY HENRY THE EIGHTH IN PRAISE OF CONSTANCY

' As the holy grouth grene with ivie all alone
Whose flowerys cannot be seen and grene wode levys be gone,
Now unto my lady, promyse to her I make
From all other only to her I me betake.
Adew myne owne ladye, adew my specyall
Who hath my hart trewly, be sure, and ever shall.'

So, with songs and music of his own composition,
comes the richest man in Europe to the throne
of England. Gay, brave, tall, full of conceit in
his own strength, Henry, a king, a Tudor, a
handsome man, abounding in excellence of craft
and art, the inheritance from his father and

247

mother, figures in our pageant a veritable symbol of the Renaissance in England.

He had, in common with the marvellous characters of that Springtime of History, the quick intelligence and all the personal charm that the age brought forth in abundance. In his reign the accumulated mass of brain all over the world budded and flowered; the time gave to us a succession of the most remarkable people in any historical period, and it is one of the triumphs of false reasoning to prove this, in England, to have been the result of the separation from the Catholic Church. For centuries the Church had organized and prepared the ground in which this tree of the world's knowledge was planted, had pruned, cut back, nursed the tree, until gradually it flowered, its branches spread over Christian Europe, and when the flowering branch hanging over England gave forth its first-fruits, those men who ate of the fruit and benefited by the shade were the first to quarrel with the gardeners.

In these days there lived and died Botticelli, Leonardo da Vinci, Raphael, Dürer, Erasmus, Holbein, Copernicus, Luther, Rabelais, and Michael Angelo, to mention a few men of every shade of thought, and in this goodly time came Henry to the English throne, to leave, at his death, instead of the firm progress of order instituted by his father, a bankrupt country with an enormously rich Government.

You may see for the later pictures of his reign a great bloated mass of corpulence, with running ulcers on his legs and the blood of wives and people on his hands, striding in his well-known attitude over the festering slums his rule had produced in London.   Harry, *Grace à Dieu !*

The mental picture from our—costume—point of view is widely different from that of the last reign.   No longer do we see hoods and cowls, brown, gray, white, and black in the streets, no longer the throngs of fine craftsmen, of church-carvers, gilders, embroiderers, candle-makers, illuminators, missal-makers ; all these served but to swell the ranks of the unemployed, and caused a new problem to England, never since solved, of the skilled poor out of work.   The hospitals were closed—that should bring a picture to your eyes—where the streets had been thronged with the doctors of the poor and of the rich in their habits, no monks or lay brothers were to be seen.   The sick, the

blind, the insane had no home but the overhung
back alleys where the foulest diseases might
accumulate and hot-beds of vice spring up, while
in the main streets Harry Tudor was carried to
his bear-baiting, a quivering mass of jewels shaking
on his corrupt body, on his thumb that wonderful
diamond the Regale of France, stolen by him from
the desecrated shrine of St.
Thomas à Becket.

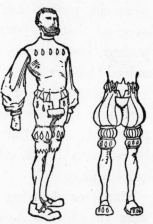

There are two distinct
classes of fashion to be seen,
the German-Swiss fashion
and the English fashion, a
natural evolution of the
national dress. The Ger-
man fashion is that slashed,
extravagant-looking crea-
tion which we know so well
from the drawings of Albert Dürer and the more
German designs of Holbein. The garments which
were known as 'blistered' clothes are excessive
growths on to the most extravagant designs of the
Henry VII. date. The shirt cut low in the neck,
and sewn with black embroidery; the little waistcoat ending at the waist and cut straight across from

shoulder to shoulder, tied with thongs of leather or coloured laces to the breeches, leaving a gap between which showed the shirt; the universal pouch on the breeches often highly decorated and jewelled. From the line drawings you will see that the sleeves and the breeches took every form, were of any odd assortment of colours, were cut, puffed, and slashed all over, so that the shirt might be pushed through the holes, looking indeed ' blistered.'

The shoes were of many shapes, as I have shown, agreeing in one point only—that the toes should be cut very broad, often, indeed, quite square.

Short or hanging hair, both were the fashion, and little flat caps with the rim cut at intervals, or the large flat hats of the previous reign, covered with feathers and curiously slashed, were worn with these costumes.

Cloaks, as you may see, were worn over the dress, and also those overcoats shaped much like the modern dressing-gown.

It is from these 'blistered,' padded breeches that we derive the trunks of the next reign, the slashings grown into long ribbon-like slits, the hose puffed at the knee.

Separate pairs of sleeves were worn with the waistcoats, or with the petti-cotes, a favourite sleeve trimming being broad velvet bands.

The invention sprang, as usual, from necessity, by vanity to custom. In 1477 the Swiss beat and routed the Duke of Burgundy at Nantes, and the soldiers, whose clothes were in rags, cut and tore up his silk tents, his banners, all material they could find, and made themselves clothes of these odd pieces—clothes still so torn and ragged that their shirts puffed out of every hole and rent. The arrival of the victorious army caused all the non-fighters to copy this curious freak in clothes, and the courtiers perpetuated the event by proclaiming blistering as the fashion.

The other and more usual fashion springs from the habit of clothes in bygone reigns.

Let us first take the shirt A. It will be seen how, in this reign, the tendency of the shirt was to come close about the neck. The previous reign showed us, as a rule, a shirt cut very low in the neck, with the hem drawn together with laces; these laces pulled more tightly together, thus rucking the material into closer gathers, caused the cut of the shirt to be altered and made so that the hem frilled out round the neck—a collar, in fact. That this collar took all forms under certain limitations will be noticed, also that thick necked gentlemen—Henry himself must have invented this—wore the collar of the shirt turned down and tied with strings of linen. The cuffs of the shirt, when they showed at the wrist, were often, as was the collar, sewn with elaborate designs in black thread or silk.

Now we take the waistcoat B. As you may see from the drawing showing the German form of dress, this waistcoat was really a petti-cote, a waist-coat with sleeves. This waist-coat was generally of richly ornamented material (Henry in purple satin, embroidered with his initials and the Tudor rose; Henry in brocade covered with posies made in letters of fine gold bullion). The material was slashed and puffed or plain, and dependent for its effect on the richness of its embroidery or design of the fabric. It was worn with or without sleeves; in most cases the sleeves were detachable.

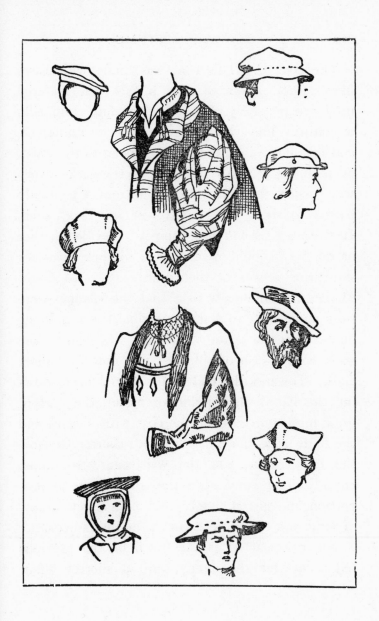

The coat C. This coat was made with bases like a frock, a skirted coat, in fact; the material used was generally plain, of velvet, fine cloth, silk, or satin. The varieties of cut were numerous, and are shown in the drawings—open to the waist, open all the way in front, close to the neck—every way; where the coat was open in front it generally parted to show the bragetto, or jewelled pouch. It was a matter for choice spirits to decide whether or no they should wear sleeves to their coats, or show the sleeves of their waistcoats. No doubt Madame Fashion saw to it that the changes were rung sufficiently to make hay while the sun shone on extravagant tastes. The coat was held at the waist with a sash of silk tied in a bow with short ends. Towards the end of the reign, foreshadowing the Elizabethan jerkin or jacket, the custom grew more universal of the coat with sleeves and the high neck, the bases were cut shorter to show the full trunks, and the waistcoat was almost entirely done away with, the collar grew in proportion, and spread, like the tail of an angry turkey, in ruffle and folded pleat round the man's neck.

The overcoat D is the gown of the previous reign cut, for the dandy, into a shorter affair, reaching not far below the knee; for the grave man it remained long, but, for all, the collar had changed to a wide affair stretching well over the shoulders. It was made, this collar, of such stuff as lined the cloak, maybe it was of fur, or of satin, of silk, or of cloth of gold. The tremendous folds of these overcoats gave to the persons in them a sense of splendour and dignity; the short sleeves of the fashionable over-coats, puffed and swollen, barred with rich *appliqué* designs or bars of fur, reaching only to the elbow, there to end in a hem of fur or some rich stuff, the collar as wide as these padded

shoulders, all told in effect as garments which gave a great air of well-being and richness to their owner.

Of course, I suppose one must explain, the sleeves varied in every way: were long, short, full, medium full, according to taste. Sometimes the overcoats were sleeveless. Beneath these garments the trunks were worn—loose little breeches, which, in the German style, were bagged, puffed, rolled, and slashed in infinite varieties. Let it be noticed that the cutting of slashes was hardly ever a straight slit, but in the

curve of an elongated S or a double S curve. Other slashes were squared top and bottom.

All men wore tight hose, in some cases puffed at the knee; in fact, the bagging, sagging, and slashing of hose suggested the separate breeches or trunks of hose.

The shoes were very broad, and were sometimes stuffed into a mound at the toes, were sewn with precious stones, and, also, were cut and puffed with silk.

The little flat cap will be seen in all its varieties in the drawings.

The Irish were forbidden by law to wear a shirt, smock, kerchor, bendel, neckerchor, mocket (a handkerchor), or linen cap coloured or dyed with saffron; or to wear in shirts or smocks above seven yards of cloth.

To wear black genet you must be royal; to wear sable you must rank above a viscount; to wear martin or velvet trimming you must be worth over two hundred marks a year.

Short hair came into fashion about 1521.

So well known is the story of Sir Philip Calthrop and John Drakes the shoemaker of Norwich, who tried to ape the fashion, that I must here allude to this ancestor of mine who was the first of the dandies of note, among persons not of the royal blood. The story itself, retold in every history of costume, is to this

effect: Drakes, the shoemaker, seeing that the
county talked of Sir Philip's clothes, ordered a
gown from the same tailor. This reached the ears
of Sir Philip, who then ordered his gown to be
cut as full of slashes as the shears could make it.
The ruin of cloth so staggered the shoemaker

that he vowed to keep to his own humble fashion
in future. No doubt Sir Philip's slashes were
cunningly embroidered round, and the gown made
rich and sparkling with the device of seed pearls so
much in use. This man's son, also Sir Philip, married
Amy, daughter of Sir William Boleyn, of Blickling,
Norfolk. She was aunt to Queen Anne Boleyn.

THE WOMEN

One cannot call to mind pictures of this time without, in the first instance, seeing the form of Henry rise up sharply before us followed by his company of wives. The fat, uxorious giant comes straight to the front of the picture, he dominates the age pictorially; and, as a fitting background, one sees the six women who were sacrificed on the political altar to pander to his vanity. Katherine of Aragon—the fine and noble lady —a tool of political desires, cast off after Henry had searched his precious conscience, after eighteen years of married life, to find that he had scruples as to the spirituality of the marriage. Anne Boleyn, tainted with the life of the Court, a pitiful figure in spite of all her odious crimes; how often must a ghost, in a black satin night-dress edged with black velvet, have haunted the royal dreams. And the rest of them, clustered round the vain king, while in the background the great figures of the time loom hugely as they play with the crowned puppets.

The note of the time, as we look at it with our eyes keen on the picture, is the final evolution

of the hood. Bit by bit, inch by inch, the plain
fabric has become enriched, each succeeding step
in an elaboration of the simple form; the border
next to the face is turned back, then the hood is

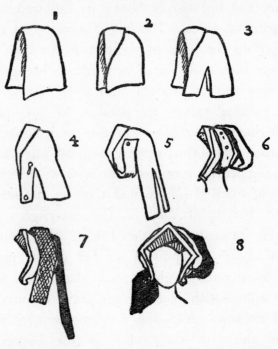

lined with fine stuff and the turnover shows this
to advantage; then the sides are split and the
back is made more full; then a tag is sewn on
to the sides by which means the cut side may

be fastened off the shoulders. The front is now
stiffened and shaped at an angle, this front is
sewn with jewels, and, as the angle forms a gap
between the forehead and the point of the hood,
a pad is added to fill in the vacant space. At
last one arrives at the diamond-shaped head-dress
worn in this reign,
and, in this reign,
elaborated in every
way, elaborated, in
fact, out of existence.
In order to make the
head-dress in its 1509
state you must make
the white lining with
the jewelled turnover
as a separate cap.
However, I think
that the drawings speak for themselves more
plainly than I can write.

Every device for crowding jewels together was
used, criss-cross, in groups of small numbers, in
great masses. Pendants were worn, hung upon
jewelled chains that wound twice round the neck,
once close to the neck, the second loop loose

and passed, as a rule, under the lawn shift. Large brooches decorated the bodices, brooches with drop ornaments, the body of the brooch of fine gold workmanship, many of them wrought in Italy. The shift, delicately embroidered with black silk, had often a band of jewellery upon it, and this shift was square cut, following the shape of the bodice.

The bodice of the gown was square cut and much stiffened to a box-like shape. The sleeves of the gown were narrow at the shoulders, and after fitting the arm for about six inches down from the shoulders, they widened gradually until, just below the elbow, they became square and very full; in this way they showed the false under-sleeve. This under-sleeve was generally made of a fine rich-patterned silk or brocade, the same stuff which formed the under-gown; the sleeve was a binding for the very full lawn or cambric sleeve which showed in a ruffle at the wrist and in great puffs under the forearm. The under-sleeve was really more like a gauntlet, as it was generally held together by buttoned tags; it was puffed with other coloured silk, slashed to show the shift, or it might be plain.

Now the sleeve of the gown was subject to much alteration. It was, as I have described, made very square and full at the elbow, and over this some ladies wore a false sleeve of gold net— you may imagine the length to which net will go, studded with jewels, crossed in many ways, twisted into patterns, sewn on to the sleeve in sloping lines — but, besides this, the sleeve was turned back to form a deep square cuff which was often made of black or coloured velvet, or of fur.

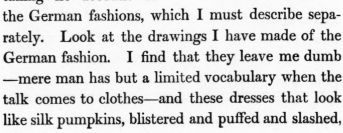

In all this I am taking no account of the German fashions, which I must describe separately. Look at the drawings I have made of the German fashion. I find that they leave me dumb —mere man has but a limited vocabulary when the talk comes to clothes—and these dresses that look like silk pumpkins, blistered and puffed and slashed, sewn in ribs, swollen, and altogether so queer, are beyond the furious dashes that my pen makes at truth and millinery. The costumes of the people of this age have grown up in the minds of most artists as being inseparable from the drawings of Holbein and Dürer.

Surely, I say to myself, most people who will read this will know their Holbein and Dürer,

between whom there lies a vast difference, but who between them show, the one, the estate of England, and the other, those most German fashions which had so powerful an influence upon our own. Both these men show the profusion of richness, the extravagant follies of the dress of their time, how, to use the words of Pliny: 'We penetrate into the bowels of the earth, digging veins of gold and silver, and ores of brass and lead; we seek also for gems and certain little pebbles. Driving galleries into the depths, we draw out the bowels of the earth, that the gems we seek may be worn on the finger. How many hands are wasted in order that a single joint may sparkle! If any hell there were, it had assuredly ere now been disclosed by the borings of avarice and luxury!'

Or in the writings of Tertullian, called by Sigismund Feyera-bendt, citizen and printer of Frankfort, a 'most strict censor who most severely blames women:' 'Come now,' says Tertullian, 'if from the first both the Milesians sheared sheep, and the Chinese spun from the tree, and the  Tyrians dyed and the Phrygians embroidered, and the Babylonians inwove; and if pearls shone and rubies flashed, if gold itself, too, came up from the earth with the desire for it; and if now, too, no lying but the mirror's were allowed, Eve, I suppose, would have desired these things on her expulsion from Paradise, and when spiritually dead.'

One sees by the tortured and twisted German fashion that the hair was plaited, and so, in curves and twists, dropped into coarse gold-web nets, thrust into web nets with velvet pouches to them, so that the hair stuck out behind in a great knob, or at the side in two protuberances; over all a cap like to the man's, but that it was infinitely more feathered and jewelled. Then, again, they wore those hideous barbes or beard-like linen cloths, over the chin, and an infinite variety of caps of linen upon their heads—caps which showed always the form of the head beneath.

In common with the men, their overcoats and cloaks were voluminous, and needed to be so if those great sleeves had to be stuffed into them; **fur** collars or silk collars, with facings to match, were rolled over to show little or great expanses of these materials.

Here, to show what dainty creatures were our lady ancestors, to show from what beef and blood and bone we come, I give you (keep your eye meanwhile upon the wonderful dresses) the daily allowance of a Maid of Honour.

Every morning at breakfast one chyne of beef from the kitchen, one chete loaf and one maunchet at the pantry bar, and one gallon of ale at the buttery bar.

For dinner a piece of beef, a stroke of roast and a reward from the kitchen. A caste of chete bread from the pantry bar, and a gallon of ale at the buttery bar.

Afternoon — should they suffer the pangs of hunger—a maunchet of bread from the pantry bar, and a gallon of ale at the buttery bar.

Supper, a messe of pottage, a piece of mutton and a reward from the kitchen. A caste of chete bread from the pantry bar, and a gallon of ale at the buttery bar.

After supper—to insure a good night's rest —a chete loaf and a maunchet from the pantry bar, and half a gallon of ale from the seller bar.

Four and a half gallons of ale! I wonder did they drink it all themselves? All this, and down in the mornings in velvets and silks, with faces as fresh as primroses.

It is the fate of all articles of clothing or adornment, naturally tied or twisted, or folded and pinned by the devotees of fashion, to become, after some little time, made up, ready made, into the shapes which had before some of the owner's mood and personality about them. These hoods worn by the women, these wide sleeves to the gowns, these hanging sleeves to the overcoats, the velvet slip of underdress, all, in their time, became falsified into ready-made articles. With the hoods you can see for yourselves how they lend themselves by their shape to personal taste ; they were made up, all ready sewn ; where pins had been used, the folds of velvet at the back were made steadfast, the crimp of the white linen was determined, the angle of the side-flap ruled by some unwritten law of mode. In the end, by a process of evolution, the diamond shape disappeared, and the cap was placed further back on the head, the contour being circular where it had previously been pointed. The velvet hanging-piece remained at the back of the head, but was smaller, in one piece, and was never pinned up, and the entire shape gradually altered towards, and finally into, the well-known Mary Queen of Scots head-dress, with which every reader must be familiar.

It has often occurred to me while writing this book that the absolute history of one such head-dress would be of more help than these isolated remarks, which have to be dropped only to be taken up in another reign, but I have felt that, after all, the arrangement is best as it  stands, because we can follow, if we are willing, the complete wardrobe of one reign into the next, without mixing the two up. It is difficult to keep two interests running together, but I myself have felt, when reading other works on the subject, that the way in which the various articles of clothing are mixed up is more disturbing than useful.

The wide sleeve to the gown, once part and parcel of the gown, was at last made separate from it—as a cuff more than a sleeve naturally widening—and in the next reign, among the most fashionable, left out altogether. The upper part of the dress, once cut low and square to show the under-dress, or a vest of other stuff, was now made, towards the end of the reign, with a false top of other stuff, so replacing the under-dress.

Lacing was carried to extremes, so that the body was pinched into the hard roll-like appearance always identified with this time ; on the other hand, many, wiser women I should say, were this the place for morals, preferred to lace loose, and show, beneath the lacing, the colour of the under-dress.

Many were the varieties of girdle and belt, from plain silk sashes with tasselled ends to rich jewelled chain girdles ending in heavy ornaments.

For detail one can do no better than go to Holbein, the master of detail, and to-day, when photographs of pictures are so cheap, and lives of painters, copiously illustrated, are so easily

A MAN OF THE TIME OF HENRY VIII.   1509-1547

A WOMAN OF THE TIME OF HENRY VIII. 1509-1547

attainable at low prices, it is the finest education, not only in painting, but in Tudor atmosphere and in matters of dress, to go straightway and study the master—that master who touched, without intention, on the moral of his age when he painted a miniature of the Blessed Thomas More on the back of a playing card.

EDWARD THE SIXTH

Reigned six years: 1547—1553.
Born, 1537.

THE MEN AND WOMEN

 HERE we have a reign which, from its very shortness, can hardly be expected to yield us much in the way of change, yet it shows, by very slight movements, that form of growth which preludes the great changes to come.

I think I may call a halt here, and proceed to tell you why this volume is commenced with Henry VII., called the Tudor and Stuart volume, and ends with the Cromwells. It is because, between these reigns, the tunic achieves maturity, becomes a doublet, and dies,

274

practically just in the middle of the reign of Charles II. of pungent memory. The peculiar garment, or rather, this garment peculiar to a certain time, runs through its various degrees of cut. It is, at first, a loose body garment with skirts; the skirts become arranged in precise folds, the folds on the skirt are shortened, the shorter they become the tighter becomes the coat; then we run through with this coat in its periods of puffings, slashings, this, that, and the other sleeve, all coats retaining the small piece of skirt or basque, and so to the straight, severe Cromwellian jerkin with the piece of skirt cut into tabs, until the volume ends, and hey presto! there marches into history a Persian business —a frock coat, straight, trim, quite a near cousin to our own garment of afternoon ceremony.

For a sign of the times it may be mentioned that a boy threw his cap at the Host just at the time of the Elevation.

To Queen Elizabeth has been given the palm for the wearing of the first silk stockings in England, but it is known that Sir Thomas Gresham gave a pair of silk stockings to Edward VI.

We now see a more general appearance in the

streets of the flat cap upon the heads of citizens.
The hood, that eminently practical head-gear, took
long to die, and, when at last it went out of fashion,
except among the labouring classes, there came in
the cap that now remains to us in the cap of the

Beefeaters at
the Tower of
London.

It is the
time of jerkin
or jacket,
doublet or
coat, and hose
—generally
worn with
trunks, which
were puffed,
short knicker-
bockers.

The flat cap, afterwards the statute cap as ordered
by Elizabeth, became, as I say, the ordinary head-
wear, though some, no doubt, kept hoods upon
their heavy travelling cloaks. This cap, which some
of the Bluecoat Boys still wear, was enforced upon
the people by Elizabeth for the encouragement

of the English trade of cappers.   'One cap of wool, knit, thicked, and dressed in England,' was to be worn by all over six years of age, except such persons as had 'twenty marks by year in lands, and their heirs, and such as have borne office of worship.

Edward, according to the portraits, always wore a flat cap, the base of the crown ornamented with bands of jewels.

The Bluecoat Boys, and long may they have the sense to keep to their dress, show us exactly the ordinary dress of the citizen, except that the modern knickerbocker has taken the place of the trunks.   Also, the long skirts of these blue coats were, in Edward's time, the mark of the grave man, others wore these same skirts cut to the knee.

That peculiar fashion of the previous reign— the enormously broad-shouldered appearance—still held in this reign to some extent, though the collars of the jerkins, or, as one may more easily know them, overcoats or jackets, open garments, were not so wide, and allowed more of the puffed shoulder of the sleeve to show.   Indeed, the collar became quite small, as in the Windsor Holbein painting of Edward, and the puff in the shoulders not so rotund.

The doublet of this reign shows no change, but the collar of the shirt begins to show signs of the ruff of later years. It is no larger, but is generally left untied with the ornamental strings hanging.

Antiquarian research has, as it often does, muddled us as to the meaning of the word 'partlet.' Fairholt, who is very good in many ways, puts down in his glossary, 'Partlet: A gorget for women.' Then he goes on to say that a partlet may be goodness knows what else. Minshein says they are 'part of a man's attire, as the loose collar of a doublet, to be set on or taken off by itself, without the bodies, as the picadillies now a daies, or as mens' bands, or womens' neckerchiefs, which are in some, or at least have been within memorie, called partlets.'

Sir F. Madden says: 'The partlet evidently appears to have been the corset or habit-shirt worn at that period, and which so commonly occurs in the portraits of the time, generally made of velvet and ornamented with precious stones.'

Hall, the author of 'Satires,' 1598, speaks of a

man, an effeminate dandy, as wearing a partlet
strip. It appears to me, who am unwillingly
forced into judging between so many learned
persons, that, from all I have been able to gather
from contemporary records and papers, the partlet

is indeed, as Minshein says, 'the loose collar of a
doublet,' in reality the same thing as a shirt band.

Henry VIII. wore a band about his neck, the
forerunner of the ruff. Some of his bands were
of silver cloth with ruffs to them, others, as I
have shown, were wonderfully embroidered.

In this case, then, the partlet is head of the family tree to our own collar, 'to be set on or taken off by itself,' and so by way of ruff, valued at threescore pound price apiece, to plain bands, to falling bands, laced neckcloth, stock—to the nine pennyworth of misery we bolt around our necks.

Dress, on the whole, is much plainer, sleeves are not so full of cuts and slashes, and they fit more closely to the arm. The materials are rich, but the ornament is not so lavish; the portrait of Edward by Gwillim Stretes is a good example of ornament, rich but simple. Shoes are not cut about at the toe quite with the same splendour, but are still broad in the toe.

For the women, it may be said that the change towards simplicity is even more marked. The very elaborate head-dress, the folded, diamond-shaped French hood has disappeared almost entirely, and, for the rich, the half hoop, set back from the forehead with a piece of velvet or silk to hang down the back, will best describe the head-gear From that to the centre-pointed hoop shows the trend of the shape. This latest form of woman's head apparel was born, I think, out of the folds

A MAN AND WOMAN OF THE TIME OF EDWARD VI. 1547-1553

of the linen cap worn in the house, and this, being repeated in the velvet nightcaps, became the extreme of fashion. The drawing will show how the square end of the linen cap, falling in the centre of the circular cap-shape, cut the semi-

circle and overlapped it, thus giving the appearance later to become exaggerated into a form cut especially to that shape. (I try to be as lucid as I can manage, but the difficulties of describing such evolutions in any but tangled language I leave the reader to imagine.)

The women are also wearing cloth hoods, rather baggy cap-like hoods, with a hanging-piece behind.

The most notable change is the collar of the gown, which suddenly springs into existence. It is a high collar and very open in front, showing a piece of the under-dress. On this collar is sewn—what I shall call—the woman's partlet, as the embroidery is often detachable and answers the same purpose as the man's partlet; this later became a separate article, and was under-propped with wires to hold it out stiffly.

The same stiff-bodied appearance holds good, but in more simple dresses the skirts were not quite as voluminous as heretofore.

With overcoats in general the hanging sleeve is being worn, the arm of the wearer coming out just below the puffed shoulder-piece.

With these remarks we may safely go on to the reign of Mary; another reign which does not yield us much in the way of clothes.

MARY

Reigned five years: 1553—1558.
Born, 1516.   Married, 1554, Philip of Spain.

THE MEN AND WOMEN.

I CANNOT do better than commence this chapter
by taking you back to the evening of August 3,
1553.   Mary, with her half-sister Elizabeth, entered
London on this date.   At Aldgate she was met
by the Mayor of London, who gave her the City
sword.   From the Antiquarian Repertory comes
this account:

'First, the citizens' children walked before her
magnificently dressed; after followed gentlemen
habited in velvets of all sorts, some black, others
in white, yellow, violet, and carnation; others
wore satins or taffety, and some damasks of all
colours, having plenty of gold buttons; afterwards
followed the Mayor, with the City Companies, and
the chiefs or masters of the several trades; after

them, the Lords, richly habited, and the most considerable knights; next came the ladies, married and single, in the midst of whom was the Queen herself, mounted on a small white ambling nag, the housings of which were fringed with gold thread; about her were six lacqueys, habited in vests of gold.

'The Queen herself was dressed in violet velvet, and was then about forty years of age, and rather fresh coloured.

'Before her were six lords bareheaded, each carrying in his hand a yellow mace, and some others bearing the arms and crown. Behind her followed the archers, as well of the first as the second guard.

'She was followed by her sister, named Madame Elizabeth, in truth a beautiful Princess, who was also accompanied by ladies both married and single.'

In the crowds about the city waiting to stare at the new Queen as she passed by, one could recognise the various professions by their colours. The trained bands in white doublets with the City arms before and behind; lawyers in black; sheriffs and aldermen in furred gowns with satin sleeves; citizens in brown cloaks and workers in cloth or leather doublets; citizens' servants in blue liveries; gentlemen's servants in very gorgeous liveries of their masters' colours. Here is a description of a gentleman's page and his clothes :

'One doublet of yelow million fustian, th'one halfe buttoned with peche-colour buttons, and the other half laced downwards; one payer of peche-colour, laced with smale tawnye lace; a graye hat with a copper edge rounde about it, with a band p'cell of the same hatt; a payer of watchet (blue) stockings. Likewise he hath twoe clokes, th'one of vessey colour, garded with twoe yards of black clothe and twisted lace of carnacion colour, and lyned with crymsone bayes; and th'other is a red shipp russet colour, striped about th'cape and down the fore face, twisted with two rows of twisted lace, russet and gold buttons afore and uppon the shoulder, being of the clothe itself, set with the said twisted lace and the buttons of russet silk and gold.'

This will give some notion of the elaborate liveries worn, and also it will show how, having understood the forms of the garments and the material which may be used, the rest, ornament and fancy, depend on the sense of the reader.

A change has come over the streets, the town is full of Spaniards come over with Philip, and these bring with them many innovations in dress. The most noticeable is the high-peaked Spanish hat, a velvet bag with a narrow brim, worn on  one side of the head. There is, also, a hard-crowned hat, round the crown-base of which is a gold cord clasped by a jewel; a feather is stuck into this hat. Yet the mass of citizens wear the flat cap, some of them, the older men, have a coif tied under their chins, and over this the flat cap. Again, older men wear black velvet skull caps.

With these Spaniards comes, also, the first appearance of the ruff, very neat and small.

Although the overcoats of Henry's and Edward's reigns still form the principal wear, the short Spanish cloak has come in, cut in full folds, and reaching not far below the waist. They also brought in the cloak with a turned up high collar; and some had sleeves to their cloaks.

One sees more beards and moustaches, short clipped beards, and beards with two points.

Shoes are now more to the shape of the foot, and high boots strapped up over the knee, also half-boots with the tops turned over to be seen. Often, where the hose meet the trunks, these are turned down.

The doublets become shaped more closely to the body, all showing the gradual change towards the Elizabethan costume, but still retaining the characteristics of earlier times, as the long skirt to the doublet, and the opening to show the collar of the shirt, or partlet strip.

Ladies now show more hair, parted, as before, in the centre, but now puffed out at the sides.

The new shape of head-dress becomes popular, and the upstanding collar to the gown is almost universal.

The gowns themselves, though retaining the same appearance as before, full skirts, no trains, big sleeves, and split to show the under-gown, have the top part of the gown covering the bosom made of a separate material, as, for instance, a gown of fine cloth will have collar and yoke of velvet.

Women wear neat linen caps, made very plain and close to the head, with small ear-pieces.

On the shoulders there is a fashion of wearing

kerchiefs of linen or silk, white as a rule; white, in fact, is frequently used for dresses, both for men and women.

The custom of carrying small posies of flowers comes in, and it is interesting to see the Queen, in her portrait by Antonio More, carrying a bunch

A MAN OF THE TIME OF MARY 1553-1558

A WOMAN OF THE TIME OF MARY   1553-1558

of violets arranged exactly as the penny bunches sold now in our streets.

There was, in most dresses, a great profusion of gold buttons, and the wearing of gold chains was common—in fact, a gold chain about the

neck for a man, and a gold chain girdle for a woman, were part of the ordinary everyday dress.

You will realize that to one born in the reign of Henry VIII. the appearance of people now was very different, and, to anyone as far away as we are now, the intervening reigns of Edward and Mary are interesting as showing the wonderful

19

quiet change that could take place in those few years, and alter man's exterior from the appearance of a playing-card, stiff, square, blob-footed, to the doublet and hose person with a cartwheel of a ruff, which recalls to us Elizabethan dress.

ELIZABETH

Reigned 45 years : 1558-1603.

THE MEN

HERE we are in the middle of
great discoveries with adventurers,
with Calvin and Michael Angelo,
living and dying, and Galileo and
Shakespeare seeing light—in the very
centre and heart of these things, and
we and they discussing the relations
of the law to linen.   How, they and
we ask, are breeches, and slop-hose
cut in panes, to be lined ?   In such
writings we are bound to concern
ourselves with the little things that
matter, and in this reign we meet
a hundred little things, little fussy things, the
like of which we leave alone to-day.   But this
is not quite true.   To-day a man, whether he cares

to admit it or no, is for ever choosing patterns, colours, shades, styles to suit his own peculiar personality. From the cradle to the grave we are decked with useless ornaments—bibs, sashes, frills, little jackets, neat ties, different coloured boots, clothes of ceremony, clothes supposed to be in harmony with the country, down, at last, to the clothes of an old gentleman, keeping a vague reminder of twenty, thirty years ago in their style, and then—grave clothes.

How well we know the Elizabethan! He is a stock figure in our imagination; he figured in our first schoolboy romances, he strutted in the first plays we saw. Because it was an heroic time we hark back to it to visualize it as best we may so that we can come nearer to our heroes—Drake, Raleigh, and the rest. The very names of the garments arouse associations—ruff, trunks, jumper, doublet, jerkin, cloak, bone-bobbin lace, and lace of Flanders —they almost take one's breath away.

Here comes a gentleman in a great ruff, yellow-starched, an egg-shaped pearl dangles from one ear. One hand rests on his padded hip, the other holds a case of toothpicks and a napkin; he is going to his tavern to dine. His doublet is bellied like a

pea's cod, and his breeches are bombasted, his little
hat is stuck on one side and the feather in it curls
over the brim. His doublet is covered with a
herring-bone pattern in silk stitches, and is slashed
all over. He is exaggerated, monstrous; he is tight-
laced; his trunks stick out a foot all round him,
and his walk is, in consequence,
a little affected; but, for all
that, he is a gallant figure.

Behind him comes a gentleman in loose knee - breeches
barred with velvet; at the knee
he has a frill of lace. His jerkin
is not stuffed out, and his ruff
is not starched to stick up round
his head. His hair is cut in
three points, one over each ear
and the third over the centre of
his forehead, where we see a twisted lock tied with
ribbon. We seem to know these people well—
very well. The first, whose clothes are of white
silk sewn with red and blue, whose trunk hose have
clocks of silk sewn on them, reminds us of whom?
And the second gentleman in green and red, with
heels of red on his shoes? Suddenly there flashes

across our memory the picture of a lighted stage, a row of shops, a policeman, and then a well-known voice calling, ' Hello, Joey, here we are again !'

Here we are again after all these centuries—clown and pantaloon, the rustic with red health on his face, the old man in Venetian slops—St. Pantaloone—just as Elizabethan, humour included, as anything can well be.

Then, enter Harlequin in his clothes of gorgeous patches; the quick, almost invisible thief, the instigator of all the evil and magic. His patches and rags have grown to symmetrical pattern, his loose doublet has become this tight-fitting lizard skin of flashing gold and colours, but his atmosphere recalls the great days.

To these enter 1830—Columbine—an early Victorian lady, who contrives to look sweetly modest in the shortest and frilliest of skirts; she looks like a rose, a rose on two pink stalks. She, being so different, gives the picture just the air of magic incongruity. Once, years ago, she was dressed in rags like Harlequin, but I suppose that the age of sentiment clothed her in her ballet costume rather than see her in her costly tatters.

We are a conservative nation, and we like our own

old jokes so much that we have kept through the ages this extraordinary pleasing entertainment straight down, clothes and all, from the days of Queen Elizabeth.

Even as we dream of this, and the harlequinade dazzles our eyes, the dream changes—a new sound is heard, a sound from the remote past, too. We listen eagerly, clown, pantaloon, harlequin, and columbine vanish to the sound of the pan-pipes and the voice of Punch.

'Root-ti-toot, rootity-toot!' There, by the corner of the quiet square, is a tall box covered with checkered cloth. Above a man's height is an opening, and on a tiny stage are two figures, one in a doublet stiffened out like a pea pod, with a ruff hanging loose about his neck, bands at his wrists, a cap on his head—Punch. The other with a linen cap and a ruff round her neck—Judy. Below, on the ground by the gentleman who bangs a drum and blows on the pan-pipes stuck in his muffler, is a dog with a ruff round his neck—Toby. And we know—delightful to think of it—that a box hidden by the check covering, contains many curiously dressed figures—all friends of ours, The world is certainly curious, and I suppose that an Elizabethan

revisiting us to-day would find but one thing the
same, the humour of the harlequinade and the
Punch and Judy show.

Now let us get to the dull part. If you wish to
swim in a sea of allusions there are a number of
books into which you may dive—

'Microcynicon.'
'Pleasant Quippes for Upstart Newfangled Gentlewomen.'
Hall's 'Satires.'
Stubbes' 'Anatomie of Abuses.'
'The Cobbler's Prophesie.'
'The Debate between Pride and Lowliness.'
'The Letting of Humours Blood in the Head Vaine.'
'The Wits Nuserie.'
Euphues' 'Golden Legacie.'
'Every Man out of his Humour.'

If you do not come out from these saturated
with detail then you will never absorb anything.

For the shapes, the doublet was a close-fitting
garment, cut, if in the Italian fashion, down to
a long peak in front. They were made without
sleeves, like a waistcoat, and an epaulette overhung
the armhole. The sleeves were tied into the
doublet by means of points (ribbons with metal
tags). These doublets were for a long time

stuffed or bombasted into the form known as
'pea's cod bellied' or 'shotten-bellied.'

The jerkin was a jacket with sleeves, and was
often worn over the doublet. The sleeves of the
jerkin were often open from shoulder to wrist to

show the doublet sleeve underneath. These sleeves
were very wide, and were ornamented with large
buttons.

The jornet was a loose travelling cloak.

The jumper a loose jerkin, worn for comfort or
extra clothing in winter.

Both doublet and jerkin had a little skirt or base. The very wide breeches known as trunks were worn by nearly everybody in the early part of the reign, until they vied with Venetian breeches for fashion. They were sometimes made of a series of wide bands of different colours placed alternately;

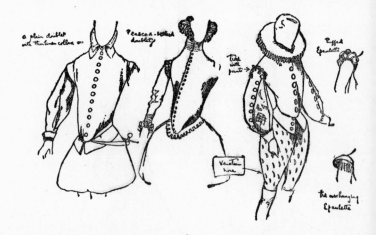

sometimes they were of bands, showing the stuffed trunk hose underneath. They were stuffed with anything that came handy—wool, rags, or bran— and were of such proportions that special seats were put in the Houses of Parliament for the gentlemen who wore them. The fashion at its height appears to have lasted about eight years.

The Venetian breeches were very full at the top and narrowed to the knee; they were slashed and puffed, or paned like lattice windows with bars of coloured stuffs or gold lace.

The French breeches were tight and ruffled in puffs about the thighs.

The stockings were of yarn, or silk, or wool. They were gartered about the knee, and pulled up over the breeches; but the man most proud of his leg wore no garters, but depended on the shape of his leg and the fit of his stocking to keep the position. These stockings were sewn with clocks at the ankles, and had various patterns on them, sometimes of gold or silver thread. Open-work stockings were known.

The stockings and breeches were called, if the breeches were short and the stockings all the way up the leg, trunk hose and trunks; if the breeches came to the knee and the stockings just came over them, they were known as upper stocks and nether stocks.

The shoes were shaped to the foot, and made of

various leathers or stuffs ; a rose of ribbon sometimes decorated the shoes.　There were shoes with
high cork soles called moyles.　Of course, there
were gallants who did things no one else thought
of doing—wearing very square-toed shoes, for
instance, or cock feathers in their hair.

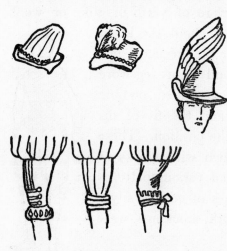

The sturtops
were boots to
the ankle.

As for the
hair, we have
the love - lock
tied with rib-
bons, the very
same that we
see caricatured
in the wigs of
clown and pan-
taloon.　We have, also, hair left fairly long and
brushed straight back from the forehead, and short-
cropped hair.　Beards and moustaches are worn by
most.

They wore little cloaks covered with embroidery,
lace, sometimes even with pearls.　For winter or for
hard travelling the jornet or loose cloak was worn.

The older and more sedate wore long stuff
gowns with hanging sleeves; these gowns, made
to fit at the waist and over the trunks, gave an
absurd Noah's ark-like appearance to the wearers.
Those who cared nothing for the fashions left
their gowns open and wore them
loose.

The common people wore simple
clothes of the same cut as their lords
—trunks or loose trousers, long hose,
and plain jerkins or doublets. In the
country the fashions alter, as a rule,
but little; however, in this reign
Corydon goes to meet Sylvia in somewhat fashionable clothes. Lodge
says: 'His holiday suit marvellous
seemly, in a russet jacket, welted with
the same, and faced with red worsted,
having a pair of blue camblet sleeves,
bound at the wrists with four yellow laces, closed
before very richly with a dozen pewter buttons.
His hose of gray kersey, with a large slop barred
all across the pocket holes with three fair guards,
stitched on either side with red thread.' His
stockings are also gray kersey, tied with different

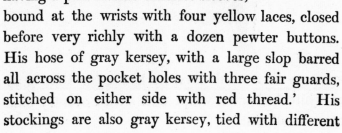

coloured laces; his bonnet is green, and has a
copper brooch with the picture of St. Dennis
'And to want nothing that might make him

amorous in his old days, he had a fair shirt-band
of white lockeram, whipt over with Coventry blue
of no small cost.'

The hats worn vary in shape from steeple-crowned, narrow-brimmed hats, to flat, broad-crowned hats ; others show the coming tendency towards the broad-brimmed Jacobean hat. Round these hats were hatbands of every sort, gold chains, ruffled lace, silk or wool.

I think we may let these gallants rest now to

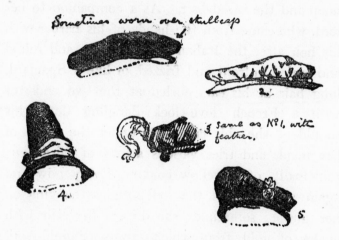

walk among the shades—a walking geography of clothes they are, with French doublets, German hose, Spanish hats and cloaks, Italian ruffs, Flemish shoes ; and these with chalked faces, fuzzed peri-wigs of false hair, partlet strips, wood busks to keep straight slim waists, will make the shades laugh perhaps, or perhaps only sigh, for there are many in that dim wardrobe of fashions who are still more foolish, still more false, than these Elizabethans.

THE WOMEN

Now this is the reign of the ruff and the monstrous hoop and the wired hair. As a companion to her lord, who came from the hands of his barber with his hair after the Italian manner, short and round and curled in front and frizzed, or like a Spaniard, long hair at his ears curled at the two ends, or with a French love - lock dangling down his shoulders, she—his lady—sits under the hands of her maid, and tries various attires of false *hair*, principally of a yellow colour. Every now and again she consults the looking-glass hanging on her girdle; sometimes she dresses her hair with chains of gold, from which jewels or gold-work tassels hang; sometimes she, too, allows a love-lock to rest upon her shoulder, or fall negligently on her ruff.

Even the country girl eagerly waits for news of the town fashions, and follows them as best she may.

In the early part of the reign the simple costume of the previous reign was still worn, and even the court ladies were quietly, though richly, dressed.

In the first two years the ruff remained a fairly small size, and was made of holland, which remained stiff, and held the folds well; but later there entered several Dutch ladies, headed by Mistress Dingham Vander Plasse, of Flanders, in 1564, who taught her pupils the art of starching cambric, and the art of folding, cutting, and pinching ruffs at five pounds a head, and the art of making starch, at the price of one pound.

First, the lady put on her underproper of wire and holland, and then she would place with a great nicety her ruff of lace, or linen, or cambric. One must understand that the ruff may be great or small, that only the very fashionable wore such a ruff as required an underproper, and that the starched circular ruff would stand by itself without the other appliance.

Before the advent of the heavily-jewelled and embroidered stomacher, and the enormous spread of skirt, the dress was a modification of that worn by the ladies in the time of Henry VIII. First, a gown cut square across the bosom and low over

20

the shoulders, full sleeves ending in bands of cambric over the hands (these sleeves slit to show puffs

of cambric from the elbow to the wrist), the skirt full and long, but without any train; the whole fitted

well to the figure as far as the waist, and very
stiff in front. Over this a second gown, generally
of plain material, split above in a V-shape, split
below at the waist, and cut away to show the
undergown. The sleeves of this gown were wide,
and were turned back or cut away just by the
elbow. Both gowns were laced up the back.
This second gown had, as a rule, a high, standing

collar, which was lined with some rich silk or with
lace.

This shape gave way to a more exaggerated
form, and finally to many varieties of exaggeration.
The lady might wear a jerkin like in shape to a
man's, except that often it was cut low and square
over the bosom, and was not stuffed quite so much
in front ; every variety of rich material was used
for this jerkin, and the sleeves were as varied as

were the man's, split and tied with ribbons.
False sleeves attached at the shoulders, and left
to hang loose, puffed, slashed all over, with or
without bands of cambric or lace at the wrists ;
these bands sometimes were frills, sometimes stiffened and turned back. No person except royalty
might wear crimson except in under-garments, and
the middle class were not allowed to wear velvet
except for sleeves.

This jerkin was sometimes worn buttoned up,
like a man's, to the neck, and when the hoops came
into fashion and were worn high up near the waist,
the basque or flounce at the bottom of the jerkin
was made long, and pleated full to the top of
the hooped petticoat.

The plainer fashion of this was a gown buttoned
high—up to the ruff—and opened from the waist
to the feet to show a full petticoat of rich material;
this was the general wear of the more sober-
minded.

Sometimes a cape was worn over the head and
shoulders, not a shaped cape, but a plain, oblong
piece of stuff. The ladies sometimes wore the shaped
cape, with the high collar that the men wore. The
French hood with a short liripipe was worn by

country ladies; this covered the hair, showing
nothing but a neat parting in front.

The openwork lace bonnet, of the shape so well
known by the portraits of Queen Mary of Scotland, is not possible to exactly describe in writing;
one variety of it may be seen in the line drawing
given. It is made of cambric and cut lace sewn on

to wires bent
into the shape
required.

In such a
time of ex-
travagance in
fashion the
additions one
may make to
any form of
dress in the

way of ribbons, bows, sewn pearls, cuts, slashes,
and puffs are without number, and I can only give
the structure on which such ornamental fripperies
can be placed. The hair, for example, can be
dressed with pearls, rings of gold, strings of pearls,
feathers, or glass ornaments. Men and women
wore monstrous earrings, but curiously enough

this fashion was more common to men than women. Hats were interchangeable, more especially the trim hat with a feather, in shape like those worn by the Yeoman of the Guard, but smaller.

The shoulder pinions of the jerkins were puffed, slashed, and beribboned in every way. The wing sleeves, open from the shoulder all the way down, were so long sometimes as to reach the ground, and were left hanging in front, or thrown back over the shoulders, the better to display the rich undersleeve.

The ladies shoes were cork-soled, high-heeled, and round-toed. The girdles were of every stuff, from gold cord, curiously knotted, to twisted silk; from these hung looking-glasses, and in them were stuck the embroidered and scented gloves.

Ladies went masked about the streets and in the theatres, or if they wished to be unconventional, they sat in the playing booths unmasked, their painted faces exposed to the public gaze.

The shoes with the high cork soles, to which I have just alluded, were in common use all over Europe, and were of all heights—from two inches to seven or eight—and they were called *chopines*. They were not such a foolish custom as might appear, for they protected the wearer from the appalling filth of the streets. The tall chopines that Hamlet mentions were really very high-soled slippers, into which the richly-embroidered shoes were placed to protect them when the ladies walked abroad. The shoes were made of leather and velvet stitched with silk, embroidered with gold, or stamped with patterns, slashed sometimes, and sometimes laced with coloured silk laces.

Some ladies wore bombazines, or a silk and cotton stuff made at Norwich, and bone lace made at Honiton, both at that time the newest of English goods, although before made in Flanders ; and they imported Italian lace and Venetian shoes, stuffed their stomachers with bombast, and wore a frontlet on their French hoods, called a *bongrace*, to keep their faces from sunburn.

Cambric they brought from Cambrai in France, and calico from Calicut in India—the world was hunted high and low for spoil to deck these gorgeous, stiff, buckramed people, so that under all this load of universal goods one might hardly hope to find more than a clothes prop ; in fact, one might more easily imagine the overdressed figure to be a marvellous marionette than a decent Englishwoman.

Falstaff will
not wear coarse
dowlas shirts,
dandies call for
ostrich feathers,
ladies must have
Coventry blue
gowns   and
Italian flag-
shaped   fans;
everybody is in
the fashion from
milkmaids to ladies of the court, each as best as they
may manage it.   The Jew moves about the streets
in his long gaberdine and yellow cap, the lady pads

about her garden in tall chopines, and the gentleman sits down as well as he may in his bombasted breeches and smokes Herbe de la Reine in a pipe of clay, and the country woman walks along in her stamell red petticoat guarded or strapped with black, or rides past to market in her over-guard skirts.

Let us imagine, by way of a picture of the times, the Queen in her bedchamber under the hands of her tiring-women: She is sitting before a mirror in her embroidered chemise of fine Raynes linen, in her under-linen petticoat and her silk stockings with the gold thread clocks. Over these she wears a rich wrap. Slippers are on her feet. In front of her, on a table, are rouge and chalk and a pad of cotton-wool—already she has made up her face, and her bright bird-like eyes shine in a painted mask, her strong face, her hawk-like nose and her expressionless mouth reflect back at her from the mirror. Beside the rouge pot is a Nuremberg egg watch, quietly ticking in its crystal case. One of the women brings forward a number of attires of false hair, golden and red, and from these the Queen choses one. It is a close periwig of tight red curls, among which pearls and pieces of burnished metal shine. With great care this wig is fastened on to the Queen's head, and she watches the process with her bright eyes and still features in the great mirror.

Then, when this wig is fixed to her mind, she rises, and is helped into the privie coat of bones and buckram, which is laced tightly by the women at her back. Now comes the moment when they are about to fasten on her whalebone hips the great farthingale—over which her voluminous petticoats and skirts will fall. The wheel of bone is tied with ribbons about her waist, and there securely fastened. After some delay in choosing an undergown, she then puts on several linen petticoats, one over another, to give the required fulness to her figure ; and then comes the stiffly-embroidered undergown—in this case but a petticoat with a linen bodice which has no sleeves.

With great care she seats herself on a broad chair, and a perfect army of ruffs is laid before her. As the tire-woman is displaying the ruffs she talks to the Queen, and tells her that peculiar story, then current, of the Lady of Antwerp, who was in a great way because she could not get her ruff to set aright, and when in a passion she called upon the devil to take it, as if in answer to the summons a young and handsome gentleman appeared. Together they tried the ruff, and the young gentleman suddenly strangled the lady and vanished. Now when they came to carry away the coffin of the lady some days later, it was found that no one could lift it, so, in the end, it was opened, and there, to the surprise of everybody, sat a great black cat setting a ruff. The Queen's eyes twinkle on this story, for she has a great fund of dry humour—and so, to the business of the ruffs. First one and then another is discarded; and finally the choice falls between one of great size, shaped like a catherine wheel and starched blue, and the other of three depths but not of such great circumference, starched yellow, after the receipt of Mrs. Turner, afterwards hung at Tyburn in a ruff of the same colour.

The Queen wavers, and the tire-woman recommends the smaller bands: 'This, madame, is one of those ruffs made by Mr. Higgins, the tailor near to St. James's, where he has set up an establishment for the making of such affairs—it is a picadillie, and would——'

The Queen stops her and chooses the ruff; it is very much purled into folds, and it bristles with points.

The women approach with a crimson over-gown and slips it over the Queen's head—it is open in front to show the rich petticoat, and it has great stuffed wings, epaulettes, or mahoitres on the shoulders. The tight-fitting bodice of the gown is buttoned up to the throat, and is stuffed out in front to meet the fall of the hoops; it has falling sleeves, but the real sleeves are now brought and tied to the points attached to the shoulders of the gown. They are puffed sleeves of the same material as the under-gown, and the falling sleeves of the upper gown are now tied with one or two bows across them so that the effect of the sleeves is much the same as the effect of the skirts; an embroidered stuff showing in the opening of a plain material. These are called virago sleeves.

This done, the strings of pearls are placed around the Queen's neck, and then the under-propper or supportasse of wire and holland is fastened on her neck, and the picadillie ruff laid over it. The Queen exchanges her slippers for cork-soled shoes, stands while her girdle is knotted, sees that the looking-glass, fan, and pomander are hung upon it, and then, after a final survey of herself in the glass, she calls for her muckinder or handkerchief, and—Queen Elizabeth is dressed.

So in this manner the Queen struts down to posterity, a wonderful woman in ridiculous clothes, and in her train we may dimly see Mr. Higgins, the tailor, who named a street without knowing it, a street known in every part of the civilized world; but, nowadays, one hardly thinks of connecting Piccadilly with a lace ruff. . . .

SHAKESPEARE AND CLOTHES.

There are not so many allusions to Elizabethan dress in the plays of Shakespeare as one might suppose upon first thought. One has grown so accustomed to Shakespeare put on the stage in elaborate dresses that one imagines, or one is apt to imagine, that there is a warrant for some of the dresses in the plays. In some cases he confounds the producer and the illustrator by introducing garments of his own date into historical plays, as, for example, Coriolanus. Here are the clothes allusions in that play :

> ' When you cast your stinking greasy caps,
>   You have made good work,
>   You and your apron-men.'

> ' Go to them with this bonnet in your hand.'

> ' Enter Coriolanus in a gown of humility.'

' Matrons fling gloves, ladies and maids their scarfs and handkerchers.'

' The kitchen malkin pins her richest lockram * 'bout her reechy neck.'

' Our veiled dames.'

' Commit the war of white and damask in their nicely gawded cheeks to the wanton and spoil of Phœbus' burning kisses.'

' Doublets that hangmen would bury with these that wore them.'

I have not kept the lines in verse, but in a convenient way to show their allusions.

In ' Pericles ' we have mention of ruffs and bases. Pericles says :

> ' I am provided of a pair of bases.'

Certainly the bases might be made to appear Roman, if one accepts the long slips of cloth or

* ' Lockram ' is coarse linen.

leather in Roman military dress as being bases;
but Shakespeare is really—as in the case of the
ruffs—alluding to the petticoats of the doublet of
his time worn by grave persons. Bases also apply
to silk hose.

In 'Titus Andronicus' we have:

> 'An idiot holds his bauble for his God.'

Julius Cæsar is mentioned as an Elizabethan:

> 'He plucked ope his doublet.'

The Carpenter in 'Julius Cæsar' is asked:

> 'Where is thy leather apron and thy rule?'

The mob have 'sweaty night-caps.'

Cleopatra, in 'Antony and Cleopatra,' says:

> 'I'll give thee an armour all of gold.'

The 'Winter's Tale,' the action of which occurs
in Pagan times, is full of anachronisms. As, for
instance, Whitsun pastorals, Christian burial, an
Emperor of Russia, and an Italian fifteenth-century
painter. Also:

> 'Lawn as white as driven snow;
> Cyprus* black as ere was crow;
> Gloves as sweet as damask roses;
> Masks for faces and for noses;

---

* Thin stuff for women's veils.

> Bugle-bracelet, necklace amber,
> Perfume for a lady's chamber;
> Golden quoifs and stomachers,
> Pins and polking-sticks of steel.'

So, you see, Autolycus, the pedlar of these early times, is spoken of as carrying polking-sticks with which to stiffen ruffs.

Shylock, in 'The Merchant of Venice,' should wear an orange-tawny bonnet lined with black taffeta, for in this way were the Jews of Venice distinguished in 1581.

In 'The Tempest' one may hear of rye-straw hats, of gaberdines, rapiers, and a pied fool's costume.

In 'The Two Gentlemen of Verona' we hear:

> 'Why, then, your ladyship must cut your hair.'
>
> 'No, girl; I'll tie it up in silken strings
> With twenty odd conceited true-love knot;
> To be fantastic may become a youth
> Of greater time than I shall show to be.'

Also:

> 'Since she did neglect her looking-glass,
> And threw her sun-expelling mask away.'

Many ladies at this time wore velvet masks 'The Merry Wives of Windsor' gives us a

A MAN OF THE TIME OF ELIZABETH   1558-1603

A WOMAN OF THE TIME OF ELIZABETH   1558-1603

thrummed hat, a muffler or linen to hide part of the face, gloves, fans. Falstaff says:

> 'When Mistress Bridget lost the handle of her fan,
> I took it up my honour thou had'st it not.'

Also:

'The firm fashion of thy foot would give an excellent motion to thy fait in a semicircled farthingale.'

'Twelfth Night' is celebrated for us by Malvolio's cross garters. Sir Toby, who considers his clothes good enough to drink in, says:

'So be these boots too: an they be not, let them hang themselves in their own straps.'

Sir Toby also remarks to Sir Andrew upon the excellent constitution of his leg, and Sir Andrew replied that:

'It does indifferent well in a flame-coloured stock.'

The Clown says:

'A sentence is but a cheveril* glove to a good wit.'

In 'Much Ado About Nothing' we learn of one who lies awake ten nights, 'carving the fashion of his doublet.' Also of one who is

'in the shape of two countries at once, as a German from the waist downwards all slops, and a Spaniard from the hip upward, no doublet.'

---

* 'Cheveril' is kid leather.

Again of a gown :

'Cloth of gold, and cuts, and laced with silver set with pearls down sides, side sleeves, and skirts, round under borne with a bluish tinsel.'

In 'As You Like It' one may show a careless desolation by ungartered hose, unbanded bonnet, unbuttoned sleeve, and untied shoe.

'The Taming of the Shrew' tells of serving-men :

'In their new fustian and their white jackets. . . . Let their blue coats be brushed, and their garters of an indifferent knit.'

Also we have a cap 'moulded on a porringer.'

'Love's Labour's Lost' tells of :

'Your hat penthouse-like o'er the shop of your eyes; with your arms crossed on your thin belly doublet like a rabbit on a spit; or your hands in your pocket like a man after the old painting.'

'All's Well that Ends Well' :

'Why dost thou garter up thy arms o' this fashion ? Dost make a hose of thy sleeves ?'

'Yonder's my lord your son with a patch of velvet on's face : whether there be a scar under't or no, the velvet knows. . . . There's a dozen of 'em, with delicate fine hats and most courteous feathers, which bow the head and nod at every man.'

In 'Henry IV.,' Part II., there is an allusion to the blue dress of Beadles.   Also :

' About the satin for my short cloak and slops.'
'The smooth-pates do now wear nothing but high shoes, and bunches of keys at their girdles.'
' To take notice how many pair of silk stockings thou hast, or to bear the inventory of thy shirts.'

There are small and unimportant remarks upon dress in other plays, as dancing-shoes in ' Romeo and Juliet ' and in ' Henry VIII.' :

' The remains of fool and feather that they got in France.'
>   ' Tennis and tall stockings,
Short blistered breeches and those types of travel.'

But in ' Hamlet ' we find more allusions than in the rest.   Hamlet is ever before us in his black :

>   ' 'Tis not alone my inky cloak, good mother,
>   Nor customary suits of solemn black.'

>   ' Lord Hamlet, with his doublet all unbraced ;
>   No hat upon his head ; his stockings fouled,
>   Ungartered, and down-goes to his ancle ;
>   Pale as his shirt.'

' Your ladyship is nearer to heaven than when I saw you last, by the altitude of a chopine.'*

' O, it offends me to the soul to hear a robustious periwig-pated fellow tear a passion into tatters.'

---

* Shoes with very high soles.

' With two provincial roses on my ragged shoes,
     My sea-gown scarfed about me.'

Having read this, I think it will be seen that
there is no such great difficulty in costuming any
play, except perhaps this last. There have been
many attempts to put ' Hamlet' into the clothes
of the date of his story, but even when the rest
of the characters are dressed in skins and cross-
gartered trousers, when the Viking element is
strongly insisted upon, still there remains the absolutely Elizabethan figure in inky black, with his
very Elizabethan thoughts, the central figure,
almost the great symbol of his age.

JAMES THE FIRST

Reigned twenty-two years: 1603—1625.
Born 1566.   Married 1589, Anne of Denmark.

THE MEN.

THIS couplet may give a little sketch of the man
we should now see before us:

> ' His ruffe is set, his head set in his ruff;
> His reverend trunks become him well enough.'

We are still in the times of the upstanding ruff;
we are watching, like sartorial gardeners, for the
droop of this linen flower.   Presently this pride of
man, and of woman too, will lose its bristling,
super-starched air, and will hang down about the
necks of the cavaliers; indeed, if we look very
carefully, we see towards the end of the reign the
firstfruits of elegance born out of Elizabethan
precision.

Now in such a matter lies the difficulty of pre-
senting an age or a reign in an isolated chapter.

325

In the first place, one must endeavour to show how
a Carolean gentleman, meeting a man in the street,
might say immediately, 'Here comes one who still
affects Jacobean clothes.' Or how an Elizabethan
lady might come to life, and, meeting the same
man, might exclaim, 'Ah! these are evidently
the new fashions.' The Carolean gentleman would
notice at first a certain air of stiffness, a certain
padded arrangement, a stiff hat, a crisp ornament
of feathers. He would see that the doublet varied
from his own in being more slashed, or slashed in
many more degrees. He would see that it was
stiffened into an artificial figure, that the little
skirt of it was very orderly, that the cut of the
sleeves was tight. He would notice also that the
man's hair was only half long, giving an appearance not of being grown long for beauty, but
merely that it had not been cut for some time.
He would be struck with the preciseness, the correct air of the man. He would see, unless the
stranger happened to be an exquisite fellow, that
his shoes were plain, that the 'roses' on them were
small and neat. His trunks, he would observe,
were wide and full, but stiff. Mind you, he would
be regarding this man with seventeenth-century

eyes—eyes which told him that he was himself an elegant, careless fellow, dressed in the best of taste and comfort—eyes which showed him that the Jacobean was a nice enough person in his dress, but old-fashioned, grandfatherly.

To us, meeting the pair of them, I am afraid that a certain notion we possess nowadays of cleanliness and such habits would oppress us in the company of both, despite the fact that they changed their linen on Sundays, or were supposed to do so. And we, in our absurd clothes, with hard hats on our heads, and stiff collars tight about our necks, creases in our trousers, and some patent invention of the devil on our feet, might feel that the Jacobean gentleman looked and was untidy, to say the least of it, and had better be viewed from a distance.

To the Elizabethan lady the case would be reversed. The man would show her that the fashions for men had been modified since her day; she would see that his hair was not kept in, what she would consider, order; she would see that his ruff was smaller, and his hat brim was larger. She would, I venture to think, disapprove of him, thinking that he did not look so 'smart.'

For ourselves, I think we should distinguish
him at once as a man who wore very large knickerbockers tied at the knee, and, in looking at a
company of men of this time. we should be struck
by the padding of these garments to a preposterous
size.

There has come into fashion a form of ruff cut
square in front and tied under the chin, which can

be seen in the drawings better than it can be
described; indeed, the alterations in clothes are
not easy to describe, except that they follow the
general movement towards looseness. The trunks
have become less like pumpkins and more like
loose, wide bags. The hats, some of them stiff and

hard, show in other forms an inclination to slouch. Doublets are often made loose, and little sets of slashes appear inside the elbow of the sleeves, which will presently become one long slash in Cavalier costumes.

We have still:

> ' Morisco gowns, Barbarian sleeves,
>   Polonian shoes, with divers far fetcht trifles;
>   Such as the wandering English galant rifles
>   Strange countries for.'

But we have not, for all that, the wild extravaganza of fashions that marked the foregoing reign. Indeed, says another writer, giving us a neat picture of a man:

> ' His doublet is
> So close and pent as if he feared one prison
> Would not be strong enough to keep his soul in,
> But his taylor makes another;
> And trust me (for I knew it when I loved Cupid)
> He does endure much pain for poor praise
> Of a neat fitting suit.'

To wear something abnormally tight seems to be the condition of the world in love, from James I. to David Copperfield.

Naturally, a man of the time might be riding

down the street across a Scotch plaid saddle
cloth and pass by a beggar dressed in clothes of
Henry VIII.'s time, or pass a friend looking truly

Elizabethan — but he would
find generally that the short,
swollen trunks were very little
worn, and also—another point
—that a number of men had
taken to walking in boots,
tall boots, instead of shoes.

As he rides along in his
velvet cloak, his puffed and
slashed doublet, his silken
hose, his hands gloved with
embroidered gloves, or bared
to show his rings, smelling of
scents, a chain about his neck, he will hear the
many street cries about him:

'Will you buy any sand, mistress?'
'Brooms, brooms for old shoes! Pouch-rings, boots, or
buskings!   Will ye buy any new brooms?'
'New oysters, new oysters!   New, new cockles!'
'Fresh herrings, cockels nye!'
'Will you buy any straw?'
'Hay yee any kitchen stuff, maids?'
'Pippins fine!   Cherrie ripe, ripe, ripe!'

And he will pass apprentices, most of them still in flat caps, blue doublets, and white cloth breeches and stockings, sewn all in one piece, with daggers on their backs or at their sides. And then, travelling with his man, he will come to his inn. For the life of me, though it has little to do with dress,

I must give this picture of an inn from Fynes Moryson, which will do no harm, despite the fact that Sir Walter Besant quoted some of it.

'As soon as a passenger comes to an Inn, the servants run to him' (these would be in doublet and hose of some plain colour, with shirt-collars to the doublets turned down loose; the trunks would be wide and to the knee, and there buttoned), 'and one takes his horse and walks him till he be cool, then rubs him and gives him meat, yet I must say that they are not much to be trusted in this last point, without the eye of the Master or his servant to oversee them. Another servant gives the passenger his private chamber, and kindles his fire, the third pulls off his boots and makes them clean' (these two servants would be wearing aprons). 'Then the Host or Hostess visits him, and if he will eat with the Host, or at a common table with the others, his meal will cost him sixpence, or in some places but fourpence, yet this course is less honourable and not used by Gentlemen; but if he will eat in his chamber' (he will retain his hat within the house), 'he commands what meats he will according to his appetite, and as much as he thinks fit for him and his company, yea, the kitchen is open to him, to command the meat to be dressed as he likes best; and when he sits at table, the Host or Hostess will accompany him, if they have many guests, will at least visit him, taking it for courtesy to be bid sit down; while he eats, if he have company especially, he shall be offered music, which he may freely take or refuse, and if he be solitary the musicians will give him good day with music in the morning.

'It is the custom and in no way disgraceful to set up part of supper for his breakfast.

'Lastly, a Man cannot more freely command at home in his own house than he may do in his Inn, and at parting if he give some few pence to the Chamberlin and Ostler they wish him a happy journey.'

Beyond this and the drawings I need say no more.

The drawings will show how the points of a

doublet may be varied, the
epaulette left or taken away,
the little skirts cut or left
plain. They show you how
a hat may be feathered and
the correct shape of the hat;
how breeches may be left
loose at the knee, or tied, or
buttoned; of the frills at the
wrist and the ruffs at the
neck—of everything, I hope,
that is necessary and useful.

THE WOMEN

'What fashion will make a woman have the best body,
tailor?'

'A short Dutch waist, with a round Catherine-wheel
fardingale, a close sleeve, with a cartoose collar, or a
pickadell.'

I think, with a little imagination, we can see the
lady: add to our picture a feather fan, a man's
beaver hat with a fine band round it stuck with a
rose or a feather, shoes with ribbons or roses, and
jewels in the hair—and I think the lady walks.

Yet so difficult do I find it to lead her tripping out of the wardrobe into the world, I would remind myself of the laws for servants in this time:

'And no servant may toy with the maids under pain of fourpence.'

It is a salutary warning, and one that must be kept in the mind's eye, and as I pluck the lady  from the old print, hold her by the Dutch waist, and twirl her round until the Catherine-wheel fardingle is a blurred circle, and the pickadell a mist of white linen, I feel, for my prying, like one who has toyed under pain of fourpence.

There are many excellent people with the true historical mind who would pick up my lady and strip her in so passionless a way as to leave her but a mass of Latin names —so many bones, tissues, and nerves—and who would then label and classify her wardrobe under so many old English and French, Dutch and Spanish names, bringing to bear weighty arguments several pages long over the derivation of

the word 'cartoose' or 'pickadell,' write in note-
books of her little secret fineries, bear down on one
another with thundering eloquence upon the rela-
tion of St. Catherine and her wheel upon seventeenth-century dressmaking, and so confuse and
bewilder the more simple and less learned folk that
we should turn away from the Eve of the seven-
teenth century and from the heap of clothes upon
the floor no whit the wiser for all their pains.

Not that I would laugh, even smile, at the dili-
gence of these learned men who in their day
puzzled the father of Tristram Shandy over the
question of breeches, but, as it is in my mind impossible to disassociate the clothes and the woman,
I find it difficult to follow their dissertations, however enlightening, upon Early English cross-stitch.
And now, after I have said all this, I find myself
doing very nearly the same thing.

You will find, if you look into the lady's wardrobe, that she has other fashions than the close
sleeve : she has a close sleeve as an under sleeve,
with a long hanging sleeve falling from the elbow ;
she has ruffs at her wrist of pointed lace, more
cuffs than ruffs, indeed. She does not always follow
the fashion of the short Dutch waist as she has, we

can see, a dress with a long waist and a tapering front to the bodice. Some dresses of hers are divided in the skirts to show a barred petticoat, or a petticoat with a broad border of embroidery. Sometimes she is covered with little bows, and at others with much gold lacing; and now and again she wears a narrow sash round her waist tied with a bow in front.

She is taking more readily to the man's hat, feathered and banded, and in so doing is forced to dress her hair more simply and do away with jewellery on her forehead; but, as is often the case, she dresses her hair with plumes and jewels and little linen or lace ruffs, and atop of all wears a linen cap with side wings to it and a peak in the centre.

Her ruff is now, most generally, in the form of an upstanding collar to her dress, open in front, finishing on her shoulders with some neat bow or other ornament. It is of lace of very fine workmanship, edged plain and square, or in all manner of fancy scallops, circles, and points.

Sometimes she will wear both ruff and collar, the ruff underneath to prop up her collar at the back to the required modish angle. Sometimes

A MAN OF THE TIME OF JAMES I.   1603-1625

A WOMAN OF THE TIME OF JAMES I.   1603-1625

her bodice will finish off in a double Catherine-
wheel.

Her maid is a deal more simple; her hair is
dressed very plainly, a loop by the ears, a twist
at the nape of the neck. She has a shawl over her
shoulders, or a broad falling collar of white linen,
She has no fardingale, but her skirts are full. Her
bodice fits, but is
not stiffened arti-
ficially; her sleeves
are tight and neat,
and her cuffs plain.
Upon her head is
a broad - brimmed
plain hat.

She has a piece
of gossip for her
mistress: at Chelsea they are making a satin dress
for the Princess of Wales from Chinese silkworm's
silk. On another day comes the news that the Constable of Castille when at Whitehall subscribed very
handsomely to the English fashion, and kissed the
Queen's hands and the cheeks of twenty ladies of
honour.

The fashion for dresses of pure white, either in

22

silk, cloth, or velvet has affected both men and
women ; and the countries which gave a name to
the cuts of the garments are evidenced in the
literature of the time. How a man's breeches or
slops are Spanish ; his waist, like the lady's, Dutch ;
his doublet French ; his and her sleeves and wings
on the shoulders French ; their boots Polonian,
cloaks German, hose Venetian, hats from everywhere. These spruce coxcombs, with looking-
glasses set in their tobacco boxes, so that they
may privately confer with them to see—

> ' How his band jumpeth with his piccadilly,
> Whether his band-strings balence equally,
> Which way his feather wags,'

strut along on their high-heeled shoes, and ogle
any lady as she passes.

Another fashion common to those in the high
mode was to have the bodice below the ruff cut so
low as to show all the breast bare, and this, together with the painting of the face, gave great
offence to the more sober-minded.

The ruffs and collars of lace were starched in
many colours—purple, goose-green, red and blue,
yellow being completely out of the fashion since
the murder of Sir Thomas Overbury by Mrs. Anne

Turner, the friend of the Countess of Somerset ; and this because Mrs. Turner elected to appear at the gallows in a yellow ruff.

As for the fardingale, it was having its last fling. This absurd garment had its uses once—so they say who write scandal of a Spanish Princess, and served to conceal her state upon a certain time ; but when ladies forsook the fashion, they wore a loose, al- most shapeless, gown, open from the waist to the feet, and a plain, unstiffened jerkin or jacket underneath.

Such a conglomera- tion is needed (if you remember we are look- ing over a lady's wardrobe) to make a lady of the time : such stuffs as rash, taffeta paropa, novats, shagge, filizetta, damask, mochado. Rash is silk and stuff, taffeta is thin silk, mochado is mock velvet. There, again, one may fall into an antiquarian trap ; whereas mochado is a manufacture of silk to imitate velvet, mokkadoe is a woollen cloth, and so on ; there is no end to it.   Still, some may read and ask themselves what is a rebatoe. It is the collar-like ruff worn at this time.   In this medley of things we shall see purles, falles, squares, buskes, tires, fans, palisadoes (this is a wire to hold the hair next to the first or duchess knot), puffs, ruffs, partlets, frislets, fillets, pendulets, bracelets, busk-points, shoe-ties, shoe roses, bongrace bonnets, and whalebone wheels—Eve !

All this, for what purpose ? To turn out one of those extraordinary creatures with a cart-wheel round the middle of their persons.

As the reign died, so did its fashions die also : padded breeches lost some of their bombast, ruffs much of their starch, and fardingales much of their circumference, and the lady became more Elizabethan in appearance, wore a roll under her hair in front, and a small hood with a jewelled frontlet on her forehead.   It was the last of the Tudor dress, and came, as the last flicker of a candle, before the new mode, Fashion's next footstep.

CHARLES THE FIRST

Reigned twenty-four years: 1625—1649.
Born 1600. Married 1625, Henrietta of France.

THE MEN.

THIS surely is the age of
elegance, if one may trust
such an elegant and graceful
mind as had Vandyck. In all
the wonderful gallery of portraits he has left, these silvery
graceful people pose in garments of ease.

The main thing that I must
do is to show how, gradually,
the stiff Jacobean dress became unfrozen from its clutch
upon the human form, how
whalebones in men's jackets melted away, breeches
no longer swelled themselves with rags and bran,

341

collars fell down, and shirts lounged through great open spaces in the sleeves.

It was the time of an immaculate carelessness; the hair was free, or seemed free, to droop in languid tresses on men's shoulders, curl at pretty will on men's foreheads. Shirts were left open at the neck, breeches were loosed at the knee. Do

I revile the time if I say that the men had an air, a certain supercilious air, of being dukes disguised as art students?

We know, all of us, the Vandyck beard, the Carolean moustache brushed away from the lips; we know Lord Pembroke's tousled — carefully tousled—hair; Kiligrew's elegant locks.

From the head to the neck is but a step—a

sad step in this reign—and here we find our friend
the ruff utterly tamed; 'pickadillies, now out of
request,' writes one, tamed into the falling band,
the Vandyck collar, which form of neck-dress has
never left the necks and shoulders of our modern
youthful prodigies, indeed, at one time, no youthful
genius dare be without one.   The variations of
this collar are too well known; of such lace as
edged them and of
the manner of their
tying, it would waste
time to tell, except
that in some in-
stances the strings
are secured by a ring.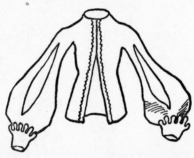
   Such a change has
come over the doublet as to make it hardly the same
garment; the little slashes have become two or three
wide cuts, the sleeves are wide and loose with, as a
rule, one big opening on the inside of the arm, with
this opening embroidered round.   The cuffs are like
little collars, turned back with point-lace edges.
The actual cut of the doublet has not altered a
great deal, the ordinary run of doublet has the
pointed front, it is tied round the waist with a

little narrow sash; but there has arrived a new jacket, cut round, left open from the middle of the breast, sometimes cut so short as to show the shirt below bulged out over the breeches. Sometimes you will see one of these new short jackets with a slit in the back, and under this the man

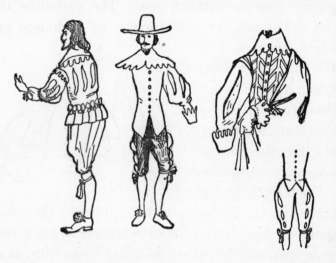

will be wearing the round trunks of his father's time.

The breeches are mostly in two classes—the long breeches the shape of bellows, tied at the knee with a number of points or a bunch of coloured ribbons; or the breeches cut the same width all the way down, loose at the knee and there ornamented with a row of points (ribbons tied in bows with tags on them).

A new method of ornamentation was this notion of coloured ribbons in bunches, on the breeches, in front, at the sides, at the knees—almost anywhere—and also upon the coats.

For some time the older fashioned short round cape or cloak prevailed, but later, large silk cloaks used as wraps thrown across the shoulders were used as well. The other cloaks had straps, like the modern golf cape, by which the cloak might be allowed to fall from the shoulders.

A custom arrived of wearing boots more frequently, and there was the tall, square-toed, high-heeled boot, fitting up the leg to just below the knee, without a turn-over; the stiff, thick leather, blacking boot with broad, stiff tops, also not turned back; and there was also the result of the extraordinary melting, crumpled dismissal of all previous stiffness, whereby the old tall boot drooped down until it turned over and fell into a wide cup, all creases and wrinkles, nearly over the foot, while across the instep was a wide, shaped flap of leather. This last falling boot-top was

turned in all manner of ways by those who cared to give thought to it.

The insides of the tops of these boots were lined with lace or silk, and the dandy turned them down to give full show to the lining—this turning of broad tops was such an inconvenience that he was forced to use a straddled walk when he wore his boots thus.

Canes were carried with gold, silver, or bone heads, and were ornamented further by bunches of ribbon.

Coming again to the head, we find ribbon also in use to tie up locks of hair; delicate shades of ribbon belonging to some fair lady were used to tie up locks to show delicate shades of love. Some men wore two long love-locks on either side of the face, others wore two elaborately-curled locks on one side only.

The hats, as the drawings will show, are broad in the brim and of an average height in the crown, but a dandy, here and there, wore a hat with next to no brim and a high crown. Most hats were feathered.

There is a washing tally in existence of this time belonging, I think, to the Duke of Rutland, which is very interesting. It is made of beech-wood covered with linen, and is divided into fifteen squares. In the centre of each square there is a circle cut, and in the circle are numbers. Over the number is a plate with a pin for pivot in the centre, a handle to turn, and a hole to expose a number. Above each circle are the names of the articles in this order:

Ruffs.	Bandes.	Cuffes.	Handkercher.	Cappes.
Shirtes.	Halfshirts.	Boote Hose.	Topps.	Sockes.
Sheetes.	Pillowberes.	Table Clothes.	Napkins.	Towells.

Topps are linen boot-frills, and halfshirts are stomachers.

There remains little to be said except that black was a favourite dress for men, also light blue and cream-coloured satin. Bristol paste diamonds were in great demand, and turquoise rings were very fashionable.

For the rest, Vandyck's pictures are available to most people, or good reproductions of them, and those, with a knowledge of how such dress came into being, are all that can be needed.

THE WOMEN.

There is one new thing you must be prepared to meet in this reign, and that will best be described by quoting the title of a book written at this time: 'A Wonder of Wonders, or a Metamorphosis of Fair Faces into Foul Visages; an invective against black-spotted faces.'

By this you may see at once that every humour was let loose in the shapes of stars, and moons, crowns, slashes, lozenges, and even a coach and horses, cut in black silk, ready to be gummed to the faces of the fair.

Knowing from other histories of such fads that the germ of the matter lies in a royal indisposition, we look in vain for the conceited history of the Princess and the Pimple, but no doubt some more earnest enquirer after truth will hit upon the story —this toy tragedy of the dressing-table.

For the dress we can do no better than look at the 'Ornatus Muliebris Anglicanus,' that wonderfully careful compilation by Hollar of all the dresses in every class of society.

It is interesting to see how the Jacobean costume lost, by degrees, its formal stiffness, and first fardingale and then ruff vanished.

Early in the reign the high-dressed hair was abandoned, and to take its place the hair was dressed so that it was gathered up by the ears, left parted on the crown, and twisted at the back to hold a plume or feather. Time went on, and hairdressing again altered; the hair was now taken in four parts: first the hair was drawn well back off the forehead, then the two side divisions were curled neatly and dressed to fall over the ears, the fourth group of hair was neatly twisted and so made into a small knot holding the front hair in its place. Later on came the fringe of small curls, as in the portrait of Queen Henrietta at Windsor by Vandyck.

We see at first that while the ruff, or rather the rebatoe—that starched lace high collar—remained, the fardingale having disappeared, left, for the upper gown, an enormous quantity of waste loose material that had previously been stretched over the fardingale and parted in front to show the satin petticoat. From this there sprung, firstly, a wide, loose gown, open all the way down and tied about the middle with a narrow sash, the opening showing the boned bodice of the under-dress with its pointed protruding

stomacher, the woman's fashion having retained
the form of the man's jerkin.   Below this showed
the satin petticoat with its centre strip or band
of embroidery, and the wide border of the same.
In many cases the long hanging sleeves were kept.

Then there came the fall of the rebatoe and
the decline of the protruding figure, and with
this the notion of tying back the full upper skirt
to show more plainly the satin petticoat, which
was now losing the centre band of ornament and
the border.

With this revolution in dress the disappearing
ruff became at first much lower and then finally
vanished, and a lace collar, falling over the
shoulders, took its place.   This gave rise to two
distinct fashions in collars, the one as I have
described, the other a collar from the neck, like
a large edition of the man's collar of that time.
This collar came over the shoulders and in two
points over the breast, sometimes completely hiding
the upper part of the dress.

The stiff-boned bodice gave place to one more
easily cut, shorter, with, in place of the long
point, a series of long strips, each strip ornamented
round the hem.

At this time the sleeves, different from the old-fashioned tight sleeves, were very full indeed, and the sleeve of the loose over-gown was made wider in proportion, and was tied across the under-sleeve above the elbow by a knot of ribbons, the whole ending in a deep cuff of lace. Then the over-gown disappeared, the bodice became a short jacket laced in front, openly, so as to show the sleeveless bodice of the same material and colour as the petticoat; the sleeves were not made so wide, and they were cut to come just below the elbow, leaving the wrists and forearm bare.

In winter a lady often wore one of those loose Dutch jackets, round and full, with sleeves just long enough to cover the under-sleeves, the whole lined and edged with fur; or she might wear a short circular fur-lined cape with a small turned-over collar. In summer the little jacket was often discarded, and the dress was cut very simply but very low in the bust, and they wore those voluminous silk wraps in common with the men.

The little sashes were very much worn, and ornaments of knots of ribbon or points (that is, a ribbon with a metal tag at either end) were universal.

The change of fashion to short full sleeves gave

rise to the turned back cuff of the same material
as the sleeve, and some costumes show this short
jacket with its short sleeves with cuffs, while under
it shows the dress with tight sleeves reaching to
the wrists where were linen or lace cuffs, a com-
bination of two fashions.

Part of the lady's equipment now was a big
feather fan, and a big fur muff for winter; also the
fashion of wearing long gloves to reach to the
elbow came in with the advent of short sleeves.

Naturally enough there was every variety of
evolution from the old fashion to the new, as
the tight sleeves did not, of course, become
immediately wide and loose, but by some common
movement, so curious in the history of such
revolutions, the sleeve grew and grew from puffs
at the elbow to wide cuffs, to wide shoulders,
until the entire sleeve became swollen out of all
proportion, and the last little pieces of tightness
were removed.

The form of dress with cuffs to the jackets,
lacing, sashes, bunches of ribbon, and looped up
skirts, lasted for a great number of years. It
was started by the death of the fardingale, and
it lived into the age of hoops.

23

These ladies wore shoe-roses upon their shoes, and these bunches of ribbon, very artificially made up, cost sometimes as much as from three to thirty pounds a pair, these very expensive roses being ornamented with jewels. From these we derive the saying, 'Roses worth a family.'

In the country the women wore red, gray, and black cloth homespun, and for riding they put on safeguards or outer petticoats. The wide-brimmed beaver hat was in general wear, and a lady riding in the country would wear such a hat or a hood and a cloak and soft top boots.

Women's petticoats were called plackets as well as petticoats.

With the careless air that was then adopted by everybody, which was to grow yet more carefully careless in the reign of Charles II., the hair was a matter which must have undivided attention, and centuries of tight dressing had not improved many heads, so that when the loose love-locks and the dainty tendrils became the fashion, many good ladies and gentlemen had recourse to the wigmaker. From this time until but an hundred years ago, from the periwig bought for Sexton, the fool of Henry VIII., down to the scratches and bobs of one's grandfather's youth, the wigmaker lived and prospered. To-day, more secretly yet more surely, does the maker of transformations live and prosper, but in the days when to be wigless was to be undressed the perruquier was a very great person.

This was the day, then, of satins, loosened hair, elbow sleeves, and little forehead curls. The stiffness of the older times will pass away, but it had left its clutch still on these ladies; how far it vanished, how entirely it left costume, will be seen in the next royal reign, when Nell Gwynne was favourite and Sir Peter Lely painted her.

A MAN OF THE TIME OF CHARLES I.   1625-1649

A WOMAN OF THE TIME OF CHARLES I.   1625 1649

ENGRAVINGS BY HOLLAR

THESE excellent drawings by Hollar need no explanation. They are included in this book because of their great value as accurate contemporary drawings of costume.

1

2

4

Marchants daughter

Marchants wife of London.

Cittizens wife

Country woman

7

English: Gentle: woman

Noble Gentle woman
of England

Lady of the Court of
England

An English Lady
of quality

THE CROMWELLS

1649—1660.

THE MEN AND WOMEN.

‘ I left my pure mistress for a space,
  And to a snip-snap barber straight went I;
  I cut my hair, and did my corps uncase
  Of ’parel’s pride that did offend the eye;
  My high crowned hat, my little beard also,
  My pecked band, my shoes were sharp at toe.

‘ Gone was my sword, my belt was laid aside,
  And I transformed both in looks and speech;
  My ’parel plain, my cloak was void of pride,
  My little skirts, my metamorphosed breech,
  My stockings black, my garters were tied shorter,
  My gloves no scent; thus marched I to her porter.’

IT is a question, in this time of restraint, of
formalism, where anything could be made plain,
cut in a cumbrous fashion, rendered inelegant,
it was done. The little jackets were denuded of
all forms of frippery, the breeches were cut straight,

359

and the ornaments, if any, were of the most severe order. Hats became broader in the brim, boots wider in the tops, in fact, big boots seemed almost a sign of heavy religious feeling. The nice hair, love-locks, ordered negligence all vanished, and  plain crops or straight hair, not over long, marked these extra-ordinary people. It was a natural revolt against extravagance, and in some more sensible minds it was not carried to excess; points and bows were allowable, though of sombre colours. Sashes still held good, but of larger size, ruffs at the wrists were worn, but of plain linen. The bands or collars varied in size according to the religious enthusiasm of the wearers, but all were plain with-out lace edgings, and were tied with plain strings. Black, dark brown, and dull gray were the common colours, relieved some-times, if the man was wearing a sleeveless coat, by the yellow and red-barred sleeves of the under-jacket, or possibly by coloured sleeves sewn into

the coat under the shoulder-wings. Overcoats
were cut as simply as possible, though they did
not skimp the material but made them wide and
loose.

The women dressed their hair more plainly,
the less serious retained the little bunches of side

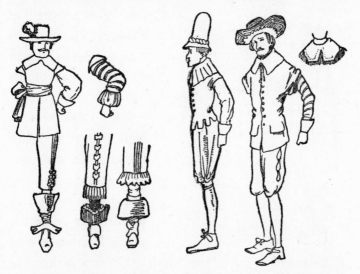

curls, but the others smoothed their hair away
under linen caps or black hoods tied under their
chins. Another thing the women did was to cut
from their bodices all the little strips but the
in the middle of the back, and this they left, like
a tail, behind. Some, of course, dressed as before

with the difference in colour and in ornament that made for severity. It had an effect on the country insomuch as the country people ceased to be extravagant in the materials for garments and in many like ways, and so lay by good fortunes for their families—these families coming later into

the gay court of Charles II. had all the more to lavish on the follies of his fashions.

The Puritan is as well-known a figure as any in history; an intelligent child could draw you a picture or describe you a Puritan as well as he could describe the Noah of Noah's Ark. He has become part of the stock for an Academy humourist, a thousand anecdote pictures have been painted of him; very often his nose is red, generally he has a book in his hand, laughing maids bring him jacks of ale, jeering Cavaliers swagger past him: his black cloak, board shoes, wide Geneva bands are as much part of our national picture as Punch or Harlequin.

The Puritaness is also known. She is generally represented as a sly bird in sombre clothes; her town garments, full skirts, black hood, deep linen collar are shown to hide a merry-eyed lady, her country clothes, apron, striped petticoat, bunched up skirt, linen cap, her little flaunt of curls show her still mischievous. The pair of them, in reality religious fanatics, prepared a harvest that they little dreamt of—a harvest of extravagant clothes and extravagant manners, when the country broke loose from its false bondage of texts, scriptural shirts, and religious petticoats, and launched into a bondage, equally false, of low cut dresses and enormous periwigs.

In the next reign you will see an entirely new
era of clothes—the doublet and jerkin, the trunks
and ruffs have their last eccentric fling, they
become caricatures of themselves, they do all the
foolish things garments can do, and then, all
of a sudden, they vanish—never to be taken up
again. Hair, long-neglected, is to have its full
sway, wigs are the note for two centuries, so
utterly different did the man become in the short
space of thirty-five years, that the buck of the
Restoration and the beau of the Jacobean order
would stare helplessly at each other, wondering
each to himself what manner of fool this was
standing before him.

A CROMWELLIAN MAN   1649-1660

A WOMAN OF THE TIME OF THE CROMWELLS   1649-1660

CHARLES THE SECOND

Reigned twenty-five years : 1660—1685.
Born 1630.   Married, 1662, Katherine of Portugal.

THE MEN AND WOMEN

ENGLAND, apparently with a sigh of relief, lays aside her hair shirt, and proves that she has been wearing a silk vest under it. Ribbon - makers and wig - makers, lace-makers, tailors, and shoemakers, pour out thankful offerings at the altar of Fashion. One kind of folly has replaced another ; it is only the same goddess in different clothes.   The lamp

365

that winked and flickered before the stern black
figure in Geneva bands and prim curls is put to
shame by the flare of a thousand candles shining
on the painted face, the exposed bosom, the
flaunting love-locks of this Carolean deity.

We have burst out into periwigs, monstrous,
bushy; we have donned petticoat breeches ruffled
like a pigeon; we have cut our coats till they
are mere apologies, serving to show off our fine
shirts; and we have done the like with our coat-
sleeves, leaving a little cuff glittering with buttons,

and above that we have cut
a great slit, all to show the
marvel of our linen.

Those of us who still
wear the long wide breeches
adorn them with heavy
frills of deep lace, and sew
bunches of ribbons along
the seams.   We tie our
cravats in long, stiff bows or knot them tight,
and allow the wide lace ends to float gracefully.

Our hats, broad-brimmed and stiff, are loaded
with feathers; our little cloaks are barred with
silk and lace and gold cord; our shoes are square-

toed and high-heeled, and are tied with a long-ended bow of ribbon.

Ribbon reigns triumphant: it ties our periwigs into bunches at the ends; it hangs in loops round our waists; it ties our shirt-sleeves up in several places; it twists itself round our knees. It is on our hats and heads, and necks and arms, and legs and shoes, and it peers out of the tops of our boots. Divines rave, moralists rush into print, to no purpose. The names seem to convey a sense of luxury: dove-coloured silk brocade, Rhingrave breeches, white lutestring seamed all over with scarlet and silver lace, sleeves whipt  with a point lace, coat trimmed and figured with silver twist or satin ribbon; canvas, camblet, galloon and shamey, vellam buttons and taffety ribbons. The cannons, those bunches of ribbons round our knees, and the confidents, those bunches of curls by our ladies' cheeks, do not shake at the thunderings of Mr. Baxter or other moral gentlemen who regard a Maypole as a stinking idol. Mr. Hall writes on 'The Loathsomeness of Long Hair,' Mr. Prynne on 'The Unloveliness of Lovelocks,' and we do not care a pinch of rappe.

Little moustaches and tiny lip beards grow under careful treatment, and the ladies wear a solar system in patches on their cheeks.

The ladies soon escaped the bondage of the broad Puritan collars, and all these had hid was exposed. The sleeves left the arms bare to the elbow, and, being slit above and joined loosely by ribbons, showed the arm nearly to the shoulder. The sleeves of these dresses also followed the masculine fashion of little cuffs and tied-up linen under-sleeves. The bodices came to a peak in front and were round behind. The skirts were full, satin being favoured, and when held up showed a satin petticoat with a long train. The ladies, for a time, indulged in a peculiar loop of hair on their foreheads, called a 'fore-top,' which gave rise to another fashion, less common, called a 'taure,' or bull's head, being an arrangement of hair on the forehead resembling the close curls of a bull. The loose curls on the forehead were

MEN OF THE TIME OF CHARLES II.   1660-1685

The picture on the right shows the dress during the first half of the reign.
That on the left indicates the change which came over men's dress in or
about October, 1666.

A WOMAN OF THE TIME OF CHARLES II.   1660-1685

called ' favorites '; the long locks arranged to hang away from the face over the ears were called 'heart-breakers'; and the curls close to the cheek were called 'confidents.' Ladies wore cloaks with baggy hoods for travelling, and for the Mall the same hats as men, loaded with feathers.

I am going to leave the change in dress during this reign to the next chapter, in which you will read how it struck Mr. Pepys. This change separates the old world of dress from the new; it is the advent of frocked coats, the ancestor of our frock-coat. It finishes completely the series of evolutions beginning with the old tunic, running through the gown stages to the doublet of Elizabethan times, lives in the half coat, half doublet of Charles I., and ends in the absurd little jackets of Charles II., who, sartorially, steps from the end of the Middle Ages into the New Ages,

24

closes the door on a wardrobe of brilliant eccentricity, and opens a cupboard containing our first frock-coat.

PEPYS AND CLOTHES

It is not really necessary for me to remind the reader that one of the best companions in the world, Samuel Pepys, was the son of a tailor. Possibly—I say possibly because the argument is really absurd—he may have inherited his great interest in clothes from his father. You see where the argument leads in the end: that all men to take an interest in clothes must be born tailors' sons. This is no more true of Adam, who certainly did interest himself, than it is of myself.

Pepys was educated at St. Paul's School, went to Trinity College, Cambridge, got drunk there, and took a scholarship. He married when he was twenty-two a girl of fifteen, the daughter of a Huguenot. He was born in 1633, three years after the birth of Charles II., of outrageous but delightful memory, and he commenced his Diary in 1660, the year in which Charles entered London, ending it in 1669, owing to his increasing weakness of sight. He was made Secretary to the

Admiralty in 1672, in 1673 he became a member of Parliament, was sent to the Tower as a Papist in 1679, and released in 1680. In 1684 he became President of the Royal Society, and he died in 1703, and is buried in St. Olave's, Crutched Friars.

Pepys mentions, in 1660, his coat with long skirts, fur cap, and buckles on his shoes. The coat was, doubtless, an old-fashioned Cromwellian coat with no waist.

Later he goes to see Mr. Calthrop, and wears his white suit with silver lace, having left off his great skirt-coat. He leaves Mr. Calthrop to lay up his money and change his shoes and stockings.

He mentions his scarlet waistclothes, presumably a sash, and regards Mr. John Pickering as an ass because of his feathers and his new suit made at the Hague. He mentions his linning stockings and wide cannons. This mention of wide cannons leads me to suppose that at this time any ornament at the knee would be called cannons, whether it was a part of the breeches or the stockings, or a separate frill or bunch of ribbons to put on.

On July 1, still in the same year, comes home his fine camlett cloak and gold buttons; also a silk suit. Later he buys a jackanapes coat with

24—2

silver buttons. Then he and Mr. Pin, the tailor agree upon a velvet coat and cap ('the first I ever had'). He buys short black stockings to wear over silk ones for mourning.

On October 7 he says that, long cloaks being out of fashion, he must get a short one. He speaks of a suit made in France for My Lord costing £200. He mentions ladies' masks.

In 1662 his wife has a pair of peruques of hair and a new-fashioned petticoat of sancenett with

black, broad lace. Smocks are mentioned, and linen petticoats.

He has a riding-suit with close knees.

His new lace band is so neat that he is resolved they shall be his great expense. He wears a scallop. In 1663 he has a new black cloth suit, with white linings under all—as the fashion is—to appear under the breeches.

The Queen wears a white-laced waistcoat and a

crimson short petticoat. Ladies are wearing hats covered with feathers.

God willing, he will begin next week to wear his three-pound periwig.

He has spent last month (October) £12 on Miss Pepys, and £55 on his clothes. He has silk tops for his legs and a new shag gown. He has a close-bodied coat, light-coloured cloth with a gold edge. He sees Lady Castlemaine in yellow satin with a pinner on.

In 1664 his wife begins to wear light-coloured locks.

In 1665 there is a new fashion for ladies of yellow bird's-eye hood. There is a fear of the hair of periwigs during the Plague. Even in the middle of the Plague Pepys ponders on the next fashion.

In 1666 women begin to wear buttoned-up riding-coats, hats and periwigs.

On October 8 the King says he will set a thrifty fashion in clothes. At this momentous date in history we must break for a minute from

our friend Pepys, and hear how this came about.
Evelyn had given the King his pamphlet entitled

'Tyrannus, or the
Mode.' The King reads
the pamphlet, and is
struck with the idea
of the Persian coat.
A long pause may be
made here, in which
the reader may float
on a mental cloud back
into the dim ages in
the East, and there
behold a transmogrified
edition of his own frock-
coat gracing the back
of some staid philosopher. Evelyn had also
published 'Mundus Muliebris; or, the Ladies'
Dressing-Room Unlocked.'

So, only one month after the Great Fire of
London, only a short time before the Dutch burnt
ships in the Medway, only a year after the Plague,
King Charles decides to reform the fashion. By
October 13 the new vests are made, and the King
and the Duke of York try them on. On the

fifteenth the King wears his in public, and says he will never change to another fashion. 'It is,' says Pepys, ' a long cassocke close to the body, of black cloth and pinked with white silk under it, and a coat over it, and the legs ruffled with black ribband like a pigeon's legs.'

The ladies, to make an alteration, are to wear short skirts. Nell Gwynne had a neat ankle, so I imagine she had a hand in this fashion.

On October 17 the King, seeing Lord St. Alban in an all black suit, says that the black and white makes them look too much like magpies. He bespeaks one of all black velvet.

Sir Philip Howard increases in the Eastern fashion, and wears a nightgown and a turban like a Turk.

On November 2 Pepys buys a vest like the King's.

On November 22 the King of France, Louis XIV., who had declared war against England earlier in the year, says that he will dress all his footmen in vests like the King of England. However, fashion is beyond the power of royal command, and the world soon followed in the matter of the Persian coat and vest, even to the present day.

Next year, 1667, Pepys notes that Lady Newcastle, in her velvet cap and her hair about her ears, is the talk of the town. She wears a number of black patches because of the pimples about her mouth, she is naked-necked (no great peculiarity), and she wears a *just au corps*, which is a close body-coat.

Pepys notices the shepherd at Epsom with his wool-knit stockings of two colours, mixed. He wears a new camlett cloak. The shoe-strings have given place to buckles, and children wear long coats.

In 1668 his wife wears a flower tabby suit ('everybody in love with it'). He is forced to lend the Duke of York his cloak because it rains. His barber agrees to keep his periwig in order for £1 a year.   He buys a black bombazin suit.

In 1669 his wife wears the new French gown called a sac; he pays 55s. for his new belt.   His wife still wears her old flower tabby gown.   So ends the dress note in the Diary.

JAMES THE SECOND

Reigned four years: 1685—1689.
Born 1633. Married, 1661, Anne Hyde; 1673,
Mary of Modena.

THE MEN AND WOMEN

In such a short space of time as this reign occupies it is not possible to show any great difference in the character of the dress, but there is a tendency, shown over the country at large, to discard the earlier beribboned fashions, and to take more seriously to the long coat and waistcoat. There is a tendency, even, to become more buttoned up—to present what I can only call a frock-coat figure. The coat became closer to the

378

body, and was braided across the front in many rows, the ends fringed out and held by buttons. The waistcoat, with the pockets an arm's length down, was cut the same length as the coat. Breeches were more frequently cut tighter, and were buttoned up the side of the leg. The cuffs of the sleeves were wide, and were turned back well over the wrist.

Of course the change was gradual, and more men wore the transitional coat than the tight one. By the coat in its changing stages I mean such a coat as this: the short coat of the early Charles II. period made long, and, following the old lines of cut, correspondingly loose. The sleeves remained much the same, well over the elbow, showing the white shirt full and tied with ribbons. The shoe-strings had nearly died out, giving place to a buckle placed on a strap well over the instep.

There is a hint of growth in the periwig, and of fewer feathers round the brim of the hat; indeed, little low hats with broad brims, merely ornamented with a bunch or so of ribbons, began to become fashionable.

Swords were carried in broad baldricks richly ornamented.

The waistclothes of Mr. Pepys would, by now, have grown into broad sashes, with heavily fringed ends, and would be worn round the outside coat; for riding, this appears to have been the fashion, together with small peaked caps, like jockey caps, and high boots.

The ladies of this reign simplified the dress into a gown more tight to the bust, the sleeves more

like the men's, the skirt still very full, but not quite so long in the train.

Black hoods with or without capes were worn, and wide collars coming over the shoulders again came into fashion. The pinner, noticed by Pepys, was often worn.

But the most noticeable change occurs in the dress of countryfolk and ordinary citizens. The men began to drop all forms of doublet, and

take to the long coat, a suit of black grogram below
the knees, a sash, and a walking-stick; for the cold,
a short black cloak. In the country the change
would be very noticeable. The country town, the
countryside, was, until a few years back, distinctly
Puritanical in garb; there were Elizabethan doublets on old men, and wide Cromwellian breeches,
patched doubtless, walked the market-place. Hair
was worn short. Now the russet brown clothes
take a decided character in the direction of the
Persian coat and knickerbockers closed at the knee.

The good-wife of the farmer knots a
loose cloth over her head, and pops a
broad-brimmed man's hat over it. She
has the sleeves of her dress made with
turned-back cuffs, like her husband's,
ties her shoes with strings, laces her
dress in front, so as to show a bright-
coloured under-bodice, and, as like as
not, wears a green pinner (an apron with
bib, which was pinned on to the dress),
and altogether brings herself up to date.

One might see the farmer's wife riding to market
with her eggs in a basket covered with a corner of
her red cloak, and many a red cloak would she meet

on the way to clep with on the times and the
fashions. The green apron was a mark of a Quaker
in America, and the Society of Friends was not by
any means sad in colour until late in their history.

Most notable was the neckcloth in this unhappy
reign, which went by the name of Judge Jeffreys'
hempen cravat.

WILLIAM AND MARY

Reigned thirteen years: 1689—1702.
The King born in 1650; the Queen born in 1662;
    married in 1677.

THE MEN

FIRST and foremost, the wig.
Periwig, peruke, campaign wig
with pole-locks or dildos, all
the rage, all the thought of
the first gentlemen. Their
heads loaded with curl upon
curl, long ringlets hanging
over their shoulders and down
their backs, some brown, some
covered with meal until their
coats looked like millers' coats;
scented hair, almost hiding the
loose-tied cravat, 'most agree-
ably discoloured with snuff
from top to bottom.'

283

My fine gentleman walking the street with the square-cut coat open to show a fine waistcoat, his stick hanging by a ribbon on to his wrist and rattling on the pavement as it dragged along, his hat carefully perched on his wig, the crown made wide and high to hold the two wings of curls, which formed a negligent central parting. His pockets, low down in his coat, show a lace kerchief half dropping from one of them. One hand is in a small muff, the other holds a fine silver-gilt box filled with Vigo snuff. He wears high-heeled shoes, red heeled,

perhaps, and the tongue of his shoe sticks up well above the instep. Probably he is on his way to the theatre, where he will comb his periwig in public, and puff away the clouds of powder that come from it. The fair lady in a side box, who hides her face behind a mask, is delighted if Sir Beau will bow to her.

We are now among most precise people. One must walk here with just such an air of artificiality as will account one a

A MAN OF THE TIME OF JAMES II.   1685-1689

A WOMAN OF THE TIME OF JAMES II.   1685-1689

fellow of high tone. The more enormous is our wig, the more frequently we take a pinch of Violet Strasburg or Best Brazil, Orangery, Bergamotte, or Jassamena, the more shall we be followed by persons anxious to learn the fashion. We may even draw a little silver bowl from our pocket, place it on a seat by us, and, in meditative mood, spit therein.

We have gone completely into skirted coats and big flapped waistcoats; we have adopted the big cuff buttoned back; we have given up altogether the wide knee-breeches, and wear only breeches not tight to the leg, but just full enough for comfort.

The hats have altered considerably now; they are cocked up at all angles, turned off the forehead, turned up one side, turned up all round; some are fringed with gold or silver lace, others are crowned with feathers.

We hear of such a number of claret-coloured suits that we must imagine that colour to be all the rage, and, in contrast to other times not long gone by, we must stiffen ourselves in buckram-lined skirts.

These powdered Absaloms could change themselves into very fine fighting creatures, and look twice as sober again when occasion demanded. They rode about the country in periwigs, certainly, but not quite so bushy and curled; many of them took to the travelling or campaign wig with

the dildos or pole-locks. These wigs were full over the ears and at the sides of the forehead, but they were low in the crown, and the two front ends were twisted into single pipes of hair; or the pipes of hair at the side were entirely removed, and one single pipe hung down the back. The custom of thus twisting the hair at the back, and there holding it with a ribbon, gave rise to the later pigtail. The periwigs so altered were known as short bobs, the bob being the fullness of the hair by the cheeks of the wig.

The cuffs of the coat-sleeve varied to the idea and taste of the owner of the coat; sometimes the sleeve was widened at the elbow to 18 inches, and the cuffs, turned back to meet the sleeves, were wider still. Two, three, or even more buttons held the cuff back.

The pockets on the coats were cut vertically and

horizontally, and these also might be buttoned up.
Often the coat was held by only two centre buttons,
and the waistcoat flaps were
not buttoned at all. The
men's and women's muffs were
small, and often tied and slung
with ribbons.

Plain round riding - coats
were worn, fastened by a clasp
or a couple of large buttons.

The habit of tying the neck-
cloth in a bow with full
hanging ends was dying out,
and a more loosely tied cravat

was being worn ; this was
finished with fine lace
ends, and was frequently
worn quite long.

Stockings were pulled
over the knee, and were
gartered below and rolled
above it.

The ordinary citizen
wore a modified edition
of these clothes—plain in cut, full, without half the

25—2

number of buttons, and without the tremendous periwig, wearing merely his own hair long.

For convenience in riding, the skirts of the coats were slit up the back to the waist; this slit could be buttoned up if need be.

Now, let us give the dandy of this time his pipe, and let him go in peace. Let us watch him stroll down the street, planting his high heels carefully, to join two companions outside the tobacco shop. Here, by the great carved wood figure of a smoking Indian with his kilt of tobacco leaves, he meets his fellows. From the hoop hung by the door one chooses a pipe, another asks for a quid to chew and a spittoon, the third calls for a paper of snuff newly rasped. Then they pull aside the curtains and go into the room behind the shop, where, seated at a table made of planks upon barrels, they will discuss the merits of smoking, chewing, and snuffing.

> ' We three are engaged in one cause,
> I snuffs, I smokes, and I chaws.'

A MAN OF THE TIME OF WILLIAM AND MARY   1689-1702

A WOMAN OF THE TIME OF WILLIAM AND MARY   1689 1702

THE WOMEN

Let me picture for you a lady of this time in the language of those learned in dress, and you will see how much it may benefit.

'We see her coming afar off; against the yew hedge her weeds shine for a moment. We see her figuretto gown well looped and puffed with the monte-la-haut. Her échelle is beautiful, and her pinner exquisitely worked. We can see her commode, her top-not, and her fontage, for she wears no rayonné. A silver pin holds her meurtriers, and the fashion suits better than did the crève-cœurs. One hand holds her Saxon green muffetee, under one arm is her chapeau-bras. She is beautiful, she needs no plumpers, and she regards us kindly with her watchet eyes.'

A lady of this date would read this and enjoy it, just as a lady of to-day would understand modern dress language, which is equally peculiar to the mere man. For example, this one of the Queen of Spain's hats from her trousseau (curiously enough a trousseau is a little bundle):

'The hat is a paille d'Italie trimmed with a profusion of pink roses, accompanied by a pink chiffon

ruffle fashioned into masses bouillonnée arranged
at intervals and circled with wreaths of shaded
roses.'

The modern terms so vaguely used are shocking,
and the descriptive names given to colours by

dress-artists are horrible
beyond belief — such as
Watteau pink and ele-
phant grey, not to speak
of Sèvres-blue cherries.

However, the female
mind delights in such
jargon and hotch-potch.

Let me be kind enough
to translate our William
and Mary fashion language.

'Weeds' is a term still in use in 'widow's weeds,'
meaning the entire dress appearance of a woman.
A 'figuretto gown looped and puffed with the monte-
la-haut' is a gown of figured material gathered into
loops over the petticoat and stiffened out with wires
'monte-la-haut.' The 'échelle' is a stomacher
laced with ribbons in rungs like a ladder. Her
'pinner' is her apron. The 'commode' is the wire
frame over which the curls are arranged, piled up in

high masses over the forehead. The 'top-not' is a large bow worn at the top of the commode; and the 'fontage' or 'tower' is a French arrangement of alternate layers of lace and ribbon raised one above another about half a yard high. It was invented in the time of Louis XIV., about 1680, by Mademoiselle Fontage. The 'rayonné' is a cloth hood pinned in a circle. The 'meurtriers,' or murderers, are those twists in the hair which tie or unloose the arrangements of curls; and the 'crève-cœurs' are the row of little forehead curls of the previous reign. A 'muffetee' is a little muff, and a 'chapeau-bras' is a hat never worn, but made to be carried under the arm by men or women; for the men hated to disarrange their wigs.

'Plumpers' were artificial arrangements for filling out the cheeks, and 'watchet' eyes are blue eyes.

The ladies have changed a good deal by the middle of this reign: they have looped up the gown

till it makes side-panniers and a bag-like droop at
the back ; the under-gown has a long train, and the

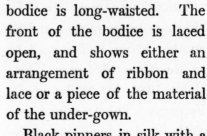

bodice is long-waisted.   The
front of the bodice is laced
open, and shows either an
arrangement of ribbon and
lace or a piece of the material
of the under-gown.

Black pinners in silk with a
deep frill are worn as well as
the white lace and linen ones.

The ladies wear short black
capes of this
stuff with a
deep frill.

Sometimes,
instead of the
fontage, a lady
wears a lace shawl over her head
and shoulders, or a sort of lace cap
bedizened with coloured ribbons.

Her sleeves are like a man's,
except that they come to the elbow
only, showing a white under-sleeve of lace gathered
into a deep frill of lace just below the elbow.

She is very stiff and tight-laced, and very long in
the waist; and at the waist where the gown opens
and at the loopings of it the
richer wear jewelled brooches.

Later in the reign there began
a fashion for copying men's
clothes, and ladies wore wide
skirted coats with deep-flapped
pockets, the sleeves of the coats
down below the elbow and with
deep-turned overcuffs. They
wore, like the men, very much
puffed
and ruf-

fled linen and lace at the
wrists. Also they wore
men's waistcoat fashions,
carried sticks and little arm-
hats — chapeau - bras. To
complete the dress the hair
was done in a bob-wig style,
and the cravat was tied
round their necks and

Country Folk.

pinned. For the winter one of those loose Dutch
jackets lined and edged with fur, having wide sleeves.

The general tendency was to look Dutch, stiff, prim, but very prosperous; even the country maid in her best is close upon the heel of fashion with her laced bodice, sleeves with cuffs, apron, and high-heeled shoes.

QUEEN ANNE

Reigned twelve years : 1702—1714.
Born 1665.   Married, 1683, Prince George of
Denmark.

THE MEN AND WOMEN

WHEN I turn to the opening of the eighteenth
century, and leave Dutch William and his Hollands
and his pipe and his bulb-gardens behind, it seems
to me that there is a great noise, a tumultuous
chattering. We seem to burst upon a date of
talkers, of coffee-houses, of snuff and scandal. All
this was going on before, I say to myself—people
were wearing powdered wigs, and were taking snuff,
and were talking scandal, but it did not appeal so
forcibly.

We arrive at Sedan-chairs and hoops too big for
them ; we arrive at red-heeled shoes. Though both
chairs and red heels belong to the previous reign,
still, we arrive at them now—they are very much

in the picture. We seem to see a profusion, a confused mass of bobbins and bone lace, mourning hatbands, silk garters, amber canes correctly conducted, country men in red coats, coxcombs, brass and looking-glass snuff-boxes.

Gentlemen walk past our mental vision with seals curiously fancied and exquisitely well cut.

Ladies are sighing at the toss of a wig or the tap on a snuff-box, falling sick for a pair of striped garters or a pair of fringed gloves. Gentlemen are sitting baldheaded in elegant dressing-gowns, while their wigs are being taken out of roulettes. The peruquier removes the neat, warm clay tube, gives a last pat to the fine pipes of the hair, and then gently places the wig on the waiting gentlemen. If you can look through the walls of London houses you will next see regiments of gentlemen, their faces pressed into glass cones, while the peruquier tosses powder over their newly-put-on periwigs. The bow at the end of the

A MAN OF THE TIME OF QUEEN ANNE 1702 1714

A WOMAN OF THE TIME OF QUEEN ANNE 1702-1714

long pigtail on the Ramillies wig is tied—that is over.

Running footmen, looking rather like Indians from the outsides of tobacco shops, speed past. They are dressed in close tunics with a fringed edge, which flicks them just above the knee. Their legs are tied up in leather guards, their feet are strongly shod, their wigs are in small bobs. On their heads are little round caps, with a feather stuck in them. In one hand they carry a long stick about 5 feet high, in the top knob of which they carry some food or a message. A message to whom?

A Running Footman.

The running footman knocks on a certain door, and delivers to the pretty maid a note for her ladyship from a handsome, well-shaped youth who frequents the coffee-houses about Charing Cross. There is no answer to the note: her ladyship is too disturbed with household affairs. Her Welsh maid has left her under suspicious circumstances, and has carried off some articles. The lady is even now writing to Mr. Bickerstaff of the *Tatler* to implore his aid.

This is the list of the things she has missed—at least, as much of the list as my mind remembers as it travels back over the years :

A thick wadded Calico Wrapper.
A Musk-coloured Velvet Mantle lined with Squirrels' Skins.

Eight night shifts, four pairs of stockings curiously darned.

Six pairs of laced Shoes, new and old, with the heels of half 2 inches higher than their fellows.

A quilted Petticoat of the largest size, and one of Canvas, with whalebone hoops.

Three pairs of Stays boulstered below the left shoulder. Two pairs of Hips of the newest fashion.

Six Roundabout Aprons, with Pockets, and four strip'd Muslin night rails very little frayed.

A silver Cheese toaster with three tongues.

A silver Posnet to butter eggs.

A Bible bound in Shagreen, with guilt Leaves and Clasps, never opened but once.

Two Leather Forehead Cloathes, three pair of oiled Dogskin Gloves.

Two brand new Plumpers, three pair of fashionable Eyebrows.

Adam and Eve in Bugle work, without Fig-
leaves, upon Canvas, curiously wrought
with her Ladyship's own hand.

Bracelets of braided Hair, Pomander, and Seed
Pearl.

A large old Purple Velvet Purse, embroidered,
and shutting with a spring, containing two
Pictures in Miniature, the Features visible.

A Silver gilt box for Cashu and Carraway Com-
fits to be taken at long sermons.

A new Gold Repeating Watch made by a
Frenchman.

Together with a Collection of Receipts to make
Pastes for the Hands, Pomatums, Lip
Salves, White Pots, and Water of Talk.

Of these things one strikes the eye most curiously
—the canvas petticoat with whalebone hoops. It
dates the last, making me know that the good
woman lost her things in or about the year 1710.
We are just at the beginning of the era of the
tremendous hoop skirt.

This gentleman from the country will tell me all
about it. I stop him and remark his clothes ; by
them I guess he has ridden from the country. He
is wearing a wide-skirted coat of red with deep
flap pockets ; his coat has buttons from neck to hem,

but only two or three—at the waist—are buttoned.
One hand, with the deep cuff pushed back from the
wrist to show his neat frilled shirt, is thrust into his
unbuttoned breeches pocket, the two pockets being
across the top of his breeches. Round his neck is a
black Steenkirk cravat (a black silk tie knotted and
twisted or allowed to hang over loose). His hat is of
black, and the wide brim is turned back from his forehead. His wig is a short black periwig in bobs—that

is, it is gathered into bunches just on
the shoulders, and is twisted in a little
bob at the back of the neck. I have
forgotten whether he wore red or blue
stockings rolled above the knee, but
either is likely. His shoes are strong,
high-heeled, and have a big tongue
showing above the buckle.

He tells me that in Norfolk, where
he has come from, the hoop has
not come into fashion ; that ladies
there dress much as they did before Queen Anne
came to the throne. The fontage is lower,
perhaps, the waist may be longer, but skirts are
full and have long trains, and are gathered in
loops to show the petticoat of silk with its deep

double row of flounces. Aprons are worn long,
and have good pockets. Cuffs are deep, but are
lowered to below the elbow. The bodice of the
gown is cut high in the back and low in front,
and is decked with a deep frill of lace or linen,
which allows less bare neck to show than formerly.
A very observant gentleman! 'But you have
seen the new hoop?' I ask him.
Yes, he has seen it. As he rode into
town he noticed that the old fashions
gave way to new, that every mile
brought the fontage lower and the
hair more hidden, until short curls
and a little cap of linen or lace
entirely replaced the old high head-
dress and the profusion of curls on
the shoulders. The hoop, he noticed,
became larger and larger as he

neared the town, and the train grew shorter, and
the patterns on the under-skirt grew larger with
the hoop.

I leave my gentleman from the country and
I stroll about the streets to regard the fashions.
Here, I see, is a gentleman in one of the new
Ramillies wigs—a wig of white hair drawn back

from the forehead and puffed out full over the ears. At the back the wig is gathered into a long queue, the plaited or twisted tail of a wig,

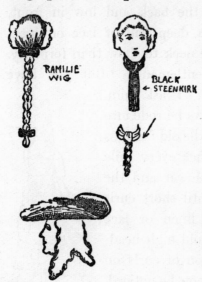

RAMILIE WIG

BLACK ← STEENKIRK

and is ornamented at the top and bottom of the queue with a black bow.

I notice that this gentleman is dressed in more easy fashion than some. His coat is not buttoned, the flaps of his waist-coat are not over big, his breeches are easy, his tie is loose. I know where this gentleman has stepped from; he has come straight out of a sampler of mine, by means of which piece of needlework I can get his story without book. I know that he has a tremendous periwig at home covered with scented powder; I know that he has an elegant suit with fullness of the skirts, at his sides gathered up to a button of silver gilt; there is plenty of lace on this coat, and deep bands of it on the cuffs. He has also, I am certain, a cane with an amber head very curiously clouded, and this cane he hangs on to his fifth button by a blue silk ribbon. This cane is never used except to lift it up at a coachman, hold it over the head of a drawer, or point out the circumstances of a story. Also, he has a single eyeglass, or perspective, which he will advance to his eye to gaze at a toast or an orange wench.

There is another figure on the sampler—a lady in one of those wide hoops; she has a fan in her hand. I know her as well as the gentleman, and know that she can use her fan as becomes a prude or a coquette. I know she takes her chocolate in bed at nine in the morning, at eleven she drinks a dish of bohea, tries a new head at her twelve o'clock toilette, and at two cheapens fans at the Change.

I have seen her at her mantua-makers; I have watched her embroider a corner of her flower handkerchief, and give it up to sit before her

26—2

glass to determine a patch. She is a good coach-woman, and puts her dainty laced shoe against the opposite seat to balance herself against the many jolts; meanwhile she takes her mask off for a look at the passing world. If only I could ride in the coach with her! If only I could I should see the fruit wenches in sprigged petticoats

 and flat, broad-brimmed hats; the ballad-sellers in tattered long-skirted coats; the country women in black hoods and cloaks, and the men in frieze coats. The ladies would pass by in pearl necklaces, flowered stomachers, artificial nosegays, and shaded furbelows: one is noted by her muff, one by her tippet, one by her fan. Here a gentleman bows to our coach, and my lady's heart beats to see his open waistcoat, his red heels, his suit of flowered satin. I should not fail to notice the monstrous petticoats worn by ladies in chairs or in coaches, these hoops stuffed out with cordage and stiffened with whalebone, and, according to Mr. Bickerstaff, making the women look like extinguishers—'with a little knob at the

upper end, and widening downward till it ends in a
basis of a most enormous circumference.'

To finish. I quite agree with Mr. Bickerstaff,
when he mentions the great shoe-shop at the
St. James's end of Pall Mall, that the shoes there
displayed, notably the slippers with green lace and
blue heels, do create irregular thoughts in the
youth of this nation.

GEORGE THE FIRST

Reigned thirteen years : 1714—1727.
Born 1660.   Married, 1682, Sophia of Brunswick.

THE MEN AND WOMEN

720

WE cannot do better
than open Thackeray,
and put a finger on this
passage :

'There is the Lion's
Head, down whose jaws
the Spectator's own let-
ters were passed; and
over a great banker's in
Fleet Street the effigy of
the wallet, which the founder of the firm bore when
he came into London a country boy.   People this
street, so ornamented with crowds of swinging
chairmen, with servants bawling to clear the way,
with Mr. Dean in his cassock, his lacquey marching

before him; or Mrs. Dinah in her sack, tripping to chapel, her footboy carrying her ladyship's great prayer - book; with itinerant tradesmen, singing their hundred cries (I remember forty years ago, as a boy in London city, a score of cheery, familiar cries that are silent now).

'Fancy the beaux thronging to the chocolate-houses, tapping their snuff-boxes as they issue thence, their periwig appearing over the red curtains. Fancy Saccharissa beckoning and smiling from the upper windows, and a crowd of soldiers bawling and bustling at the door—gentlemen of the Life Guards, clad in scarlet with blue facings, and laced with gold at the seams; gentlemen of the Horse Grenadiers, in their caps of sky-blue cloth, with the garter embroidered on the front in gold and silver; men of the Halberdiers, in their long red coats, as bluff Harry left them, with their ruffs and velvet flat-caps. Perhaps the King's Majesty himself is going to St. James's as we pass.'

The Four Georges.

We find ourselves, very willingly, discussing the shoes of the King of France with a crowd of powdered beaux; those shoes the dandyism of

which has never been surpassed, the heels, if you
please, painted by Vandermeulen with scenes from

Rhenish victories! Or we go to
the toy-shops in Fleet Street,
where we may make assignations
or buy us a mask, where loaded
dice are slyly handed over the
counter. Everywhere—the beau.
He rides the world like a cock-
horse, or like Og the giant rode
the Ark of Noah, steering it with
his feet, getting his washing for
nothing, and his meals passed up
to him out by the chimney. Here
is the old soldier begging in his
tattered coat of red; here is a
suspicious-looking character with a
black patch over his eye; here the
whalebone hoop of a petticoat takes
up the way, and above the monstrous hoop is the tight bodice,
and out of that comes the shoulders
supporting the radiant Molly —

patches, powder, paint, and smiles. Here a woman
passes in a Nithsdale hood, covering her from head

A MAN OF THE TIME OF GEORGE I.   1714-1727

A WOMAN OF THE TIME OF GEORGE I. 1714-1727

to foot—this great cloak with a piquant history of
prison-breaking ; here, with a clatter of high red
heels, the beau, the everlasting beau, in gold lace,
wide cuffs, full skirts, swinging cane. A scene of
flashing colours. The coats embroidered with
flowers and butterflies, the cuffs a mass of fine
sewing, the three-cornered hats cocked at a jaunty
angle, the stockings rolled above the
knee. Wigs in three divisions of loops
at the back pass by, wigs in long
queues, wigs in back and side bobs.
Lacquer-hilted swords, paste buckles,
gold and silver snuff-boxes flashing in
the sun, which struggles through the
mass of swinging signs.

There is a curious sameness about
the clean-shaven faces surmounted by
white wigs ; there is—if we believe the
pictures—a tendency to fat due to the
tight waist of the breeches or the
buckling of the belts. The ladies wear
little lace and linen caps, their hair

escaping in a ringlet or so at the side, and flowing
down behind, or gathered close up to a small knob
on the head. The gentlemen's coats fall in full

folds on either side; the back, at present, has not begun to stick out so heavily with buckram. Aprons for ladies are still worn. Silks and satins, brocades and fine cloths, white wigs powdering velvet shoulders, crowds of cut-throats, elegant gentlemen, patched Aspasias, tavern swindlers, foreign adventurers, thieves, a highwayman, a foot-pad, a poor poet—and narrow streets and mud.

Everywhere we see the skirted coat, the big flapped waistcoat; even beggar boys, little pot-high urchins, are wearing some old laced waistcoat tied

with string about their middles—a pair of heel-trodden, buckleless shoes on their feet, more likely bare-footed. Here is a man snatched from the tripe-shop in Hanging Sword Alley by the King's men—a pickpocket, a highwayman, a cut-throat in hiding. He will repent his jokes on Jack Ketch's kitchen when he feels the lash of the whip on his naked shoulders as he screams behind the cart-tail; ladies in flowered hoops will stop to look at him, beaux will lift their quizzing glasses, a young girl will whisper behind a fan, painted with the loves of

Jove, to a gorgeous young fop in a light-buttoned coat of sky-blue.

There is a sadder sight to come, a cart on the way to Tyburn, a poor fellow standing by his coffin with a nosegay in his breast; he is full of Dutch courage, for, as becomes a notorious highwayman, he must show game before the crowd, so he is full of stum and Yorkshire stingo. Maybe we stop to see a pirate hanging in chains by the river, and we are jostled  by horse officers and watermen, revenue men and jerkers, and, as usual, the curious beau, his glass to his eye. Never was such a time for curiosity: a man is preaching mystic religion; there is a new flavour to the Rainbow Tavern furmity; there is a fellow who can sew with his toes; a man is in the pillory for publishing Jacobite ballads— and always there is the beau looking on.

Country ladies, still in small hoops, even in full

dresses innocent of whalebone, are bewildered by
the noise; country gentlemen, in plain-coloured

coats and stout shoes, have come to
London on South Sea Bubble business.
They will go to the Fair to see the Harlequin and Scaramouch dance, they will buy
a new perfume at The Civet Cat, and they
will go home—the lady's head full of the
new hoop fashion, and she will cut away
the sleeve of her old dress and put in
fresh lace ; the gentleman full of curses on
tavern bills and the outrageous
price of South Sea shares.

'And what,' says country dame to
country dame lately from town—' what
is the mode in gentlemen's hair ?' Her
own goodman has an old periwig,
very full, and a small bob for ordinary
wear.

'The very full periwig is going out,'
our lady assures her; 'a tied wig is
quite the mode, a wig in three queues
tied in round bobs, or in hair loops, and
the long single queue wig is coming in rapidly,
and will soon be all the wear.' So, with talk of

flowered tabbies and fine lutestring, are the fashions passed on.

Just as Sir Roger de Coverley nearly called a young lady in riding-dress 'sir,' because of the upper half of her body, so the ladies of this day might well be taken for 'sirs,' with their double‑breasted riding-coats like the men, and their hair in a queue surmounted by a cocked hat.

Colours and combinations of colours are very striking: petticoats of black satin covered with large bunches of worked flowers, morning gown of yellow flowered satin faced with cherry-coloured bands, waistcoats of one colour with a fringe of another, bird's-eye hoods, bodices covered with gold lace and embroidered flowers—all these gave a gay, artificial appearance to the age; but we are to become still more quaintly devised, still more powdered and patched, in the next reign.

GEORGE THE SECOND

Reigned thirty-three years: 1727—1760.
Born 1683.   Married, 1705, Caroline of Anspach.

THE MEN

JUST a few names of wigs, and you will see how
the periwig has gone into the background, how
the bobwig has superseded the campaign-wig; you
will find a veritable confusion of barbers' enthu-
siasms, half-forgotten designs, names dependent
on a twist, a lock, a careful disarrangement—
pigeon's-wing wigs with wings of hair at the sides,
comets with long, full tails, cauliflowers with a
profusion of curls, royal bind-wigs, staircase wigs,
ladders, brushes, Count Saxe wigs, cut bobs, long
bobs, negligents, chain-buckles, drop-wigs, bags.
Go and look at Hogarth; there's a world of dress
for you by the grim humorist who painted Sarah
Malcolm, the murderess, in her cell; who painted
'Taste in High Life.'   Wigs! inexhaustible subject
—wigs passing from father to son until they arrived

at the second-hand dealers in Monmouth Street, and
there, after a rough overhauling, began a new life.
There was a wig lottery at sixpence a ticket in
Rosemary Lane, and with even ordinary wigs—
Grizzle Majors
at twenty-five
shillings, Great
Tyes at a
guinea, and
Brown Bag-
wigs at fifteen
shillings —
quite a con-
siderable sav-
ing might be
made by the
lucky lottery
winner.

On wigs,
hats cocked to suit the passing fashion, broad-
brimmed, narrow-brimmed, round, three-cornered,
high-brimmed, low-brimmed, turned high off the
forehead, turned low in front and high at the back
—an endless crowd. Such a day for clothes, for
patches, and politics, Tory side and Whig to your

face, Tory or Whig cock to your hat; pockets high, pockets low, stiff cuffs, crushable cuffs, a regular

jumble of go-as-you-please. Let me try to sort the jumble.

Foremost, the coat. The coat is growing more full, more spread; it becomes, on the beau, a great spreading, flaunting, skirted

affair just buttoned by a button or two at the waist. It is laced or embroidered all over; it is flowered or plain. The cuffs are huge; they will, of course, suit the fancy of the owner, or the tailor. About 1745 they will get small—some will get small; then the fashions begin to run riot; by

A MAN OF THE TIME OF GEORGE II. 1727-1760

A WOMAN OF THE TIME OF GEORGE II.   1727-1760

the cut of coat you may not know the date of it,
then, when you pass it in the street.   From 1745
there begins the same jumble as to-day, a hopeless
thing to unravel ; in the next reign, certainly, you
may tell yourself here is one of the new Maca-
ronies, but that will be all you will mark out of the
crowd of fashions—one more remarkable, newer
than the rest, but perhaps you have been in the
country for a week, and a new
mode has come in and is dying out.

From coat let us look at waistcoat. Full flaps and long almost to
the knees ; but again, about 1756,
they will be shorter.   They are
fringed, flowered, laced, open to
show the lace cravat fall so daintily,
to show the black velvet bow-tie
that comes over from the black
velvet, or silk, or satin tie of the
queue.   Ruffles of lace, of all qualities, at the
wrists, the beau's hand emerging with his snuff-box
from a filmy froth of white lace.

In this era of costume — from George I. to
George IV.—the great thing to remember is that
the coat changes more than anything else ; from

the stiff William and Mary coat with its deep, stiff
cuffs, you see the change towards the George I.
coat, a looser cut of the same design, still simple in
embroideries ; then the coat skirts are gathered to
a button at each side of the coat just behind the
pockets. Then, in George II.'s reign, the skirt hangs
in parallel folds free from the button, and shapes to
the back more closely, the opening of the coat, from

the neck to the
waist, being so cut
as to hang over
the buttons and
show the cravat
and the waistcoat.
Then, later in the
same reign, we see
the coat with the
skirts free of buck-
ram and very full
all round, and the
cuffs also free of
stiffening and fold-
ing with the crease of the elbow.   Then, about 1745,
we get the coat left more open, and, for the beau,
cut much shorter—this often worn over a double-

breasted waistcoat. Then, arriving at George III.,
we get a long series of coat changes, with a collar on
it, turned over and standing high in the neck, with
the skirts buttoned back, then cut away; then the
front of the coat cut away like the modern dress-
coat.

In following out these really complicated changes,
I have done my best to make my meaning clear by
placing dates against those drawings where dates
are valuable, hoping by this means to show the rise
and fall of certain fashions more clearly than any
description would do.

It will be noticed that, for ceremony, the periwig
gave place to the tie-wig, or, in some few cases, to
natural hair curled and powdered. The older men
kept to the periwig no doubt from fondness of the
old and, as they thought, more grave fashion; but,
as I showed at the beginning of the chapter, the
beau and the young man, even the quite middle-
class man, wore, or had the choice of wearing,
endless varieties of false attires of hair.

The sporting man had his own idea of dress,
even as to-day he has a piquant idea in clothes, and
who shall say he has not the right? A black wig,
a jockey cap with a bow at the back of it, a very

resplendent morning gown richly laced, a morning cap, and very comfortable embroidered slippers, such mixtures of clothes in his wardrobe—his coat, no doubt, a little over-full, but of good cloth, his fine clothes rather over-embroidered, his tie-wig often pushed too far back on his forehead, and so showing his cropped hair underneath.

Muffs must be remembered, as every dandy carried a muff in winter, some big, others grotesquely small. Bath must be remembered, and the great Beau Nash in the famous Pump-Room—as Thackeray says, so say I : ' I should like to have seen the Folly,' he says, meaning Nash. ' It was a splendid em- broidered, beruffled, snuff-boxed, red-heeled, imper- tinent Folly, and knew how to make itself respected. I should like to have seen that noble old madcap Peterborough in his boots (he actually had the audacity to walk about Bath in boots !), with his blue ribbon and stars, and a cabbage under each arm, and a chicken in his hand, which he had been cheapening for his dinner.'

It was the fashion to wear new clothes on the Queen's birthday, March 1, and then the streets noted the loyal people who indulged their extrava- gance or pushed a new fashion on that day.

Do not forget that no hard-and-fast rules can be laid down ; a man's a man for all his tailor tells him he is a walking fashion plate. Those who liked short cuffs wore them, those who did not care for solitaires did without ; the height of a heel, the breadth of a buckle, the sweep of a skirt, all lay at the taste of the owner — merely would I have you remember the essentials.

There was a deal of dressing up — the King, bless you, in a Turkish array at a masque—the day of the Corydon and Sylvia : mock shepherd, dainty shepherdess was here ; my lord in silk loose coat with paste buttons, fringed waistcoat, little three-cornered hat under his arm, and a pastoral staff between his fingers, a crook covered with cherry and blue ribbons ; and my lady in such a hoop of sprigged silk or some such stuff, the tiniest of straw hat on her head, high heels

tapping the ground, all a-shepherding — what?
Cupids, I suppose, little Dresden loves, little
comfit-box jokes, little spiteful remarks about the
Germans.

Come, let me doff my Kevenhuller hat with the
gold fringe, bring my red heels together with a
smart tap, bow, with my hand on the third button
of my coat from which my stick dangles, and let
me introduce the ladies.

THE WOMEN

I will introduce the fair, painted, powdered,
patched, perfumed sex (though this would do for
man or woman of the great world then) by some
lines from the *Bath Guide*:

> ' Bring, O bring thy essence-pot,
> Amber, musk, and bergamot;
> Eau de chipre, eau de luce,
> Sanspareil, and citron juice.
> *   *   *   *
> In a band-box is contained
> Painted lawns, and chequered shades,
> Crape that's worn by love-lorn maids,
> Watered tabbies, flowered brocades;
> Straw-built hats, and bonnets green,
> Catgut, gauzes, tippets, ruffs;
> Fans and hoods, and feathered muffs,

Stomachers, and Paris nets,
Earrings, necklaces, aigrets,
Fringes, blouses, and mignionets;
Fine vermillion for the cheek,
Velvet patches à la grecque.
Come, but don't forget the gloves,
Which, with all the smiling loves,
Venus caught young Cupid picking
From the tender breast of chicken.'

Now I think it will be best to describe a lady of quality. In the first years of the reign she still wears the large hoop skirt, a circular whale-bone arrangement started at the waist, and, at intervals, the hoops were placed so that the petticoat stood out all round like a bell; over this the  skirt hung stiff and solemn. The bodice was tight-laced, cut square in front where the neckerchief of linen or lace made the edge soft. The sleeves still retained the cuff covering the elbow, and the

under-sleeve of linen with lace frills came half-way down the forearm, leaving bare arm and wrist to show.

Over the skirt she would wear, as her taste held her, a long, plain apron, or a long, tucked apron, or an apron to her knees. The bodice generally formed the top of a gown, which gown was very full-skirted, and was divided so as to hang back behind the dress, showing, often, very little in front. This will be seen clearly in the illustrations.

The hair is very tightly gathered up behind, twisted into a small knob on the top of the head, and either drawn straight back from the forehead or parted in the middle, allowing a small fringe to hang on the temples. Nearly every woman wore a small cap or a small round straw hat with a ribbon round it.

The lady's shoes would be high-heeled and pointed-toed, with a little buckle and strap.

About the middle of the reign the sacque became the general town fashion, the sacque being so named on account of the back, which fell from the shoulders into wide, loose folds over the hooped petticoat. The sacque was gathered at the back in close pleats, which fell open over the skirt part of this dress.   The front of the sacque was some-

times open, sometimes made tight in the bodice.

Now the lady would puff her hair at the sides and powder it; if she had no hair she wore false, and a little later a full wig.   She would now often discard her neat cap and wear a veil be-hind her back, over her hair, and falling over her shoulders.

In 1748, so they say, and so I believe to be true, the King, walking in the Mall, saw the Duchess of Bedford riding in a blue riding-habit with white silk facings—this would be a man's skirted coat, double-breasted, a cravat, a three-corned hat, and a full blue skirt.   He admired her dress so much and thought it so neat that he straightway ordered that the officers of the navy, who, until now, had worn scarlet, should take this coat for the model of their new uniform. So did the navy go into blue and white.

The poorer classes were not, of course, dressed in hooped skirts, but the bodice and gown over the petticoat, the apron, and the turned back cuff to the short sleeve were worn by all. The orange wench laced her gown neatly, and wore a white cloth tied over her head; about her shoulders she wore a kerchief of white, and often a plain frill of linen at her elbows. There were blue canvas, striped dimity, flannel, and ticken for the humble; for the

rich, lustrings, satins, Padesois, velvets, damasks, fans and Leghorn hats, bands of Valenciennes and Point de Dunquerque—these might be bought of Mrs. Holt, whose card Hogarth engraved, at the Two Olive Posts in the Broad part of the Strand.

Seventeen hundred and fifty-five saw the one-

horse chairs introduced from France, called
cabriolets, the first of our own extraordinary
wild-looking conveyances contrived for the mini-
mum of comfort and the maximum of danger.
This invention captivated the hearts of both men
and women. The men painted cabriolets on
their waistcoats, they embroidered them on their
stockings, they cut them out in black silk and
patched their cheeks with them, horse and all;
the women began to take up, a little later, the
cabriolet caps with round sides like linen wheels,
and later still, at the very end of the reign, there
began a craze for such head-dresses—post-chaises,
chairs and chairmen, even waggons, and this craze
grew and grew, and hair grew—in wigs—to meet
the cry for hair and straw men-of-war, for loads
of hay, for birds of paradise, for goodness knows
what forms of utter absurdity, all of which I put
down to the introduction of the cab.

I think that I can best describe the lady of
this day as a swollen, skirted figure with a pinched
waist, little head of hair, or tiny cap, developing
into a loose sacque-backed figure still whaleboned
out, with hair puffed at the sides and powdered,
getting ready to develop again into a queer figure

under a tower of hair, but that waits for the next reign.

One cannot do better than go to Hogarth's prints and pictures — wonderful records of this time—one picture especially, 'Taste in High Life,' being a fine record of the clothes of 1742; here you will see the panier and the sacque, the monstrous muff, the huge hoop, the long-tailed wig, the black boy and the monkey. In the 'Noon' of  the 'Four Parts of the Day' there are clothes again satirized.

I am trusting that the drawings will supply what my words have failed to picture, and I again—for the twenty-first time—repeat that, given the cut and the idea of the time, the student has always to realize that there can be no hard-and-fast rule about the fashions; with the shape he can take liberties up to the points shown, with colour he can do anything — patterns of the materials are obtainable, and Hogarth will give anything required in detail.

GEORGE THE THIRD

Reigned sixty years : 1760—1820.
Born 1738.   Married, 1761, Charlotte Sophia
of Mecklenburg-Strelitz.

THE MEN AND WOMEN

THROUGHOUT this long reign the changes of costume are so frequent, so varied, and so jumbled
together, that any precise account of them would
be impossible.   I have endeavoured to give a
leading example of most kind of styles in the
budget of drawings which goes with this chapter.

Details concerning this reign are so numerous :
Fashion books, fashion articles in the *London
Magazine*, the *St. James's Chronicle*, works innumerable on hair-dressing, tailors' patterns—these
are easily within the reach of those who hunt the
second-hand shops, or are within reasonable distance
of a library.

Following my drawings, you will see in the

A MAN OF THE TIME OF GEORGE III. 1760-1820

A WOMAN OF THE TIME OF GEORGE III.   1760-1820

first the ordinary wig, skirted coat, knee-breeches, chapeau-bras, cravat or waistcoat, of the man about town. I do not mean of the exquisite about town, but, if you will take it kindly, just such clothes as you or I might have worn.

In the second drawing we see a fashionable man, who might have strutted past the first fellow in the Park. His hair is dressed in a twisted roll; he wears a tight-brimmed little hat, a frogged coat, a fringed waistcoat, striped breeches, and buckled shoes.

In the third we see the dress of a Macaroni. On his absurd wig he wears a little Nevernoise hat; his cravat is tied in a bow; his breeches are loose, and beribboned at the knee. Many of these Macaronis wore coloured strings at the knee of their breeches, but the fashion died away when Jack Rann, 'Sixteen String Jack,' as he was called after this fashion, had been hung in this make of breeches.

In number four we see the development of the tail-coat and the high-buttoned waistcoat. The tail-coat is, of course, son to the frock-coat, the skirts of which, being inconvenient for riding, had first been buttoned back and then cut back to give more play.

In the fifth drawing we see the double-breasted cut-away coat.

Number six is but a further tail-coat design.

Number seven shows how different were the styles at one time. Indeed, except for the Macaroni and other extreme fashions, the entire budget of men as shown might have formed a crowd in the Park on one day about twenty years before the end of the reign. There would not be much powdered hair after 1795, but a few examples would remain.

A distinct change is shown in the eighth drawing of the long-tailed, full coat, the broad hat, the hair powdered, but not tied.

Number nine is another example of the same style.

The tenth drawing shows the kind of hat we associate with Napoleon, and, in fact, very Napoleonic garments.

In eleven we have a distinct change in the appearance of English dress. The gentleman is a Zebra, and is so-called from his striped clothes. He is, of course, in the extreme of fashion, which did not last for long; but it shows a tendency towards later Georgian appearance—the top-hat,

28—2

the shorter hair, the larger neck-cloth, the pantaloons—forerunners of Brummell's invention—the
open sleeve.

Number twelve shows us an ordinary gentleman
in a coat and waistcoat, with square flaps, called
dog's ears.

As the drawings continue you can see that the
dress became more and more simple, more like
modern evening dress as to the coats, more like
modern stiff fashion about the neck.

The drawings of the women's dresses should
also speak for themselves. You may watch the
growth of the wig and the decline of the hoop—
I trust with ease. You may see those towers of
hair of which there are so many stories. Those
masses of meal and stuffing, powder and pomatum,
the dressing of which took many hours. Those
piles of decorated, perfumed, reeking mess, by
which a lady could show her fancy for the navy
by balancing a straw ship on her head, for sport
by showing a coach, for gardening by a regular
bed of flowers. Heads which were only dressed,
perhaps, once in three weeks, and were then re-
scented because it was necessary. Monstrous
germ - gatherers of horse - hair, hemp-wool, and

powder, laid on in a paste, the cleaning of which is too awful to give in full detail. 'Three weeks,' says my lady's hairdresser, 'is as long as

a head can go well in the summer without being opened.'

Then we go on to the absurd idea which came over womankind that it was most becoming to look like a pouter pigeon. She took to a buffon, a gauze or fine linen kerchief, which stuck out pigeon-like in front, giving an exaggerated bosom to those who wore it. With this fashion of 1786 came the broad-brimmed hat.

Travel a little further and you have the mob cap.

All of a sudden out go hoops, full skirts, high hair, powder, buffons, broad-brimmed hats, patches, high-heeled shoes, and in come willowy figures and thin, nearly transparent dresses, turbans, low shoes, straight fringes.

I am going to give a chapter from a fashion book, to show you how impossible it is to deal with the vagaries of fashion in the next reign, and if I chose to occupy the space, I could give a similar chapter to make the confusion of this reign more confounded.

GEORGE THE FOURTH

Reigned ten years : 1820—1830.
Born 1762.   Married, 1795, Caroline of Brunswick.

OUT of the many fashion books of this time I have
chosen, from a little brown book in front of me, a
description of the fashions for ladies during one
part of 1827.   It will serve to show how mere
man, blundering on the many complexities of the
feminine passion for dress—I was going to say
clothes—may find himself left amid a froth of frills,
high and dry, except for a whiff of spray, standing
in his unromantic garments on the shore of the
great world of gauze and gussets, while the most
noodle-headed girl sails gracefully away upon the
high seas to pirate some new device of the Devil or
Paris.

Our wives—bless them ! — occasionally treat us
to a few bewildering terms, hoping by their gossamer
knowledge to present to our gaze a mental picture

DRAWINGS TO ILLUSTRATE THE COSTUME OF THE
REIGN OF

GEORGE THE THIRD

THE FIRST FORTY-EIGHT DRAWINGS BY THE AUTHOR, AND
THE REMAINING TWELVE BY THE DIGHTONS,
FATHER AND SON

1768.

1772

1773

1773

1773

1782

1783

1786

1775

1775

1775

1776

1777

1783

1783

1783

1786

1787

1789

1793

1794

1794

1794

1794

1803

1810

1820

1830

The King.

The Navy.

The Army.

Pensioners.

The Church.

The Law.

The Stage.

The Universities.

The Country.

The Duke of Norfolk.

The City.

The Duke of Queensbury.

of a new, adorable, ardently desired—hat. Perhaps
those nine proverbial tailors who go to make the
one proverbial man, least of his sex, might, by a
strenuous effort, confine the history of clothes
during this reign into a compact literature of forty
volumes. It would be indecent, as undecorous as
the advertisements in ladies' papers, to attempt to
fathom the language of the man who endeavoured
to read the monumental effigy to the vanity of
human desire for adornment. But is it adornment ?

Nowadays to be dressed well is not always the
same thing as to be well dressed. Often it is far
from it. The question of modern clothes is one of
great perplexity. It seems that what is beauty
one year may be the abomination of desolation the
next, because the trick of that beauty has become
common property. You puff your hair at the sides,
you are in the true sanctum of the mode ; you
puff your hair at the sides, you are for ever utterly
cast out as one having no understanding. I shall
not attempt to explain it : it passes beyond the
realms of explanation into the pure air of Truth.
The Truth is simple. Aristocracy being no longer
real, but only a cult, one is afraid of one's servants.

Your servant puffs her hair at the sides, and, hang it! she becomes exactly like an aristocrat. Our servant having dropped her *g's* for many years as well as her *h's*, it behoved us to pronounce our *g's* and our *h's*. Our servants having learned our English, it became necessary for us to drop our *g's;* we seem at present unwilling in the matter of the *h*, but that will come.

To cut the cackle and come to the clothes-horse, let me say that the bunglement of clothes which passes all comprehension in King George IV.'s reign is best explained by my cuttings from the book of one who apparently knew. Let the older writer have his, or her, fling in his, or her, words.

'CUROSY REMARKS ON THE LAST NEW FASHIONS.

' The City of London is now, indeed, most splendid in its buildings and extent ; London is carried into the country ; but never was it more deserted.

' A very, very few years ago, and during the summer, the dresses of the wives and daughters of our opulent tradesmen would furnish subjects for the investigators of fashion.

' Now, if those who chance to remain in London take a day's excursion of about eight or ten miles distance from the Metropolis, they hear the inn-keepers deprecating the steamboats, by which they declare they are almost ruined : on Sundays, which would sometimes bring them the clear profits of ten or twenty pounds, they now scarce produce ten shillings.

' No ; those of the middle class belonging to *Cockney Island* must leave town, though the days are short, and even getting cold and comfortless ; the steamboats carrying them off by shoals to Margate and its vicinity.

' The pursuit after elegant and superior modes of dress must carry us farther ; it is now from the rural retirement of the country seats belonging to the noble and wealthy that we must collect them.

' Young ladies wear their hair well arranged, but not quite with the simplicity that prevailed last month ; during the warmth of the summer months, the braids across the forehead were certainly the best ; but now, when neither in fear of heat or damp, the curls again appear in numerous clusters round the face ; and some young ladies, who seem to place their chief pride in a fine head of hair, have such a multitude of small ringlets that give to what is a natural charm all the *poodle-like* appear-ance of a wig.

'The bows of hair are elevated on the summit of the head, and confined by a comb of tortoise-shell.

'Caps of the cornette kind are much in fashion, made of blond, and ornamented with flowers, or puffs of coloured gauze ; most of the cornettes are small, and tie undɔr the chin, with a bow on one side, of white satin ribbon; those which have ribbons or gauze lappets floating loose have them much shorter than formerly.

'A few dress hats have been seen at dinner-parties and musical amateur meetings in the country, of transparent white crape, ornamented with a small elegant bouquet of marabones.

'When these dress hats are of coloured crape, they are generally ornamented with flowers of the same tint as the hat, in preference to feathers.

'Printed muslins and chintzes are still very much worn in the morning walks, with handsome sashes, having three ends depending down each side, not much beyond the hips. With one of these dresses we saw a young lady wear a rich black satin pelerine, handsomely trimmed with a very beautiful black blond ; it had a very neat effect, as the dress was light.

'White muslin dresses, though they are always worn partially in the country till the winter actually commences, are now seldom seen except on the young : the embroidery on these dresses is exquisite.

Dresses of Indian red, either in taffety or chintz,
have already made their appearance, and are expected to be much in favour the ensuing winter;
the chintzes have much black in their patterns; but
this light material will, in course, be soon laid aside
for silks, and these, like the taffeties which have
partially appeared, will no doubt be plain: with
these dresses was worn a Canezon spencer, with
long sleeves of white muslin, trimmed with narrow
lace.

'Gros de Naples dresses are very general, especially for receiving dinner-parties, and for friendly
evening society.

'At private dances, the only kind of ball that has
at present taken place, are worn dresses of the
white-figured gauze over white satin or gros de
Naples; at the theatricals sometimes performed by
noble amateurs, the younger part of the audience,
who do not take a part, are generally attired in
very clear muslin, over white satin, with drapery
scarves of lace, barège, or thick embroidered tulle.

'Cachemire shawls, with a white ground, and a
pattern of coloured flowers or green foliage, are
now much worn in outdoor costumes, especially
for the morning walk; the mornings being rather
chilly, these warm envelopes are almost indispens-
able. We are sorry, however, to find our modern

belles so tardy in adopting those coverings, which
ought now to succeed to the light appendages of
summer costume.

'The muslin Canezon spencer, the silk fichu,
and even the lighter barêge, are frequently the
sole additions to a high dress, or even to one but
partially so.

'We have lately seen finished to the order of a
lady of rank in the county of Suffolk, a very
beautiful pelisse of jonquil-coloured gros de Naples.
It fastens close down from the throat to the feet,
in front, with large covered buttons; at a suitable
distance on each side of this fastening are three
bias folds, rather narrow, brought close together
under the belt, and enlarging as they descend to
the border of the skirt. A large pelerine cape is
made to take on and off; and the bust from the
back of each shoulder is ornamented with the same
bias folds, forming a stomacher in front of the
waist. The sleeves, *à la Marie*, are puckered a few
inches above the wrist, and confined by three straps;
each with a large button. Though long ends are
very much in favour with silk pelerines, yet there
are quite as many that are quite round; such was
the black satin pelerine we cited above.

'Coloured bonnets are now all the rage; we are
happy to say that some, though all too large, are in
the charming cottage style, and are modestly tied

under the chin. Some bonnets are so excessively large that they are obliged to be placed quite at the back of the head ; and as their extensive brims will not support a veil, when they are ornamented with a broad blond, the edge of that just falls over the hair, but does not even conceal the eyes. Leghorn hats are very general ; their trimmings consist chiefly of ribbons, though some ladies add a few branches of green foliage between the bows or puffs : these are chiefly of the fern ; a great improvement to these green branches is the having a few wild roses intermingled.

'The most admired colours are lavender, Ester-hazy, olive-green, lilac, marshmallow blossom, and Indian red.

' At rural fêtes, the ornaments of the hats gene-rally consist of flowers ; these hats are backward in the Arcadian fashion, and discover a wreath of small flowers on the hair, *ex bandeau*. In Paris the most admired colours are ethereal-blue, Hortensia, cameleopard-yellow, pink, grass-green, jonquil, and Parma-violet.'—*September* 1, 1827.

Really this little fashion book is very charming : it recreates, for me, the elegant simpering ladies ; it gives, in its style, just that artificial note which conjures this age of ladies with hats—' in the charm-ing cottage style, modestly tied under the chin.'

They had the complete art of languor, these dear creatures; they lisped Italian, and were fine needle-women; they painted weak little landscapes: nooks or arbours found them dreaming of a Gothic revival —they were all this and more; but through this sweet envelope the delicate refined souls shone: they were true women, often great women; their loops of hair, their cameleopard pelerines, shall not rob them of immortality, cannot destroy their softening influence, which permeated even the outrageous dandyism of the men of their time and steered the three-bottle gentlemen, their husbands and our grandfathers, into a grand old age which we rever-ence to-day, and wonder at, seeing them as giants against our nerve-shattered, drug-taking generation.

As for the men, look at the innumerable pictures, and collect, for instance, the material for a colossal work upon the stock ties of the time, run your list of varieties into some semblance of order; commence with the varieties of macassar-brown stocks, pass on to patent leather stocks, take your man for a walk and cause him to pass a window full of Hibernian stocks, and let him discourse on the stocks worn by turf enthusiasts, and, when you are approaching the end of your twenty-third volume,

give a picture of a country dinner-party, and end
your work with a description of the gentlemen
under the table being relieved of their stocks by
the faithful family butler.

POWDER AND PATCHES

'The affectation of a mole, to set off their beauty,
    such as Venus had.'

'At the devill's shopps you buy
A dresse of powdered hayre.'

From the splendid pageant of history what figures
come to you most willingly? Does a great procession go by the window of your mind? Knights
bronzed by the sun of Palestine, kings in chains,
emperors in blood-drenched purple, poets clothed
like grocers with the souls of angels shining
through their eyes, fussy Secretaries of State, in-
formers, spies, inquisitors, Court cards come to life,
harlequins, statesmen in great ruffs, wives of Bath
in foot-mantles and white wimples, sulky Puritans,
laughing Cavaliers, Dutchmen drinking gin and
talking politics, men in wide-skirted coats and
huge black periwigs—all walking, riding, being
carried in coaches, in sedan-chairs, over the face of

29

England. Every step of the procession yields
wonderful dreams of colour; in every group there
is one who, by the personality of his clothes, can
claim the name of beau.

Near the tail of the throng there is a chattering,
bowing, rustling crowd, dimmed by a white mist
of scented hair-powder. They are headed, I think
—for one cannot see too clearly—by the cook of
the Comte de Bellemare, a man by name Legros,
the great hairdresser. Under his arm is a book,
the title of which reads, 'Art de la Coiffure des
Dames Françaises.' Behind him is a lady in an
enormous hoop; her hair is dressed *à la belle Poule ;*
she is arguing some minute point of the disposition
of patches with Monsieur Léonard, another artist
in hair. 'What will be the next wear?' she asks.
A heart near the eye—*l'assassine,* eh ? Or a star
near the lips—*la friponne?* Must I wear a *galante*
on my cheek, an *enjouée* in my dimple, or *la
majestueuse* on my forehead?' Before we can hear
the reply another voice is raised, a guttural German
voice ; it is John Schnorr, the ironmaster of Erzge-
binge. 'The feet stuck in it, I tell you,' he says—
'actually stuck ! I got from my saddle and looked
at the ground. My horse had carried me on to

what proved to be a mine of wealth. Hair-powder!
I sold it in Dresden, in Leipsic; and then, at
Meissen, what does Böttcher do but use my hair-
powder to make white porcelain!' And so the
chatter goes on. Here is Charles Fox tapping the
ground with his red heels and proclaiming, in a
voice thick with wine, on the merits of blue hair-
powder; here is Brummell, free from hair-powder,
free from the obnoxious necessity of going with his
regiment to Manchester.

The dressy person and the person who is well
dressed—these two showing everywhere. The one is
in a screaming hue of woad, the other a quiet note
of blue dye; the one in excessive velvet sleeves that
he cannot manage, the other controlling a rich
amplitude of material with perfect grace. Here a
liripipe is extravagantly long; here a gold circlet
decorates curled locks with matchless taste. Everywhere the battle between taste and gaudiness.
High hennins, steeples of millinery, stick up out
of the crowd; below these, the towers of powdered
hair bow and sway as the fine ladies patter along.
What a rustle and a bustle of silks and satins,
of flowered tabbies, rich brocades, cut velvets,
superfine cloths, woollens, cloth of gold!

See, there are the square-shouldered Tudors,
there are the steel glints of Plantagenet armour,
the Eastern-robed followers of Cœur de Lion; the
swaggering beribboned Royalists; the ruffs, trunks,
and doublets of Elizabethans; the snuffy, wide-
skirted coats swaying about Queen Anne. There
are the soft, swathed Norman ladies with bound-up
chins; the tapestry figures of ladies proclaiming
Agincourt; the dignified dames about Elizabeth of
York; the playmates of Katherine Howard; the
wheels of round farthingales and the high lace collars
of King James's Court; the beauties, bare-breasted,
of Lely; the Hogarthian women in close caps.
And, in front of us, two posturing figures in
Dresden china colours, rouged, patched, powdered,
perfumed, in hoop skirts, flirting with a fan—the
lady; in gold-laced wide coat, solitaire, bagwig,
ruffles, and red heels—the gentleman. ' I protest,
madam,' he is saying, 'but you flatter me vastly.'
' La, sir,' she replies, ' I am prodigiously truthful.'

' And how are we to know that all this is true?'
the critics ask, guarding the interest of the public.
' We see that your book is full of statements, and
there are no, or few, authorities given for your
studies. Where,' they ask, ' are the venerable

anecdotes which are given a place in every respectable work on your subject ?'

To appease the appetites which are always hungry for skeletons, I give a short list of those books which have proved most useful :

MS. Cotton, Claudius, B. iv.

MS. Harl., 603.   Psalter, English, eleventh century.

The Bayeaux Tapestry.

MS. Cotton, Tiberius, C. vi.   Psalter.

MS. Trin. Coll., Camb., R. 17, 1.   Illustrated by Eadwine, a monk, 1130-1174.

MS. Harl. Roll, Y. vi.

MS. Harl., 5102.

Stothard's 'Monumental Effigies.'

MS. C. C. C., Camb., xvi.

MS. Cott., Nero, D. 1.

MS. Cott., Nero, C. iv.   Full of drawings.

MS. Roy., 14, C. vii.

Lansdowne MS., British Museum.

Macklin's 'Monumental Brasses.'

Journal of the Archæological Association.

MS. Roy., 2, B. vii.

MS. Roy., 10, E. iv.   Good marginal drawings.

The Loutrell Psalter.   Invaluable for costume.

MS. Bodl. Misc., 264.   1338-1344.   Very full of useful drawings.

Dr. Furnivall's edition of the Ellesmere MS. of Chaucer's 'Canterbury Tales.'

Boutell's 'Monumental Brasses.'

MS. Harl., 1319. Metrical history of the close of Richard II.'s reign. Good drawings for costume.

MS. Harl., 1892.

MS. Harl., 2278.

Lydgate's ' Life of St. Edmund.'

MS. Roy., 15, E. vi. Fine miniatures.

The Bedford Missal, MS. Add., 18850.

MS. Harl., 2982. A Book of Hours. Many good drawings.

MS. Harl., 4425. The Romance of the Rose. Fine and useful drawings.

MS. Lambeth, 265.

MS. Roy., 19, C. viii.

MS. Roy., 16, F. ii.

Turberville's ' Book of Falconrie ' and ' Book of Hunting.'

Shaw's ' Dresses and Decorations.'

Jusserand's ' English Novel ' and ' Wayfaring Life.' Very excellent books, full of reproductions from illuminated books, prints, and pictures.

The Shepherd's Calendar, 1579, British Museum.

Harding's ' Historical Portraits.'

Nichols's ' Progresses of Queen Elizabeth.'

Stubbes's ' Anatomie of Abuses,' 1583.

Braun's ' Civitates orbis terrarum.'

' Vestusta Monumenta.'

Hollar's ' Ornatus Muliebris Anglicanus.'

Hollar's ' Aula Veneris.'

Pepys's Diary.

Evelyn's Diary.

Tempest's ' Cries of London.' Fifty plates.

Atkinson's ' Costumes of Great Britain.'

In addition to these, there are, of course, many other books, prints, engravings, sets of pictures, and heaps of caricatures. The excellent labours of the Society of Antiquaries and the Archæological Association have helped me enormously ; these, with wills, wardrobe accounts, ' Satires ' by Hall and others, ' Anatomies of Abuses,' broadsides, and other works on the same subject, French, German, and English, have made my task easier than it might have been.

It was no use to spin out my list of manuscripts with the numbers—endless numbers—of those which proved dry ground, so I have given those only which have yielded a rich harvest.

BEAU BRUMMELL AND CLOTHES

' A person, my dear, who will probably come and speak to us ; and if he enters into conversation, be careful to give him a favourable impression of you, for,' and she sunk her voice to a whisper, ' he is the celebrated Mr. Brummell.'—' Life of Beau Brummell,' Captain Jesse.

Those who care to make the melancholy pilgrimage may see, in the Protestant Cemetery at Caen,

the tomb of George Bryan Brummell. He died, at
the age of sixty-two, in 1840.

It is indeed a melancholy pilgrimage to view the
tomb of that once resplendent figure, to think,
before the hideous grave, of the witty, clever,
foolish procession from Eton to Oriel College,
Oxford; from thence to a captaincy in the 10th
Hussars, from No. 4 Chesterfield Street to No. 13
Chapel Street, Park Lane; from Chapel Street a
flight to Calais; from Calais to Paris; and then, at
last, to Caen, and the bitter, bitter end, mumbling
and mad, to die in the Bon Sauveur.

Place him beside the man who once pretended
to be his friend, the man of whom Thackeray spoke
so truly: 'But a bow and a grin. I try and take
him to pieces, and find silk stockings, padding,
stays, a coat with frogs and a fur coat, a star and a
blue ribbon, a pocket handkerchief prodigiously
scented, one of Truefitt's best nutty-brown wigs
reeking with oil, a set of teeth, and a huge black
stock, under-waistcoats, more under-waistcoats, and
then nothing.'

Nothing! Thackeray is right; absolutely nothing
remains of this King George of ours but a sale list
of his wardrobe, a wardrobe which fetched £15,000

second-hand—a wardrobe that had been a man. He invented a shoe-buckle 1 inch long and 5 inches broad. He wore a pink silk coat with white cuffs. He had 5,000 steel beads on his hat. He was a coward, a good-natured, contemptible voluptuary. Beside him, in our eyes, walks for a time the elegant figure of Beau Brummell. I have said that Brummell was the inventor of modern dress: it is true. He was the Beau who raised the level of dress from the slovenly, dirty linen, the greasy hair, the filthy neck-cloth, the crumbled collar, to a position, ever since held by Englishmen, of quiet, unobtrusive cleanliness, decent linen, an abhorrence of striking forms of dress.

He made clean linen and washing daily a part of English life.

See him seated before his dressing-glass, a mahogany-framed sliding cheval glass with brass arms on either sides for candles. By his side is George IV., recovering from his drunken bout of last night. The Beau's glass reflects his clean-complexioned face, his grey eyes, his light brown hair, and sandy whiskers. A servant produces a shirt with a 12-inch collar fixed to it, assists the Beau

into it, arranges it, and stands aside. The collar
nearly hides the Beau's face. Now, with his hand
protected with a discarded shirt, he folds his collar
down to the required height. Now he takes his
white stock and folds it carefully round the collar ;
the stock is a foot high and slightly starched.
A supreme moment of artistic decision, and the
stock and collar take their perfect creases. In an
hour or so he will be ready to partake of a light
meal with the royal gentleman. He will stand up
and survey himself in his morning dress, his regular,
quiet suit. A blue coat, light breeches fitting the
leg well, a light waistcoat over a waistcoat of some
other colour, never a startling contrast, Hessian
boots, or top-boots and buckskins. There was
nothing very peculiar about his clothes except, as
Lord Byron said, 'an exquisite propriety.' His
evening dress was a blue coat, white waistcoat,
black trousers buttoned at the ankle—these were
of his own invention, and one may say it was the
wearing of them that made trousers more popular
than knee-breeches—striped silk stockings, and a
white stock.

He was a man of perfect taste—of fastidious
taste. On his tables lay books of all kinds in fine

covers. Who would suspect it? but the Prince is
leaning an arm on a copy of Ellis's ' Early English
Metrical Romances.' The Beau is a rhymer, an
elegant verse-maker. Here we see the paper-
presser of Napoleon —I am flitting for the moment
over some years, and see him in his room in Calais
—here we notice his passion for buhl, his Sèvres
china painted with Court beauties.

In his house in Chapel Street he saw daily portraits of Nelson and Pitt and George III. upon his
walls. This is no Beau as we understand the term,
for we make it a word of contempt, a nickname for
a feeble fellow in magnificent garments. Rather
this is the room of an educated gentleman of
' exquisite propriety.'

He played high, as did most gentlemen ; he was
superstitious, as are many of the best of men.
That lucky sixpence with the hole in it that
you gave to a cabman, Beau Brummell, was
that loss the commencement of your downward
career ?

There are hundreds of anecdotes of Brummell
which, despite those of the ' George, ring the bell '
character, and those told of his heavy gaming, are
more valuable as showing his wit, his cleanliness,

his distaste of display—in fact, his 'exquisite propriety.'

A Beau is hardly a possible figure to-day ; we have so few personalities, and those we have are chiefly concerned with trade—men who uphold trusts, men who fight trusts, men who speak for trade in the House of Commons. We have not the same large vulgarities as our grandfathers, nor have we the same wholesome refinement; in killing the evil—the great gambler, the great men of the turf, the great prize-fighters, the heavy wine-drinkers—we have killed, also, the good, the classic, well-spoken civil gentleman. Our manners have suffered at the expense of our morals.

Fifty or sixty years ago the world was full of great men, saying, writing, thinking, great things. To-day—perhaps it is too early to speak of to-day. Personalities are so little marked by their clothes, by any stamp of individuality, that the caricaturist, or even the minute and truthful artist, be he painter or writer, has a difficult task before him when he sets out to point at the men of these our times.

George Brummell came into the world on June 7, 1778. He was a year or so late for the Macaroni style of dress, many years behind the Fribbles, after the Smarts, and must have seen the rise and fall of the Zebras when he was thirteen. During his life he saw the old-fashioned full frock-coat, bagwig, solitaire, and ruffles die away; he saw the decline and fall of knee-breeches for common wear, and the pantaloons invented by himself take their place. From these pantaloons reaching to the ankle came the trousers, as fashionable garments, open over the instep at first, and joined by loops and buttons, then strapped under the boot, and after that in every manner of cut to the present style. He saw the three-cornered hat vanish from the hat-boxes of the polite world, and he saw fine-coloured clothes give way to blue coats with brass buttons or coats of solemn black.

It may be said that England went into mourning over the French Revolution, and has not yet recovered. Beau Brummell, on his way to Eton, saw a gay-coloured crowd of powdered and patched people, saw claret-coloured coats covered with embroidery gold-laced hats, twinkling shoe-buckles. On his last walks in Caen, no doubt, he dreamed of London as a place of gay colours instead of the drab place it was beginning to be.

To-day there is no more monotonous sight than the pavements of Piccadilly crowded with people in dingy, sad clothes, with silk tubes on their heads, their black and gray suits being splashed by the mud from black hansoms, or by the scatterings of motor-cars driven by aristocratic-looking mechanics, in which mechanical-looking aristocrats lounge, darkly clad. Here and there some woman's dress enlivens the monotony ; here a red pillar-box shines in the sun ; there, again. we bless the Post-Office for their red mail-carts, and perhaps we are strengthened to bear the gloom by the sight of a blue or red bus.

But our hearts are not in tune with the picture; we feel the lack of colour, of romance, of everything but money, in the street. Suddenly a magnificent policeman stops the traffic ; there is a sound of jingling harness, of horses' hoofs beating in unison. There flashes upon us an escort of Life Guards sparkling in the sun, flashing specks of light from swords, breastplates, helmets. The little forest of waving plumes, the raising of hats, the polite murmuring of cheers, warms us. We feel young, our hearts beat ; we feel more healthy, more alive, for this gleam of colour.

Then an open carriage passes us swiftly as we stand with bared heads. There is a momentary sight of a man in uniform—a man with a wonderful face, clever, dignified, kind. And we say, with a catch in our voices :

'THE KING—GOD BLESS HIM !'

THE END

Letterpress printed in Great Britain by J. W. Arrowsmith Ltd., Bristol